Village des Sauteur
Saut S. Marie

I. au Pari Sien

Villages d'Outaouacs au lac

les Missisague

Ny les Amik

Lt Tessalons

LAC HURON

Route de P. P.

MICHIGANE

Missilimakimac

Isles et nation des Missilimakinacs

Ance Kiacnan

R Nantunagan

Outaouacs

Vieux Desertts

Planches atta

R. Marquete

Baye de Saguinam

Nat gu

LAC des ILINOIS

R Poutouatami

la Grande Riviere

Louis Hennep

Forts Sh Josep

Miscouakimina

R. de Marameg

Lac Ganatchio ou S. Claire

Outaouacs Hurons Missisague Poutouatami

Nat Ne

detrut te haut

Bagagou

R. Noire

P aux Orus

la Baye

Nellet R

Chicagou R

R J Miamis

Fort de la Salle les Poutouatamis

Miamis

Portage

LAC ERIE

R. de Macopin

Portage

Lac Sandouske

Ilinois R.

Chasse des Amis des Francois

les Miamis

les Miamis

Crevecoeur cher

Peorra

Obio ou la Belle Riviere

Riviere d Oubache ou S Hieronyme

Desert de six vingt lieues d'etendue ou les Ilinois font la Chasse de boeuf

Riviere des anciens Chaouanons ainsi nommé parceque les Chaouanons y Habitoient autrefo

les Cheraqui

Terre ma

I A N E

Tongeria

Amo bi

Elisabe

Second Rapide

Aiouache

Iahcouet

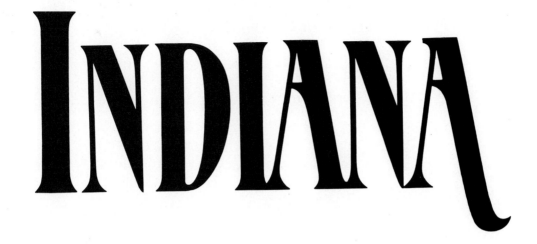

Picture Research by Mary Ellen Gadski
"Partners in Progress" by Judy Keene

Produced in cooperation with the
Historic Landmarks Foundation of
Indiana

Windsor Publications, Inc.
Northridge, California

INDIANA

An Illustrated History

Patrick J. Furlong

Windsor Publications, Inc.—History Books Division
Publisher: John M. Phillips
Editorial Director: Teri Davis Greenberg
Design Director: Alexander D'Anca

Staff for *Indiana: An Illustrated History*
Senior Editor: Julie Jaskol
Director, Corporate Biographies: Karen Story
Assistant Director, Corporate Biographies: Phyllis Gray
Editor, Corporate Biographies: Judith Hunter
Editorial Assistants: Kathy M. Brown, Patricia Cobb, Lonnie Pham, Pat Pittman,
Deena Tucker, Sharon L. Volz
Design and Layout: Christina McKibbin
Corporate Biographies Layout: Mari Priemesberger

Library of Congress Cataloging in Publication Data

Furlong, Patrick Joseph, 1940-
  Indiana : an illustrated history.

  "Produced in cooperation with the Historic
Landmarks Foundation of Indiana."
  Bibliography: p. 224
  Includes index.
  1. Indiana—History. 2. Indiana—Description and
travel. 3. Indiana—Industries. I. Gadski, Mary
Ellen. II. Title.
F526.F84   1985   977.2   85-20205
ISBN 0-89781-152-6

Facing page: *The town of Richmond sits quietly under a blanket of snow in this watercolor made in the winter of 1859-1860 by English artist Lefevre J. Cranstone. His paintings of this Indiana town are considered among his best work during his brief American sojourn. Courtesy, Indiana Historical Society*

Following pages: *It has been said of artist T.C. Steele that "no other Indiana painter has left for the enjoyment of future generations so large a number of landscapes and portraits." He is best known today for his outdoor sketching in the European Impressionist tradition. This canvas is entitled* Oaks at Vernon. *Courtesy, Indianapolis Museum of Art. John Herron Fund*

CONTENTS

Foreword

Indiana is not my native state, but through nearly twenty years as an adopted Hoosier I have come to know and appreciate its people and their fascinating history. Over many thousands of miles which have taken me to every part of the state I have learned that there is far more to the Indiana landscape than endless rows of corn and soybeans. From the hills of Brown County to the sand dunes along Lake Michigan, Indiana offers beauty in many forms to the eye of a discerning visitor. Those who rush through Indiana on an interstate highway at the maximum legal speed will not notice the prosperous and friendly small towns or even Indianapolis's new office towers and sports arenas. For those who already know about Indiana this volume offers a fresh view of the state and its history, while for anyone who has never noticed Indiana it offers an opportunity to begin understanding what it means to be a Hoosier.

No one writes a history without asking friends, librarians, archivists, and often strangers for help with a seemingly endless flow of questions. I would like to acknowledge those who have helped me understand Indiana better, particularly the resourceful and gracious staffs of the Indiana State Library, the Indiana Historical Society, the Indiana Historical Bureau, and the librarians of Indiana University at South Bend. Ralph Gray and James Madison have assisted me for years from their vast understanding of Hoosier lore, as has the elder statesman of Indiana historical studies, Professor Donald F. Carmony, whose review of my manuscript has saved me from many errors while also improving my prose. Donald B. Marti has strengthened my understanding of farming and rural life in general. Mary Ellen Gadski has encouraged me to meet deadlines, suggested improvements in coverage and in style, and cheerfully sought to locate illustrations which I assured her ought to exist "somewhere."

My wife Trudy deserves special thanks for her

support through months when it seemed that I would never finish this book. She has also saved me from sentences which seemed clear enough at the time but could only have confused readers who were not able to read my mind. Betsy and Joseph, the only native Hoosiers in the family, have often waited while I was "busy with the

book." They have helped also by reminding me that the young are curious about history, if historians will only make it interesting for them. This is what I have tried to achieve.

South Bend
June 1985

Two steamboats make their way down the Ohio River as the foreground figures hike to a fishing spot in the wooded hills. This pleasant view was glimpsed from Hanover College near Madison. Courtesy, Indiana Historical Society.

C H A P T E R 1

*As shown by this detail from a painting
called "Indians Playing the Moccasin
Game," artist George Winter recorded
the customs of the Indians before they
were driven from Indiana. The Indians
have adopted European dress in this
painting, circa 1840. Courtesy, Indiana
State Museum*

The Land, The Indians, And The French

The boundaries which separate Indiana from its neighboring states are not just arbitrary lines drawn across a map. The states of the American union develop a personality of their own, a complex blend of geography, history, and culture which dramatically distinguishes one from another. Indiana may share many elements in common with the other states of the midwestern heartland, but it is distinct. The land itself is different, the people are different, and—most important—their shared experiences over the years are different from those of neighboring states.

The name "Indiana" was used as early as 1765 by a company of colonial land speculators who hoped to make their fortunes by acquiring a great tract of land from the Indians at a very low price and then selling it in thousands of smaller parcels to would-be farmers at a much higher price. The Indiana Company was organized by Pennsylvania traders who had suffered heavy losses from Indian attacks during Pontiac's uprising two years earlier. They won compensation from the Iroquois Confederation of Six Nations in the form of 3,500,000 acres of land on the upper Ohio River in the present state of West Virginia. British authorities refused to confirm the grant, as did the revolutionary government of Virginia a few years later. The claimants tried and failed to win support from the Continental Congress, and the Supreme Court rejected their last claim in 1798. The Indiana Company left only its name.

When Congress voted in 1800 to divide the growing Northwest Territory into two jurisdictions the name "Indiana" was revived for the new western territory. The boundaries were altered as new territories were created for Illinois and Michigan, and altered again when Ohio and then Indiana were admitted to the Union. Before 1800 there was no single name to describe what became the state of Indiana, but most of it can conveniently be called the Wabash country after the celebrated Wabash River which flows across the state to the Ohio.

Artificial legal boundaries did not exist during the centuries when the Indians were the only inhabitants of what would become Indiana. For the French the Wabash country was part of the *pays d'en haut* or "upcountry," the great western backcountry rich in furs and flowing with the rivers that were the highways of that era. For the British authorities the Wabash country was a land reserved for the Indians, at least for the time being, and the Revolution came before they could alter their plans. Americans made the region their own during the Revolutionary War, and established the Northwest Territory as its government in 1787.

For many years Indiana and its neighboring states north of the Ohio were viewed by residents of the Atlantic seaboard as the Northwest, but as the nation moved ever farther westward Indiana became the Old Northwest and later still part of the Midwest. These are not merely geographical names, they have strong emotional meanings as well, ranging from the excitement and opportunity of the northwestern frontier in the early nineteenth century to the drabness of the Midwest imagined by television comedians in the late twentieth century.

Except for the hills of southwestern Indiana the land itself was largely molded by glaciers. At least three times within the past half-million years great sheets of ice stretching southward from the Canadian arctic covered most of Indiana, reshaping the very face of the earth. In the frigid depths of the ice age the glaciers were more than 1,000 feet thick over central Indiana, and the moving ice scraped away hills and filled ancient river valleys. When the ice melted, the rush of waters for thousands of years created new river systems. Only the southern third of Indiana escaped the ice and retained a pattern of frequent hills with many narrow valleys and small streams draining generally to the west and southwest.

The latest ice invasion, the Wisconsin glaciation, moved into Indiana about 25,000 years ago. The ice extended south of Indianapolis and advanced and retreated several times, leaving lines of boulders called terminal moraines to show just how far southward the ice moved before the climate altered once again. As the Wisconsin glacier retreated, the Wabash River carried an enormous volume of water from the melting ice, shaping the Wabash valley as it is known today. Centuries later the Kankakee River carried the icy water as the ice retreated into Michigan, flowing southwest from South Bend to the Illinois River. Gradually as the ice disappeared the flow diminished, and the St. Joseph River cut across the valley to feed its waters into glacial Lake Chicago, much larger than the present Lake Michigan. The wide river bed of the glacial Kankakee filled with sediment and then decaying plant matter to form the Great Kankakee Swamp, leaving the placid meandering Kankakee River to carry away its surplus waters. Lake Chicago shrank by stages into Lake Michigan, with its successive shorelines in Lake and Porter counties clearly marked by beaches and sand dunes now many miles inland.

The appearance of the land continued to change, as arctic tundra gave way to evergreen forests of spruce and fir, and then to pine which covered almost all of the region. About 8,000 years ago further warming brought deciduous hardwood forests which survived until pioneer axes cleared the land for farming in the nineteenth century. Oak and hickory forest predominated on the southwestern hills and in parts of northern Indiana, while beech-maple forest covered half the state in a broad central region, extending as far as the Ohio

River near New Albany. Along most of the Ohio and in some of the hill country mixed hardwood forest dominated, with a rich variety of basswood, buckeye, sycamore, and other species. About 87 percent of Indiana was forested before 1800, leaving 10 percent wetlands, chiefly in the northwest, and 3 percent prairie grasslands in the north and northwest. Most of the virgin forest was cut for timber or simply cleared away and destroyed to prepare the land for farming throughout the nineteenth century. The beech-maple forests grew on the rich and level lands favored by farmers, and virtually nothing survived. Remnants of the oak-hickory and mixed hardwood forests survive in remote hills, and conservationists have realized their value and worked to preserve some reminder of what Indiana had been. The Kankakee wetlands are much reduced by drainage, but enough remains to show what the region was before men began to alter the landscape. Only a few tiny relics of the tallgrass dry prairie survive, notably the Hoosier Prairie nature preserve amid the industry of Lake County.

The Ohio River forms the southern boundary of Indiana. Called *la belle riviere* or the "beautiful river" by the French explorers, today the Ohio is a great thoroughfare of commerce, as it has been for centuries. The storied steamboats are gone, but barges pushed by powerful diesel towboats carry a heavy traffic of coal, sand, gravel, and petroleum products. In the early years of the nineteenth century the Ohio was the primary route for the pioneers. Most of Indiana was settled by Americans moving down and across the Ohio and then northward. Only in the final years of settlement in northern Indiana did the flow of pioneers move directly westward.

The Wabash River, on the other hand, while scenic and storied, is too shallow for anything larger than canoes or deeper than rafts. The state song recalls summer nights on the banks of the Wabash, and the beauty of Indiana's rivers is widely recognized, but many people still envision the Indiana landscape to be endless miles of cornfields. Others are attracted to the Brown County hills and the knobs near the Ohio, particularly

when the trees turn color in the autumn, but neglect the rest of the state. Indiana lacks grandly spectacular scenery, but possesses quiet beauty.

The Wabash country has been inhabited continuously since the retreat of the last glacier, although very little is known of the earliest residents. The Paleo-Indian or Big Game Hunting Tradition describes small groups of wandering hunters who pursued large animals such as mammoths. Scattered finds of their fluted spear points show that they lived throughout Indiana. Indians of the Archaic Tradition inhabited the state from about 8,000 B.C. to about 1,000 B.C., hunting as well as gathering food, living in small villages which remained in one location for several years, before moving on. There is a good record of the Archaic presence in their stone tools, trade goods from distant regions, and, from late in the period, a considerable number of ceremonial burials. The Archaic Indians also left their refuse in the forms of shell mounds, piles of freshwater mussel shells sometimes ten feet thick and covering several acres. Bones of deer, elk, bear, and smaller mammals give evidence that their diet was not exclusively shellfish. Most of the shell mounds are in southern Indiana. To the north the inhabitants seem to have been hunters and gatherers who did not remain long in any one place, but who did bury their dead. The most characteristic Archaic artifact, often found with burials, is the "birdstone," a well-carved figure something like a bird, but of unknown significance.

The Woodland Tradition extended from about 1,000 B.C. to A.D. 900 and is characterized by the use of pottery and the construction of earthworks and burial mounds. The Woodland Indians left many remains of their culture, particularly in central and southern Indiana, although the record is often difficult to interpret. Much of their pottery was decorated in a variety of patterns made by a cord or a flat tool. They cultivated squash and perhaps other plants as well. Mounds State Park near Anderson preserves a number of burial mounds, one of them more than 350 feet across. Recent discoveries in Posey County show a group of at least sixteen mounds in a mile-long complex,

Above: *Autumn can be quietly beautiful, as it is in McCormick's Creek State Park . . .*

Left: *. . . or it can be as vibrant and dramatic as these bright leaves in Brown County. Photos by Bill Thomas*

Left: *This wintertime view shows how Sugar Creek got its name. Photo by Bill Thomas*

Below: *A spring morning is misty and cool in this southern Indiana woods. Photo by Bill Thomas*

but study of this site is only beginning. The bow and arrow appeared in the Middle Woodland period, probably before A.D. 400, and although it does not seem to have introduced any great changes it must have made hunting more successful. The last centuries of the Woodland period were a time of apparent decline, for which the reasons are unknown.

The Mississippian Tradition, from about 900 to 1600, was a complex culture based on the inten-sive cultivation of corn, beans, and squash, and marked by large permanent settlements with thousands of inhabitants. The Mississippian culture was widespread throughout the southeastern part of the United States, extending as far north as the Ohio valley and the modern city of St. Louis. The largest Mississippian settlement in Indiana was at Angel Mounds State Memorial near Evansville, a town of perhaps 3,000 Indians, with many more living in nearby villages. The site along the Ohio

Facing page: *The gently sloping contours seen in this 1891 photograph are actually earthworks excavated by Indians of the Woodland Tradition, well over 1,000 years ago. The earthworks are now part of Mounds State Park near Anderson. Courtesy, Indiana Historical Society*

River was protected by a ditch and palisade more than a mile in length, and the ceremonial focus of the town was a mound 650 feet long, 300 feet wide, and 44 feet high. The inhabitants lived chiefly on cultivated plants, but deer and small game, fish, and shellfish were consumed in considerable quantities. They also made pottery in many forms, usually without surface decoration except for occasional painting. Angel Mounds was inhabited from about 1200 to about 1600, when it was abandoned for unknown reasons. There are other Mississippian sites along the Ohio and the lower Wabash, but central and northern Indiana during this period had only smaller and less permanent Indian villages. Although the early Spanish explorers visited some southern Mississippian towns, by the time the French reached the Wabash valley around 1700 all memory of this settled agricultural

pattern of Indian life had vanished, and there is no way to trace any connection from the people of Angel Mounds to any of the historic Indian tribes of the region.

The Miami was the most powerful Indian nation in the Wabash country when French explorers arrived, but like the French they were newcomers. The Miami entered northern Indiana from their homeland in Iowa and Wisconsin dur-

Above: *The French explorer La Salle was looking for a western water route in the late 1600s when he explored a small part of Indiana along the St. Joseph River in the area around what is now South Bend. This portrait of him was engraved for the* Magazine of American History *in the nineteenth century. Courtesy, Indiana Historical Society*

Left: *This detail from a 1725 German map of the New World shows that much of the interior of the continent was still little-known. Its nomenclature reveals a strong French influence, as indeed France was extending its domination over the territory. On Lake Michigan (here "Lac des Ilinois") one can note "Chigagou" and Fort de La Salle where the Miami River (now the St. Joseph) enters the lake. To the south, the Ohio River ("la Belle Riviere") is shown flowing into the Wabash ("l'Oubache"). Courtesy, Indiana Historical Society*

ing the 1670s, and by the mid-eighteenth century they dominated the Wabash valley and the upper Maumee region, with their chief town at Kekionga, the modern Fort Wayne. The Potawatomi moved into northern Indiana from Michigan and Wisconsin at the end of the seventeenth century. In southern Indiana no single tribe matched the power of the Miami and their Wea and Piankashaw kinsmen. Kickapoo and Kaskaskia mingled with Delaware and Wyandot who had already been forced westward by the pressure of European settlement. There were also Shawnee in Indiana, a powerful tribe whose lands in Ohio came under increasing attack from the new American nation at the end of the eighteenth century.

French colonization in the St. Lawrence valley began during the early years of the seventeenth century, while the English were first settling in Virginia. French explorers, missionaries, and fur traders moved westward on the rivers and the lakes, but permanent settlements spread slowly. In 1673 Louis Joliet and Father Jacques Marquette traveled the upper part of the Mississippi River. Two years later the dying Marquette traveled along the southern and eastern waters of Lake Michigan, perhaps landing briefly in what would later be known as Indiana.

The earliest documented French visitor to Indiana was the Sieur de La Salle who traveled to the southeastern part of Lake Michigan and led his party up the St. Joseph River as far as South Bend in 1679. They then left the St. Joseph by a short portage, carrying their canoes and supplies for three or four miles to the headwaters of the Kankakee River which they followed downstream until it flowed into the Illinois River. This discovery opened a practical water route between the Great Lakes and the Mississippi which would be used by the French for years to come. In the early years of the eighteenth century the French fur traders, missionaries, and soldiers opened a new and safer route from the Great Lakes to Louisiana, bypassing the hostile Fox Indians along the Illinois River. From Lake Erie they paddled their great canoes up the Maumee River to its source at the Miami town of Kekionga. There they portaged ten miles to a tributary of the Wabash River, and then down the Wabash to the Ohio, and on to the Mississippi to New Orleans.

Because the French were trying to control a vast territory and a rich fur trade with a very small military force it was essential for them to maintain good relations with as many Indian nations as possible. In general the French were far more successful than the English in their relations with the Indians, often living among them for years and adopting many of their customs. The Sieur de Vincennes, for example, was ordered to live among the Miami and secure their continuing alliance with the French.

In 1717 the Sieur de Belestre erected the first French post in Indiana, at Ouiatanon on the banks of the Wabash not far from the modern Lafayette. Often called a fort, Ouiatanon was in truth a fortified trading post and mission station, with a customary garrison of one officer and about ten men. English influence among the Wea band of the Miami had been growing, and Ouiatanon was intended as a permanent post from which the French could exercise their influence in the Wabash country. It served the additional purpose of protecting the water route between the lakes and the Mississippi.

In 1722 Charles Du Buisson built a post at Kekionga and named it Fort Sainte Phillipe des Miamis, usually known as Fort Miami or Fort des Miamis. The young Vincennes who assumed most of the responsibility for maintaining good relations with the Miami after his father died in 1719 was ordered to Ouiatanon. Gradually Vincennes shifted his activity to the lower Wabash valley where he came under the orders of the governor of Louisiana.

There was a considerable rivalry between the Canadian authorities and those in Louisiana, and the boundary was never clearly defined, although it was understood to be somewhere on the high ground of the middle Wabash, called in French *terre haute*. In 1731-1732 Vincennes established a post on the lower Wabash called Post Vincennes, or simply Vincennes, the oldest continuously inhabited European settlement in Indiana. Vin-

Vincennes, Father and Son

Jean-Baptiste Bissot de Vincennes was born at Quebec in 1668. As a young man he sold his family property and obtained a commission in the colonial regular forces. He was ordered west by Governor Frontenac and soon made his mark as an officer of wide influence among the Miami Indians. Although never promoted he was given increasingly important duties. From 1712 until his death in 1719 he lived among the Miami, urging them to keep peace with the Illinois tribe and fight the Fox Indians instead, and always to remain loyal to France and hostile to the British.

His son Francois-Marie Bissot de Vincennes was born in Montreal in 1700. From the age of thirteen the younger Vincennes lived among the Miamis, following his father's example in winning a position of trust among the Indians. In 1722 while still a cadet he was assigned to command the post at Ouiatanon. British agents and traders were becoming increasingly troublesome, but Vincennes struggled to maintain French predominance along the Wabash. He received greater support and then promotion from the governor of Louisiana, and in 1730 shifted his residence to the lower Wabash where he was clearly within Loui-

siana jurisdiction. In 1731-1732 he built the post known as Vincennes. He had few troops and insufficient money, and on occasion had to borrow from visitors to keep up the customary gifts for the Indians. In 1736 he led a small party of Miami warriors southward to join an expedition against the Chickasaw, who were then allies of the British. The French and their Indian friends were overwhelmed, and Vincennes was captured, tortured, and burned at the stake. According to the testimony of the only French survivor, Vincennes sang a hymn as the flames rose about him.

cennes recommended a garrison of at least thirty men for his new post, but he had only ten Frenchmen with him. Like Ouiatanon and Fort Miami, Vincennes was more trading post than fort, a stronghold from which the French could buy furs from and endeavor to influence the Indians.

The French forces in the entire Great Lakes region were never strong enough to hold the vast territory with any security. In the mid-1740s, for example, there were no more than fifty French soldiers and civilians at Vincennes. At Ouiatanon there were only twenty French, along with some 600 friendly Indian warriors. The question was always how to keep the Indians friendly to the French, as British traders ventured more and more into the Ohio valley and the Wabash country. The French moved with determination in 1748 to strengthen their position in the backcountry. Their chief effort was to expel British traders from the Ohio valley, win support from additional Indian nations, and finally to build a chain of

forts from Lake Erie to the Forks of the Ohio, the modern Pittsburgh. Before the French could complete their forts the governor of Virginia sent Colonel George Washington westward to interfere. Washington was defeated in July 1754, but his campaign opened the final struggle for control of North America, a great war for empire usually known as the French and Indian War.

There was no fighting in the Wabash country. British detachments from Roger's Rangers simply occupied Fort Miami late in 1760 and Ouiatanon in the autumn of 1761. Vincennes, which was under the jurisdiction of Louisiana, was not occupied by the British until 1765. French North America was no more, except for the thousands of French people remaining in Canada. Only a small number of French men and women remained at Vincennes, but the French left their mark on much of Indiana in many of the names by which its rivers and towns are known today.

C H A P T E R II

George Rogers Clark was a young man in his late twenties when he became a hero through his Revolutionary War victory at Vincennes in 1779, which was popularly believed to have secured the Northwest Territory for the Americans. This oil portrait of Clark was done by Matthew Jouett much later in the general's life. Courtesy, The Filson Club, Louisville, Kentucky

The American Frontier

The Peace of Paris of 1763 marked the end of the French and Indian War. In North America everything east of the Mississippi River except for the city of New Orleans became British territory, while to the west the French colony of Louisiana, along with its capital of New Orleans, was transferred to Spain. The diplomats of Europe devised their treaties in the elegant comfort of Paris, but in the American backcountry there was no peace. For a century France and Britain had struggled to win the friendship of the various Indian nations, but now that the great war was ending the British believed that there was no longer any need to provide the customary gifts such as powder, shot, blankets, and ornaments for the Indians. The Indians of the Great Lakes and the Ohio valley feared the advance of settlers from the British colonies, and the Ottawa chief Pontiac led a confederacy among the northern tribes to resist white invasion.

Pontiac's Rebellion, as the British called it, began with an attack against Fort Detroit in May 1763. The British were forewarned by friendly Indians, and Pontiac lost the expected advantage of surprise. Despite this, the Indians were able to keep Detroit closely besieged for four months. Fort Pitt at Pittsburgh was also brought under siege, and all of the smaller posts of the northwestern frontier were captured by the Indians, with heavy casualties among the British regulars and the colonial frontiersmen. Fort Miami and Ouiatanon were each garrisoned by small detachments of one officer and about fifteen soldiers. Both were taken by overwhelming forces, but the prisoners were generally well treated after French traders persuaded the Indians to spare their British captives. In August a column of British regulars and colonial rangers defeated the Indians at Bushy Run near Pittsburgh, and Pontiac's uprising collapsed.

The frontier peace was an uneasy one, and the prospect of frequent and expensive Indian wars frightened British officials on both sides of the Atlantic. A royal proclamation dated October 7, 1763, announced a new policy. The Indians living in the vast region between the Appalachian ridge line and the Mississippi were placed under the protection of the British crown. To reduce the danger of conflict and to assure the Indians of British justice, all colonial settlement west of the mountains was strictly forbidden. Anyone trading with the Indians would need a license from a colonial governor. Private land purchases from the Indians were strictly forbidden, and it was this provision which threatened the dreams of colonial land speculators.

As an Indian policy the Proclamation of 1763 was remarkably fair and generous by British standards, but to colonials eager for western lands it was a direct assault against their cherished interests. For the residents of Vincennes the proclamation was an eviction notice. The problem was simple ignorance: British officials were not aware that there were any French civilians on the Wabash who might wish to remain. Pontiac himself traveled down the Wabash in early 1764, attempting without success to stir up the remaining French residents to resist British authority. His every effort frustrated, Pontiac agreed to peace terms in a conference at Ouiatanon in June and July 1765.

Ouiatanon and Fort Miami were never rebuilt, but at Vincennes there were some 400 civilians, including ten black slaves and seventeen Indian slaves, probably captured in battle. The residents owned 300 oxen, 600 cows, 250 horses, 300 hogs, and substantial crops of corn, wheat, and tobacco, but this thriving frontier settlement had no legal standing. The British commander for North America, Lieutenant General Thomas Gage, was surprised to learn of such a substantial and growing backwoods town, and he was reluctant to force so many people from their homes.

Little is known of life in Vincennes at this period, but from all accounts it was a rough and rowdy place with more than a few residents who were happy to find themselves beyond the reach of the law. A certain degree of order returned in 1769 when Father Pierre Gibault arrived, reviving both religion and a sense of social stability. Gage wished to reestablish a fort at Vincennes, but his superiors in London ordered the town abandoned. Gage issued the order in April 1772, but made no effort to enforce it. The French inhabitants, led by Father Gibault, sent a petition to Lord Dartmouth, the colonial secretary, and the evacuation order was canceled.

The Quebec Act of 1774 extended the boundaries of the Province of Quebec southward to the Ohio, a measure entirely satisfactory to the people of Vincennes, but one more cause for dispute between the British government and its unruly subjects in the thirteen colonies. Yet at Vincennes, far from the riots and tea parties of Boston, there was happiness and quiet, and finally, in 1775, a resident symbol of British authority in the presence of Lieutenant Governor Edward Abbott.

Meanwhile, hunters from the Virginia and North Carolina backcountry made their way into Kentucky despite the Proclamation of 1763, and they were soon followed by land dealers and settlers. The first permanent settlements in Kentucky were the Virginia outpost of Harrodsburg in 1774 and the Carolina fort at Boonesborough in 1775. As the Revolution undermined royal authority hundreds of eager pioneers entered Kentucky, and late in 1776 the revolutionary government of Virginia extended its legal jurisdiction with the establishment of Kentucky County. Through Cumberland Gap the settlers entered a rich land where various Indian nations hunted but none lived permanently. They naturally feared the advancing Americans who immediately competed with them for game and would soon destroy their hunting grounds for farming. Shawnee, Miami, and other war parties from the north raided Kentucky as the settlers sought refuge in stockaded "stations." British authorities in Detroit aided and encouraged the Indians in a series of bloody attacks during 1777, and Lieutenant Governor Henry Hamilton became notorious among American frontiersmen as "Hamilton the Hair-Buyer."

The inhabitants of the Kentucky settlements had to defend themselves as best they could, and some of them came to believe that it would be better to carry the battle to the enemy. The idea of an offensive across the Ohio was widely shared, but it required determined leadership to organize and lead an American invasion of the Indian country. George Rogers Clark was a young Virginian of ambition, courage, and ability, and he assumed the responsibility of leading a force of volunteer militia from Kentucky to seize the old French settlements on the Wabash and the Mississippi. From these posts north of the Ohio Clark hoped to prevent further Indian attacks on Kentucky and eventually to capture the British fort at Detroit from which the Indians were supplied. It was a daring and ambitious plan, but Clark had neither men nor supplies to put it into effect.

Clark traveled the long but familiar road to Williamsburg, where he represented Kentucky County in the Virginia House of Delegates. He persuaded Governor Patrick Henry to support his plan, and on January 2, 1778, the newly promoted Lieutenant Colonel Clark received secret orders for an expedition against Kaskaskia on the Mississippi. Virginia had long claimed the lands north and west of the Ohio, and Governor Henry encouraged Clark to win over the French inhabitants as new citizens of Virginia. Clark received a small amount of money and a requisition for gunpowder and shot, but he was left on his own to raise 350 volunteers. It required months to recruit the troops, for many of the early volunteers deserted before the force could be completed, and Clark set out with only 175 men. The expedition

left the Falls of the Ohio, a location later named Louisville, on June 26, 1778, dramatically launching their boats during an eclipse of the sun.

Clark's tiny army moved down the Ohio without incident, marched overland across southern Illinois, and surprised Kaskaskia on July 4. The old French post fell without resistance, for there were no British troops present. Clark skillfully used the new alliance between the United States and France to win the French inhabitants to his cause, promising to protect their property rights and to safeguard their Catholic faith. He marched northward sixty miles to capture Cahokia without firing a shot. Father Gibault and a number of residents of Vincennes were visiting in Cahokia, and at Clark's eloquent urging they returned home and persuaded the people of Vincennes to swear allegiance to Virginia. George Rogers Clark had taken three towns at very little cost, but his campaign was only beginning, for the British at Detroit were certain to counterattack. Colonel Henry Hamilton, the hated "Hair-Buyer," moved with a force of only 35 British regulars and 130 Canadian militia, supported by an unknown number of Indian allies, to recapture Vincennes on December 17.

Cold weather made further campaigning impossible, and Hamilton settled in at Vincennes to spend the winter in idle comfort. Most of his Indians and many of the French Canadians of the militia soon wandered away, and Hamilton made himself unpopular by his arrogant manners and harsh policies. He did make some effort to repair the old fort, which he renamed Fort Sackville, but there was no urgency in the work. Clark fully understood the danger of his position at Kaskaskia, hundreds of miles from assistance with the enemy between him and the Kentucky settlements. Clark decided that his only hope was to act boldly and quickly, to take Hamilton by surprise before the British could improve their position. As Clark later told Governor Henry: "Great things have been affected by a few Men well Conducted."

In the best military tradition Colonel Clark secured fresh intelligence about the British position from Francis Vigo, a St. Louis fur trader and one of Clark's supporters, who had recently visited

Vincennes. Clark set out with 172 men, about half of them French volunteers from Kaskaskia and Cahokia. His route was directly across country, amid heavy winter rains and through four flooded river valleys for 180 miserable miles, which he covered in sixteen days.

On the afternoon of February 23, 1779, Clark's little army reached dry ground within a mile of Vincennes. Clark sent a warning to the French inhabitants to remain in their homes and away from the fort. Then just at dusk he paraded his troops near the western bank of the Wabash, skillfully using the ground to conceal their actual strength while showing enough battle flags for an army of a thousand men. Clark crossed the river and came up to the walls of the fort without meeting any resistance, for the French had told the British commander nothing. Not until the Americans began to fire through the gaps in the fort's stockade did the British soldiers realize that they were under attack. The shooting continued through the night until the early light of morning when Clark sent a flag of truce to demand Hamilton's surrender. The British commander refused and the firing resumed for another two hours, until Hamilton asked for a parley. Hamilton wanted a three-day cease-fire while Clark demanded immediate surrender, but they did agree to speak face-to-face at the church. Clark considered Hamilton a murderer for his methods of frontier warfare, and told him bluntly that he hoped for a proper excuse to execute him, his officers, and his Indian allies.

After conferring with his officers Colonel Hamilton returned with conditions which Clark rejected, and so he was compelled to accept Clark's harsh terms. The surrender was signed and Fort Sackville handed over on February 25. Like most frontiersmen, Clark believed that the only way to eliminate the Indian menace was "to excel them in barbarity." While the truce talks dragged on through the day, the Americans tomahawked four Indian prisoners in plain sight of the British, scalped them, and threw their bodies into the Wabash. Hamilton said afterwards that Clark himself had killed the captives and rubbed his hands in their blood, but Clark's account did not mention

the incident at all. Hamilton was sent in chains to Virginia where even Thomas Jefferson proposed to treat him as a criminal rather than a prisoner of war.

George Rogers Clark recaptured Vincennes, but he had not conquered the northwestern wilderness for the United States. Neither Virginia nor the Continental Congress could send sufficient supplies or reinforcements. Clark used his eloquence and his reputation for ferocity to dominate the Indians, but he was never able to carry out his cherished plan to attack Detroit. He had to use his own credit and that of the friendly New Orleans merchant Oliver Pollock to supply his troops, and both suffered great losses when Virginia refused repayment. Virginia did establish Illinois County in December 1778, with boundaries taking in the entire northwest country, but the Old Dominion was never able to make its claim over the region effective and the county government lapsed in 1781. Clark renamed the fort at Vincennes in honor of Patrick Henry and left a garrison of forty men to defend it. He returned to the Falls of the Ohio where he built Fort Nelson on the Kentucky side of the river, which would become the flourishing city of Louisville.

Facing page: *Fur trader Francis Vigo became one of Vincennes' most prosperous residents. Although he never learned to read or write, he was a founder of Vincennes University and a shareholder of the Vincennes Library Company. Courtesy, Indiana State Library, Indiana Division*

Although admirers of George Rogers Clark believe that his victory at Vincennes in 1779 secured the Northwest for the new American nation, there is no evidence that the peace commissioners at Paris even knew of his exploits. There was little argument about the western boundary of the United States which, except near the Gulf Coast, extended to the Mississippi River. The Northwest was part of the original territory of the United States as defined by the Peace of Paris of 1783, but there was already a serious dispute in the Continental Congress about which states would benefit from this vast territory. Massachusetts, Connecticut, and New York all claimed portions of the Northwest, and Virginia claimed the entire territory as its own. Land speculators living in states such as Pennsylvania and Maryland which had no western claims believed that they would be excluded from opportunities that rightfully belonged to all Americans, and they argued that the unsettled western lands should be placed under the jurisdiction of Congress. The arguments were long and complex, but by 1781 all of the states agreed to give up their western land claims. Virginia carried out its promise in 1784, deeding the territory north and west of the far bank of the Ohio River to the United States. The full width of the Ohio remained under Virginia jurisdiction, a right still jealously guarded by Kentucky and West Virginia. Because Virginia had already used all of the land in Kentucky to pay some of its troops, it retained the right to grant certain lands in the northwest, the military lands of Ohio, and also a tract reserved for George Rogers Clark and his followers just across the river from Louisville. The first settlement on this Clark grant was appropriately named Clarksville in 1784.

The Continental Congress struggled to devise a suitable policy for the west. The Ordinance of 1784 set forth the principle that new states equal in every respect to the original thirteen would be established as soon as there was a sufficient population in any area. The Land Ordinance of 1785 provided for survey of the land before settlement and set the terms for its eventual sale. The Northwest Ordinance of 1787, passed by the Congress in New York while the Constitutional Convention was sitting in Philadelphia, finally established a territorial government for the region north and west of the Ohio River. The Northwest Ordinance included a number of significant safeguards for the rights of the white inhabitants, including trial by jury and freedom of religion, as well as the complete exclusion of slavery. It also provided a legal framework for the support of public education, although sufficient money for schools would not become available for many years. Arthur St. Clair, president of the Continental Congress when the ordinance was adopted, was chosen as the first governor of the territory, and he established its government at Marietta in July 1788. The only officer of the territory in what would become Indiana was a single justice of the peace at Clarksville.

Winthrop Sargent, secretary of the territory, traveled to Vincennes in 1790 and established Knox County, which survives with much-reduced boundaries and with Vincennes still its county seat. All of the original county officers were appointed by Governor St. Clair, but French as well as American residents were named to the offices of sheriff, coroner, clerk, recorder, treasurer, and justices of the peace. Division of the county into civil townships began in 1791, and under a 1795 law the township tax assessors were elected, the first officers of government to be chosen by the people of the territory.

For several years the Northwest Territory was the scene of bloody warfare, as the Indians of the Great Lakes region struggled, with British encouragement, to halt the spread of American settlement. The Miami and Potawatomi were important members of this new Indian confederacy, and from Fort Knox at Vincennes Major John Francis Hamtramck endeavored with his few troops to

William Wells And Little Turtle

When Miami war chief Little Turtle visited Washington, D.C., in 1797, he sat for a portrait by famed American artist Gilbert Stuart. Although the original painting is now lost (reputedly burned in the Capitol fire during the War of 1812), it is known from an engraving made from it. This particular illustration is copied from the 1868 History of Fort Wayne by William Brice. Courtesy, Indiana State Library, Indiana Division

William Wells lived for nearly twenty years partly as a white American and partly as a Miami Indian, trying to explain his two peoples to one another. Wells came west from Pennsylvania with his family when he was nine to settle near Louisville. He lived the normal life of a frontier boy until he was captured by a Miami raiding party when he was fourteen. Like other likely young captives he was adopted as an Indian and given the name Apekonit, meaning "carrot" because of his red hair. He was a brave warrior and lured many river travelers into ambush by pretending to call for help. He soon became a friend of the Miami war chief Little Turtle and married the chief's daughter Sweet Breeze. Wells visited Vincennes from time to time, but he preferred life among the Miami and fought under Little Turtle in the victories over Harmar and St. Clair.

In 1792, however, Wells decided to live as an American once again, probably because he wanted to raise his children in a peaceful and settled society. He soon became an interpreter for the army and tried without success to persuade the Miami to talk peace. In 1793-1794 he commanded a company of scouts for "Mad Anthony" Wayne and combined intelligence-gathering with raids against the Indian confederacy. Wells became Wayne's chief interpreter for the Greenville peace conference in the summer of 1795. The following year he escorted a number of Indian leaders including Little Turtle to Philadelphia, where they received great attention and met President Washington.

Wells and Little Turtle visited the capital again in 1797, when Wells was named deputy Indian agent for Fort Wayne. For years he worked along with Quaker missionaries to persuade the now-peaceful Miami to live as settled farmers, with little success. He tried also to protect the Miami lands from Governor Harrison's efforts to open additional territory for American settlement, a conflict beyond any hope of peaceful solution.

Little Turtle died just as the United States went to war against Britain and many of the Indians in 1812. He had argued to the last in favor of peace and against strong liquors. That year Captain Wells took about thirty friendly Miami from Fort Wayne to cover the evacuation of the threatened Fort Dearborn at Chicago. On August 15, 1812, dressed as a Miami warrior, he led the army column in a forlorn effort to reach safety. Some 500 hostile Potawatomi ambushed the Americans within a few miles of the fort, and Wells died along with thirty-eight soldiers and fourteen women and children. In tribute to his bravery the Potawatomi cut off Wells' head and paraded it on a spear point, then removed his heart and ate it to gain the dead hero's courage for themselves.

protect the town and to assist the expeditions based at Fort Washington at Cincinnati. In 1790 Brigadier General Josiah Harmar led a force of regulars and Kentucky militia to the Miami towns on the Wabash and the Maumee. Harmar destroyed several villages and took a number of women and children prisoner, but suffered such losses from the Miami, led by Little Turtle, that he was forced to resign from the army. After Harmar's defeat President George Washington determined upon another and much stronger offensive for 1791, under the command of Major General Arthur St. Clair. The army started late for its objective at the forks of the Maumee and struggled through unmapped forests until it was attacked on November 4 by Indians from many tribes. More than 900 men were killed or seriously wounded, the greatest casualties ever suffered by the U.S. Army in a battle with the Indians.

General St. Clair too was forced to resign from the army, but he retained his office as governor of the territory. President Washington found a new and more energetic commander in Anthony Wayne, called "Mad Anthony" for his daring night assault against Stony Point during the Revolutionary War. Wayne spent more than a year recruiting and training his army, and when he finally moved forward in 1793 he extended a chain of forts to support his advance. He turned back an Indian attack against Fort Recovery and shattered combined Indian forces at Fallen Timbers, near the modern Toledo, on August 20, 1794. Wayne then shifted his army up the Maumee River and built Fort Wayne upon the site of the old French Fort Miami. With this American stronghold in the midst of the Miami country, and with the British having abandoned their Indian allies in fear of American reprisal, the Indian nations of the Northwest were compelled to make peace. The Greenville treaty of 1795 forced the Indians to give up all claim to the southern half of Ohio and a narrow strip which became part of Indiana in 1803.

Until 1795 Indian wars limited migration and slowed political development, and Governor St. Clair's distrust of the ordinary citizens delayed elections for several years more. Popular demands for a territorial assembly increased, and in 1798 St. Clair finally called for an election. Knox County was entitled to one representative, who had to own at least 200 acres of land. Only adult men who owned at least fifty acres of land could vote. John Small was chosen by the men of Knox County as their representative, and he joined with the other twenty-one members of the lower house to nominate ten men for the council which acted as the upper house of the territorial assembly. Henry Vanderburgh of Vincennes was among the five appointed by President John Adams, and Vanderburgh was soon chosen president of the council. In October 1799 the assembly had its first opportunity to elect a delegate to represent the Northwest Territory in the federal House of Representatives. The candidates were Arthur St.

Clair, Jr., and William Henry Harrison, and the assembly selected Harrison over the governor's son.

William Henry Harrison, although elected president many years later as the "log cabin candidate," was descended from one of the leading families of Virginia. He was born in 1773 at the family plantation and his father Benjamin Harrison was a distinguished patriot who signed the Declaration of Independence and served as governor of Virginia. Harrison entered the army in 1791 and served on General Wayne's staff during the successful campaign against the Indians. In 1795 Harrison married Anna Symmes, daughter of John Cleves Symmes, who was both a territorial judge and a leading land speculator. With such strong political support Captain Harrison resigned from the army in 1797 and was soon appointed territorial secretary. He was a young man of considerable charm and ability, and he soon won many friends of his own beyond the circle of his father-in-law's political and speculative associates. Although territorial delegates in Congress could not vote, Harrison quickly made his mark in the new capital at Washington, and he played a major role in the passage of the Land Law of 1800. This measure reduced the minimum lot sold by the federal government from 640 acres to 320 acres, and allowed four years to complete payment, two reforms which were very popular among those who hoped to settle in the west.

In the peaceful years after 1795 the population of the eastern part of the Northwest Territory increased rapidly and there were growing demands for a division so that the more populated region could become a state. Governor St. Clair tried to keep the whole vast territory under his own rule as long as possible, but on May 7, 1800, Congress divided the Northwest Territory. A week later President John Adams named the twenty-seven-year-old William Henry Harrison as governor of the new Indiana Territory.

The lush and wild terrain of early Indiana gave way for the most part to increasing agriculture. From Parker Gilmore, Prairie Farms and Prairie Folks, *1872*

Top, right: *Henri Elouis, a native of Caen, France, painted this portrait of Anthony Wayne in 1796, the year the general died. The portrait remained in obscurity until it was rediscovered around 1910 in deplorable condition, having been painted over. After careful restoration it's been called "the most characteristic and interesting portrait of Anthony Wayne that exists." Courtesy, Indiana Historical Society*

Right: *This popular lithograph of William Henry Harrison was based on the oil painting attributed to well-known American artist Rembrandt Peale. The original portrait showed Harrison in civilian dress, but in 1813 the major general's striking uniform of blue and gold was superimposed on the canvas. Courtesy, Indiana Historical Society*

CHAPTER III

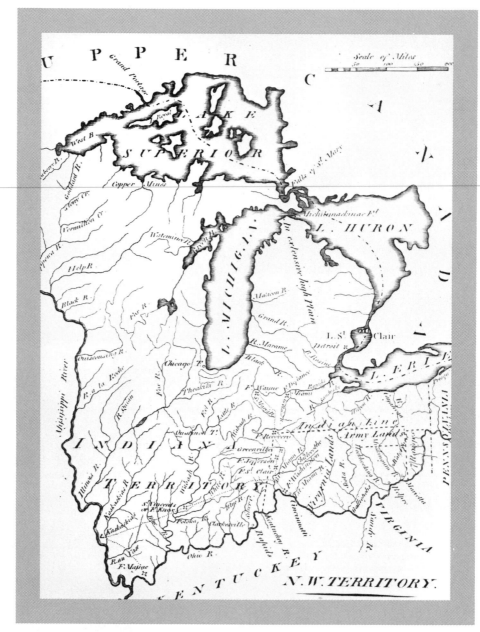

This 1801 map of the Northwest Territory was the first map to use the name "Indiana" to denote the approximate area that was later to become the state. It was published in Mathew Carey's American Pocket Atlas, *which was carried westward by many pioneers as their guide. Courtesy, Indiana Historical Society*

The Territory Becomes A State

The new Indiana Territory was a vast expanse of forest, extending from the Ohio River to Lake Superior and west to the Mississippi. There were small army posts near Vincennes, at Fort Wayne, and at Fort Michilimackinac in the far north; Detroit remained part of the Northwest Territory until Ohio became a state in 1803. Within the Indiana Territory in 1800 there were uncounted thousands of Indians of many nations but only 5,641 "civilized" persons reported by the census, including about 200 black slaves, although slavery was forbidden by the Northwest Ordinance of 1787. The largest settlement was Vincennes, with 714 residents in the town and another 819 nearby. The town boasted some 400 houses, most built of logs but a few covered with clapboards and painted. The old fort had decayed and the army had built a new Fort Knox about three miles to the north. The only road was the ancient buffalo trace to the Falls of the Ohio, over which the mail from the East arrived once a week during good weather. The French residents at Vincennes suffered from the gradual decline of the fur trade, and they mixed little with the growing number of American settlers. Second in size was Clarksville with 929 inhabitants. The southeastern gore, a triangular tract opened to settlement by the Greenville treaty of 1795, did not become part of Indiana un-

til 1803.

The second-ranking official of the territory was Secretary John Gibson, a sixty-year-old Pennsylvanian known more for his youthful captivity among the Mingo Indians than for any political achievement. The three judges, William Clark, John Griffin, and Henry Vanderburg, were undistinguished figures, untainted by the speculative and political scheming which had so troubled the Northwest Territory. Governor William Henry Harrison was the most distinguished as well as the youngest of the territorial officers, and was also the most popular. He was fair and honest, and left office in 1812 no wealthier than he had entered it twelve years earlier.

The Indiana Territory legally came into existence on July 4, 1800, but Secretary Gibson did not reach Vincennes to establish the territorial government until July 22. He soon appointed the necessary officers for Knox County, which includ- ed most of the present state of Indiana. Wayne County included most of what is now Michigan, while St. Clair County provided local government for the Illinois country. Each county had a sheriff, a treasurer, a recorder, and a court clerk, as well as a number of justices of the peace. Plural office holding was not unusual, and Gibson was both justice of the peace and recorder for Knox County as well as territorial secretary.

William Henry Harrison arrived at Vincennes just after the new year, and took his oath as governor on January 10, 1801. By virtue of his office Governor Harrison was also superintendent of Indian affairs, and he was quickly faced with complaints that unruly Americans had stolen Indian land, slaughtered game without restraint, and even murdered several Indians. Harrison learned that most of the accusations were indeed true, and that the Indians around Vincennes had been reduced to miserable conditions. Orders were issued to restrict liquor sales to the Indians, for many disputes began as drunken quarrels. Beyond this attempted safeguard, injustices against the Indians went unpunished, despite the governor's appeal for better treatment, for white juries were unwilling to convict whites accused of mistreating Indians.

Harrison purchased several hundred acres of land near Vincennes and built the finest brick mansion in the territory, naming it "Grouseland." The Harrisons and their large and growing family (eight children in Vincennes and two more later) lived well, but the governor was not a wealthy man and he did not acquire very extensive property within the territory, in sharp contrast with the vast and troubled land claims of his father-in-law Judge John Cleves Symmes in Ohio.

The Indiana Territory was too large to govern effectively, although there were only small settlements in its more remote regions—250 people at Michilimackinac, 100 at Peoria, 50 at Green Bay, and some 1,200 in and around Kaskaskia on the Mississippi. When Ohio became a state in 1803 the wedge-shaped gore was shifted to Indiana, bringing a substantial gain in population. At the same time the land north of Ohio was also transferred to Indiana, adding the 3,000 inhabitants at Detroit. The people of Michigan lived so far from Vincennes that they wanted a territorial government of their own, and early in 1805 Congress established the Michigan Territory. The residents of the Kaskaskia region soon voiced the same arguments and early in 1809 Congress created the Illinois Territory, leaving Indiana within its present boundaries except for a ten-mile adjustment in the north when it achieved statehood. As the population of the territory increased new counties were proclaimed by the governor, beginning with Clark County in the southeast in 1801, named for George Rogers Clark. A few months after the southeastern gore joined Indiana it was formed into Dearborn County, named in honor of Secretary of War Henry Dearborn. Other counties followed at frequent intervals, named usually in honor of some military hero or political figure,

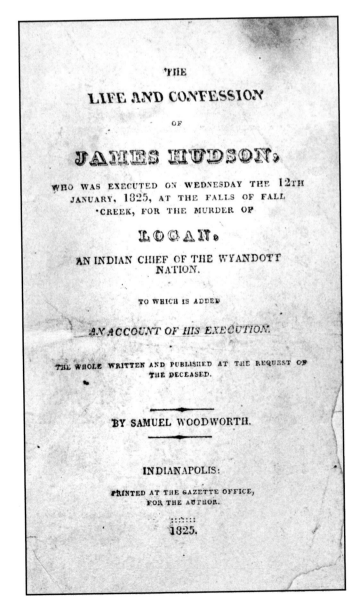

THE

LIFE AND CONFESSION

OF

JAMES HUDSON,

WHO WAS EXECUTED ON WEDNESDAY THE 12TH JANUARY, 1825, AT THE FALLS OF FALL CREEK, FOR THE MURDER OF

LOGAN,

AN INDIAN CHIEF OF THE WYANDOTT NATION.

TO WHICH IS ADDED

AN ACCOUNT OF HIS EXECUTION.

THE WHOLE WRITTEN AND PUBLISHED AT THE REQUEST OF THE DECEASED.

BY SAMUEL WOODWORTH.

INDIANAPOLIS:

PRINTED AT THE GAZETTE OFFICE, FOR THE AUTHOR.

1825.

James Hudson was one of a group of settlers who brutally murdered a band of Indians encamped near the falls of Fall Creek, Madison County, in 1824. When Hudson was executed for his crime on January 12, 1825, he became the first white man in the United States to receive capital punishment for killing an Indian. Courtesy, Indiana Historical Society

many now almost forgotten except for their names on the map.

Governor Harrison had legal discretion to inaugurate the second or elective stage of territorial government when he thought proper. Governor St. Clair had put off elections in the Northwest Territory as long as possible, but Harrison learned from his troubled example and called upon the men of Indiana to vote in September 1804 on the question of establishing a territorial assembly. Only about 400 votes were cast, but there was a modest majority in favor of an assembly and in January 1805, nine representatives were elected to establish the first general assembly for the Indiana Territory. President Jefferson allowed the governor to make his own choice of councilors for the upper house, and the new legislature elected his friend Benjamin Parke to Congress, giving Harrison a very large influence over the territorial government. The first session of the assembly reorganized the county courts, altered the tax laws, regulated fees charged by ferries, gristmills, and taverns, and prohibited sale or gifts of liquor to the Indians.

Elihu Stout came to Vincennes in 1804 to establish the *Indiana Gazette*, and its pages were soon filled with political news and controversy. Stout's printing shop burned in 1806 but he rebuilt and resumed publication as *The Western Sun*. Slavery was the question of greatest conflict.

The front page of the thirteenth issue of The Western Sun, *September 26, 1807, features the distinctive design of this early Indiana newspaper published in Vincennes. Courtesy, Indiana State Library, Newspaper Division*

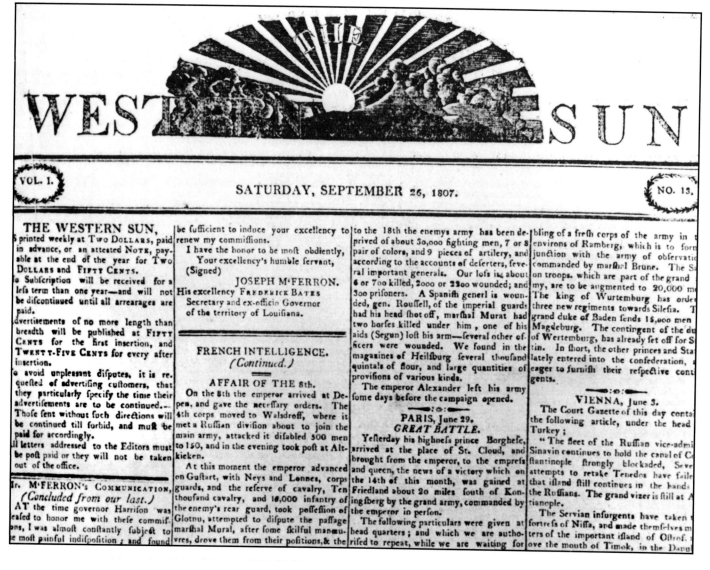

Forbidden by the Northwest Ordinance of 1787, slavery was still permitted in the territory because many prominent settlers wanted to use slave labor to clear their forest lands for farming. Governor Harrison himself owned several slaves, and he forwarded a petition to Congress asking that slavery be allowed in the territory for ten years. The petitioners also asked for more land to be opened for settlement, easier terms for purchase, and elimination of property requirements for voting. Each request was calculated to encourage settlement, for everyone except the Indians expected to benefit as the territory increased in population.

In 1805 the first session of the assembly did all it could to further slavery, permitting slaveowners to bring slaves into Indiana and hold them as indentured servants for terms as long as ninety-nine years. Children born to slave mothers would work for their masters until they reached the age of thirty for males or twenty-eight for females. About 100 indentures were registered under the law, including several by the governor, but there was already strong opposition to slavery, and Congress refused to remove the antislavery section of the Northwest Ordinance.

As superintendent of Indian affairs Harrison faced a conflict between his duty to protect the Indians from assault and cheating and his equal responsibility to persuade them to give up more and more of their land. Harrison tried to be as fair as an American frontier official of that era could be, but he was never able to stop the disruptive trade in liquor or to find a jury willing to convict a white man for a crime against an Indian. He met frequently with Indian delegations to negotiate land treaties and hear complaints.

The Wea, Piankashaw, Kickapoo, Eel River Miami, and Delaware, all living near Vincennes, had been greatly weakened by years of heavy drinking, contact with white settlers, and excessive hunting on their lands, and in 1802 they gave up their claims to a large tract near Vincennes for about $1,500 worth of presents. For a small additional payment the Miami, Shawnee, and Potawatomi gave up their opposition to the Vincennes treaty. During the summer of 1804 the Delaware

J.O. Lewis made this portrait of Potawatomi chief Sun-A-Get or "Hard Times" at the treaty of Massinnewa in 1827. Courtesy, Indiana Historical Society

and Piankashaw chiefs came to Vincennes and yielded their claims to 1,500,000 acres of southern Indiana, extending from the Wabash to Clark's Grant at the Falls of the Ohio, in return for $300 a year for ten years and farm animals and tools worth $800 to help them become settled farmers on a remnant of their old hunting grounds. President Jefferson dreamed of teaching the Indians of the Northwest to become peaceful farmers, but the poorly-funded efforts by missionaries and government agents to teach them white methods of agriculture failed dismally.

Little Turtle and William Wells were among the angry Miami and Potawatomi leaders entertained at Grouseland in 1805, where they charged that the Delaware had traded away lands they had no right to sell. Harrison was a gracious but stubborn host who eventually persuaded the northern tribes to surrender their claims to an additional 2,000,000 acres of southeastern Indiana, for the much higher price of $1,600 a year for ten years and $4,000 in presents of clothing, saddles, and rifles for the chiefs. In three years Harrison had obtained title to more than 4,500,000 acres of land in Indiana and even more in the Illinois country, all without firing a shot.

In September of 1809 Harrison called a great council at Fort Wayne to meet with some 1,400 Indians in another effort to obtain still more land for white settlement. He tried to convince them that the land was no longer rich in game and that the fur trade could bring them little profit because the long wars in Europe had disrupted commerce. The Miami leaders resisted stubbornly, but the Delaware and the Potawatomi were desperate for the rewards Harrison offered. After long and skillful negotiation Harrison persuaded the Miami to join them along with the Kickapoo and Wea and agree to the sale of 3,000,000 acres for a total cost of $10,350 in cash and gifts. The land included a strip along the "gore" and a larger tract north and east of Vincennes bounded by the "ten o'clock line," a line defined by the shadow of a stick at ten o'clock in the morning.

Many of the new settlers entered the territory with a strong dislike of slavery, particularly in the southeastern counties, and they combined with representatives from the Illinois country to work against Governor Harrison and his friends. Territorial offices were often awarded to the governor's fellow Virginians, and his opponents denounced Harrison and his wealthy and educated friends as "Virginia Aristocrats." Harrison prevented the 1808 legislature from repealing the Negro indenture law, but he was unable to halt the election of Jesse B. Thomas as congressional delegate, who pledged to secure separation of the Illinois Territory. Thomas won passage of the Illinois bill early in 1809 and also persuaded Congress to make the office of territorial delegate elective by the people

rather than the assembly. In the election Harrison favored Thomas Randolph, a Virginia friend whom he had recently appointed attorney general. Although the governor campaigned widely for Randolph, who was a very dull speaker, the young and dynamic Jonathan Jennings prevailed with a plurality of only twenty-six votes. The rejected Randolph was so angry that he challenged one of his critics to a duel, but his intended victim refused to fight and swore out a warrant against the attorney general.

William Henry Harrison remained personally popular, but he could no longer have his own way in the Indiana Territory, or put his friends into every political office. The territorial elections of 1810 confirmed the power of Harrison's opponents whose strength was among the more

Brewett, "a celebrated Miami chief," according to artist J.O. Lewis, was also present at the treaty of Massinnewa. Courtesy, Indiana Historical Society

Jonathan Jennings

This portrait of Jonathan Jennings, first governor of the state of Indiana, was painted thirty-five years after his death by James Forbes, a Scottish-born artist. It was based on a miniature painted for Jenning's fiancee around 1810, following his first year as Indiana's delegate to Congress. Courtesy, Indiana Historical Bureau, State of Indiana; Photographer: Robert Wallace, Indianapolis Museum of Art

Jonathan Jennings exemplified the new man of the frontier, working his way upward from obscure beginnings to land ownership and political prominence. Born in New Jersey, he moved with his family to western Pennsylvania and arrived in the Indiana Territory in 1807 at the age of twenty-three. He had studied the law in the office of a successful lawyer and was admitted to the bar as soon as he reached Vincennes. He worked briefly in the land office, dabbled in trade and speculated in land, trying like so many frontiersmen to find wealth. He was appointed clerk to the board of Vincennes University, and soon clashed with Governor Harrison who was president of the board of trustees. He resigned and moved to Clark County in 1808 and quickly made himself the political leader of the antislavery men in the rapidly growing settlements of southeastern Indiana. In 1809 he was elected as delegate to Congress, after an active campaign which proved his appeal to the average citizen. He was reelected regularly but made little mark in Washington, although he was always attentive to the problems of his constituents.

Jennings was the leading politician in Indiana by 1816, and he worked successfully in Congress to promote statehood. After dominating the constitutional convention he was easily chosen as the first governor of the new state. The state government, however, was not a powerful force in Indiana. Land policy was set by federal law and the people expected little from the state except a suitable court system and low taxes. Jennings was an honest and unexciting governor and he was overwhelmingly reelected in 1819 for a second three-year term. Like many of the people of Indiana he suffered financial losses in the Panic of 1819, and his salary of $1,000 did not begin to cover his expenses. Jennings was a man of the frontier, friendly, without pretense, trying always to succeed but usually finding as much trouble as profit. He achieved little as governor, but little was expected. After two terms he was ineligible for reelection as governor and so in 1822 he won election to Congress, serving in the House of Representatives for eight years. Twice he was a candidate for the Senate, but each time the legislature chose someone else. Jennings was not a strong party man, and this injured his prospects as the Jacksonian Democrats gained power.

Like so many other frontiersmen in that hard-drinking age Jennings had an increasing problem with liquor, and in 1830 he lost his seat in Congress. His last years were spent in his log house near Charlestown, entertaining his many visitors and working his farm. He died in 1834, still deep in debt, for Jonathan Jennings never found the financial success he had so long sought on the Indiana frontier.

Tenskwatawa And Tecumseh

No Indian leader in the first half of the nineteenth century had greater impact on white Americans than the Shawnee warrior Tecumseh. To white Americans he embodied the "noble savage" ideal: brave, resolute, and kind to captives but fearsome in combat. He was an enemy to be respected, even admired. Yet it was his younger brother Tenskwatawa who first distinguished himself, preaching a revival of Indian tradition that Americans could never appreciate.

Their father died in battle in 1774, and an elder brother who raised Tecumseh also fell fighting the Americans. Tecumseh fought against St. Clair and Wayne, and was a skilled hunter as well as a brave warrior. His young brother fought only one battle, often failed to find game to feed his family, and became a drunkard. But in April 1805 he fell into a trance and had a vision of the Master of Life, who revealed to him the means to restore Shawnee life to the old ways. He took a new name, Tenskwatawa or "Open Door," denounced liquor as the greatest evil destroying the Indian way of life, and preached a return to the old traditions and a rejection of the white man's tools, even returning to the bow and arrow for hunting. The Shawnee Prophet, as he was usually called by the whites, soon attracted fol-

This engraving of Tecumseh appeared in Benson Lossing's Pictorial Field Book of the War of 1812. *The cap, medallion, and uniform of a brigadier general in the British army were added to the original approximately fifty years later. Courtesy, Indiana State Library, Indiana Division*

This engraving of Tenskwatawa, known as the Shawnee Prophet, has the same origin as that of his older brother Tecumseh. They were both sketched by French trader Pierre LeDru around 1808. These drawings then served as the basis for the engravings featured in Benson Lossing's Pictorial Fieldbook of the War of 1812, *published in 1868. Courtesy, Indiana Historical Society*

lowers from as far away as Lake Superior, and vigorously opposed the Protestant missionaries among the Delaware tribe in the Whitewater valley.

When Tenskwatawa's revival failed to stop the American advance, Tecumseh's military methods and plans for a confederacy of all the northwestern tribes gained greater prominence. Tecumseh was not ready for war in 1811, but his brother sought battle at Tippecanoe in his absence, and the defeat there forever shattered the Prophet's standing as a spiri-

tual leader. He had promised victory through his magic, and the angry survivors tied him with rope and carried him away from Prophetstown. Tecumseh fought with the British and was killed in action at the Thames, his death opening the way to American expansion. Tenskwatawa lived on in Canada until the early 1820s, and then returned to the United States to help lead a band of Shawnee on the painful trek westward. The aged Prophet had lost all his influence and spent his last years in obscurity, dying in Kansas in 1836.

populated settlements at Clarksville and in the Whitewater valley. They again controlled the assembly and persuaded Congress to give the vote to any free white man who was twenty-one years of age, paid any tax at all, and had lived in the territory for one year. Jennings was easily re-elected as delegate in Congress in 1811 and his friends in the assembly showed their power by repealing the Negro indenture law.

General Anthony Wayne's victory at Fallen Timbers in 1794 had shattered the power of the Shawnee and greatly weakened the Miami and other nations of the Wabash country. But after fifteen years a new generation of Indian leaders had come of age and they inspired a renewed spirit of resistance to the advancing menace of American settlement. Governor Harrison was uncomfortably aware of the growing reputation of Tenskwatawa, a spiritual leader usually known as the Shawnee Prophet. In the spring of 1808 the Prophet moved from Ohio to the central Wabash, building "Prophetstown" near the mouth of the Tippecanoe River not far from the old French post of Ouiatanon.

In addition to the worry of a growing Indian confederacy, Harrison and most other frontiersmen were convinced that the British, who were seizing American ships and seamen on the Atlantic Ocean, were also arming and encouraging the Indians of the Northwest. By 1809 there was widespread talk of a new Indian war, and the governor strengthened the long-neglected militia while also conferring with the Prophet at Vincennes to talk of peace. The following year his warrior brother Tecumseh came to the capital for a council, meeting with the governor on the lawn of Grouseland to talk of a peaceful settlement which both men knew to be impossible.

Reports increased of attacks against isolated settlers and in June 1811 Harrison sent a message to Tecumseh accusing him of plotting war against the United States and warning that he would have to face "swarms of hunting-shirt men as numerous as the mosquitoes on the shores of the Wabash." Tecumseh came to Vincennes in July, accompanied by some 300 warriors, and Harrison paraded 700 militia to intimidate the Indians. Both Harrison and Tecumseh talked of peace, but they accomplished nothing.

Governor Harrison was now convinced that the time for forceful action had arrived, but the administration in Washington hesitated. On September 19 the regulars of the Fourth Infantry reached Vincennes, giving Harrison enough troops to venture into the forests with some prospects of success. He marched from Vincennes on September 26, with 345 regulars and 415 Indiana militia, supported by 200 mounted militia and some volunteers from Kentucky. After a march of sixty-five miles the army halted for a month at the high ground the French had known as Terre Haute to build Fort Harrison. Finally authorized by the War Department to advance on Prophetstown and "disperse" the Indians gathered there, Harrison led his troops north from Fort Harrison on October 29. He reached Prophetstown on November 6, and rejecting the advice of his officers to attack immediately, agreed instead to attend a council fire the next morning.

The army made its camp within a mile of the Indians, along the banks of a creek three miles from the mouth of Tippecanoe River. The men were cold, wet, and miserable, and the army's axes were so dull it was difficult to cut enough firewood to warm them through a rainy night.

With Tecumseh away recruiting south of the Ohio, the Prophet promised that his magic would make the American gunpowder like sand and their bullets as soft as raindrops. The inspired Indians attacked before dawn, trying to fight their way into the camp against resistance that was often hand-to-hand combat. Harrison organized the defense, rushed reinforcements to the most threatened points and encouraged his troops at great risk to himself. His horse was shot through the neck and a bullet passed through the brim of his hat, but he was untouched. As soon as there was light enough to see clearly Harrison ordered a counterattack which pushed the Indians away from the camp and into a hurried retreat. The Americans were in no condition to pursue, for the battle of Tippecanoe was costly, although less

Left: *This Currier lithograph of General Harrison at the Battle of Tippecanoe is captioned "Upon one occasion as he (Gen'l Harrison) was approaching an angle of the line, against which the Indians were advancing with horrible yells, Lieut. Emmerson seized the Bridle of his Horse, and earnestly entreated that he would not go there ... but the Governor putting spurs to his Horse, pushed on to the point of attack, where the enemy was received with firmness and driven back."*

Facing page: *Kurtz & Allison of Chicago published this inaccurate and romanticized view of the Battle of Tippecanoe in 1889. Its image of the battle mirrors the nation's view of the victory and the victorious General William Henry Harrison. Courtesy, Indiana State Library*

than two hours long. Fifty-one men were killed and 150 wounded. As many as 700 warriors from eight tribes had assaulted Harrison's camp, and they too suffered heavy losses. Only three of the American dead had been scalped, but the Kentucky volunteers in particular took many Indian scalps at leisure as soon as the fighting ended.

The Americans entered Prophetstown the next day, took away as much food as they could carry, and burned everything they left. A number of new British rifles were found, as well as a supply of high-quality gunpowder, evidence enough for frontiersmen that the stories about the British authorities in Canada encouraging the Indians were

indeed true. Harrison's victorious army returned to Vincennes to a welcome much subdued by the heavy casualties suffered at the battle of Tippecanoe. There were arguments between regular and militia officers about who deserved the greatest credit for the victory, as well as vicious political attacks against Governor Harrison for the way he had fought the campaign.

Success at Tippecanoe did not bring peace to the Indiana frontier, and attacks against settlers came as close as seven miles to Vincennes. The governor sent Mrs. Harrison and their eight children, ranging in age from fifteen years to seven months, to safety in Cincinnati. When Congress

declared war against Great Britain on June 18, 1812, the army was unprepared and the war began badly for them along the northwestern frontier, with the massacre at Fort Dearborn in July and the loss of Detroit in August. In September the Scott County village of Pigeon Roost was destroyed, and its twenty-four residents killed. While the federal government delayed, Harrison was appointed major general in command of the Kentucky militia, an extraordinary tribute to his popularity in the West. General Harrison acted quickly despite his questionable authority north of the Ohio and marched to reinforce the threatened outpost of Fort Wayne. He arrived in time to drive away Indians who had besieged the fort for four days, and sent detachments to raid the Miami villages on the upper Wabash and the Potawatomi settlements on the Elkhart River. Late in

September Harrison was placed in full command of the northwestern army, with orders to protect the frontier against the British and their Indian allies, to recapture Detroit as soon as possible, and then to invade Canada.

There was little more fighting within the Indiana Territory, except for Captain Zachary Taylor's brave defense of Fort Harrison with a handful of regulars against a large Indian force in September. Indiana militiamen patrolled the frontier and escorted supply convoys, and some of them fought with Harrison in Michigan and later in Canada. During the fall and winter of 1812-1813 General Harrison was chiefly concerned with gathering sufficient supplies—there were shortages of weapons, clothing, equipment, and of course food. With all of his military activity the governor had no time for his civilian duties, and he resolved the conflict on December 28 by resigning as governor.

New forts were built to shelter the army in northern Ohio. Harrison, like "Mad Anthony" Wayne before him, waited until he was fully prepared, beat off enemy attacks, and then recaptured Detroit in September 1813. Advancing into Canada in pursuit of the British and Indian forces, General Harrison brought them to battle on the banks of the Thames River (near the modern London, Ontario) on October 5. There he won a decisive victory, defeating the British and shattering forever the Indian resistance in the Northwest. Tecumseh and Harrison fought one another directly for the first time since Fallen Timbers in 1794, and Tecumseh, the greatest leader of Indian resistance against the westward movement of American settlers, was killed in action.

Harrison and Governor Lewis Cass of the Michigan Territory met the leaders of the northwestern tribes in July 1814, and made peace on terms which were devastating for the Indians. The chiefs of the Chippewa, Ottawa, Potawatomi, Wyandot, Delaware, Seneca, Shawnee, and Miami all made their marks on the final treaty of peace in September 1815 at Spring Wells near Detroit, while Harrison signed for the United States. The war with Britain had ended months earlier, and

This building in Corydon, Harrison County, was used by the new state government of Indiana as the capitol from 1816 until 1825, when Indianapolis became the new state seat. Built of native blue limestone, the structure was restored in 1929, a few years before this photo was taken. It is now operated as a museum by the state of Indiana. Courtesy, Indiana State Library, Indiana Division

now there was nothing to impede the thousands of Americans who hoped to find land and opportunity in the West.

A majority of the territorial assembly asked Congress for permission to organize a state government in December 1811, but the limited population and the turmoil of war, together with a grave shortage of money, put off all hopes for statehood until peace was restored. John Gibson served as acting governor when Harrison went to command the army, and he faced impossible problems. When he addressed the legislature in February 1813, Gibson warned that "Our former frontiers are now wilds and our inner settlements have become frontiers."

Tax collections were very difficult because of the war, and the territorial treasury contained only $2.47. Taxes were increased to two dollars on each black slave or servant and thirty-seven and a half cents for each horse, but the land tax was reduced to seventy-five cents for each hundred acres of first-rate land, while second- and third-rate land paid fifty and twenty-five cents for each hundred acres. The highest tax was an impossible fifty dollars for each billiard table.

After much argument the territorial capital was moved from Vincennes, on the western edge of the territory since the splitting off of Illinois, to the more centrally located Corydon, a small settlement not far west of Clarksville. Harrison and his friends had dominated life at Vincennes, but the new capital was located in a region inhabited by small landowners who opposed slavery. A new governor, Thomas Posey, arrived in April 1813, and established the government at Corydon. When the war ended General Harrison settled at North Bend, Ohio, just west of Cincinnati, and played no further part in the affairs of the Indiana Territory.

There was no significant opposition to statehood, and with the Indian menace removed settlers now rushed westward. The federal census of 1810 showed a population of 24,520, including 237 slaves, but the 1815 territorial census showed 63,897 inhabitants in Indiana's thirteen counties. Only Governor Posey resisted statehood, and that was part of his effort to secure reappointment as

Entitled Emigration Toward the West, *this engraving from an early nineteenth-century European book about the United States is representative of the way hundreds of new settlers traveled to Indiana. Note the prominence of farming tools in the central horse-drawn cart. Courtesy, Indiana Historical Society*

Frank M. Hohenberger took this photograph of the celebrated constitutional elm in Corydon around 1915. The state's constitution had been written under its boughs when the convention met in its shade to escape the heat. The tree was then fifty feet tall with a five-foot diameter and 132-foot spread. Ten years later, the tree had died, its limbs were removed, and a huge sandstone memorial was erected over the trunk by the state of Indiana. Courtesy, Indiana State Library, Indiana Division

territorial governor for another three years. In Congress Jonathan Jennings had little difficulty in winning passage of an enabling act, including a provision extending the boundary of Indiana ten miles northward to give the new state its own access to Lake Michigan. Statehood now came with a rush.

President Madison signed the enabling act on April 19, 1816, and the news reached Vincennes on May 2. Notice for the election of the constitutional convention appeared in *The Western Sun* on May 4, only nine days before the men of the territory were to vote for delegates. Political opponents accused Jennings of rushing the election so that only his friends would be prepared in time, but most of the voters seem to have been ready enough and the possibility of statehood had been discussed for months. Jennings was elected president of the convention at Corydon on June 10 and the constitution was written almost entirely by his supporters. John Baddolet of Vincennes, one of the minority of Harrison men at the convention, noted that there were "several thinking men" among the delegates, but most of them he regarded as "empty babblers, democratic to madness, having incessantly the *people* in their mouths and their dear selves in their eyes." This was a harsh political view of the generally competent Jennings faction led by James Noble, a lawyer, legislator, and veteran militia officer. The Jennings faction overwhelmed Benjamin Parke of Vincennes, the former delegate to Congress, and the remnants of the old Harrison "aristocrats."

The convention quickly compiled a suitable constitution for the new state by borrowing from the older states, particularly Kentucky and Ohio. Only 21 of the 129 sections in the constitution were newly written at Corydon, with ten other federal and state documents providing ample material to copy. The Indiana Constitution of 1816 was a typical example of northern frontier democracy. Slavery was strictly forbidden, but only white men were permitted to vote or to serve in the militia. All adult white males were allowed to vote, and there were no property requirements

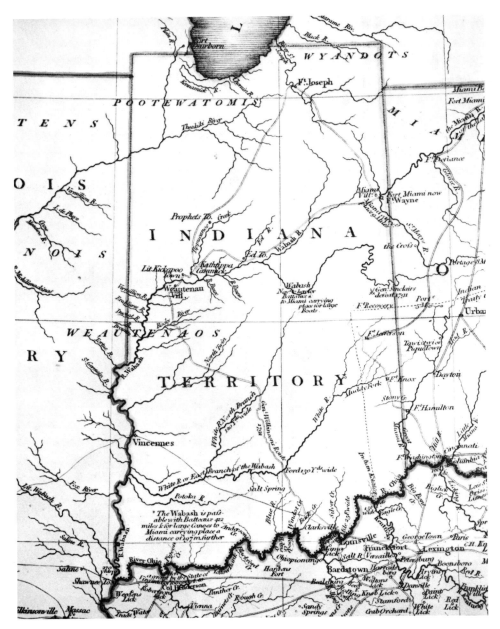

Nearly three years after Indiana gained its statehood, London mapmaker John Carey published a new map of the United States with Indiana as a territory. The dotted line along the eastern boundary from Fort Recovery south to the Ohio River approximates the Indian boundary line established by the Greenville treaty of 1795. According to this representation of the Lake Michigan shoreline, most of present-day Chicago would be in Indiana. Courtesy, Indiana State Library, Indiana Division

for voting or holding office. There was an idealistic provision for free public education from the elementary level through a state university, but there was no provision for tax funds and Indiana's schools always lacked money. The constitution was very much the work of the small landowners who opposed special privilege or claims of aristocracy.

The small farmers had taken control of the territorial legislature and now they created the state government. As John D. Barnhart described their work, this constitution "contained the ideals of the frontier." It was not expected to solve the problems of the poor, for these frontiersmen were confident that they could succeed without govern-

ment help. What they sought was freedom and opportunity, cheap land, and the chance to succeed on their own. They did not think it necessary to ask the people to ratify the constitution.

The first election of state officers was set only five weeks after the constitution was adopted on June 29, but that was time enough for a vigorous campaign. Jonathan Jennings received 5,211 votes, easily defeating Thomas Posey with 3,934. The first state general assembly convened at Corydon on November 4, 1816, and Governor Jennings was sworn into office three days later. President James Madison signed the joint resolution formally admitting Indiana on December 11, making it the nineteenth state of the Union.

CHAPTER IV

*The hardships of pioneer life are soft-
ened in this Currier & Ives lithograph of
a cozy homestead titled* A Home in the
Wilderness.

Forests To Farms, Trails To Rails

Men and women emigrated to Indiana for a variety of reasons, but the rich land itself was their most cherished goal. Men outnumbered women among the pioneer residents of Indiana, but not overwhelmingly. This was a frontier for families, particularly young families who hoped to grow up with the new state. The work of clearing the land was slow and painful, and a family of modest capital could manage through hard work and with reasonably good fortune to obtain food, shelter, clothing and eventually some of the comforts of life.

Although the legendary American pioneer was typically a farmer who came west with his wife and a milk cow and made his cabin, furniture, and farm implements with only an ax and a knife as his tools, there were also pioneers with no desire to face the backbreaking drudgery of agriculture. They came with a variety of ambitions, some hoping for easy wealth as land speculators and town promoters, others to ply their trades as millers, blacksmiths, or storekeepers. Young lawyers hoped for government appointment or dreamed of becoming brilliant orators or perhaps successful politicians. For everyone the frontier represented a hope for the future, and for some it was also an escape from demanding parents, unhappy marriages, eager creditors, or the sheriff.

Calvin Fletcher was a prominent early settler of Indianapolis. His diaries, now published, have provided important historical insight into the life of the frontier community. This portrait of him was taken in 1860. Courtesy, Indiana Historical Society

The frontier was largely a man's world in which women lived and worked and suffered, generally as part of a family. A boy of seventeen could move west on his own, but for a woman without a husband or protective relatives the frontier was a hostile land. A widow could operate her husband's farm or business without fear of gossip, but for a woman who appeared to be alone by choice there were few respectable opportunities.

There were just under 25,000 residents of Indiana in 1810, but ten years later the census showed a population of 147,000, an increase of 488 percent. The growing number of young families soon produced large numbers of children. During the 1820s the population of Indiana doubled, and during the 1830s it doubled again, reaching a total of 686,000 in 1840. The growth rate declined from these pioneer levels during the 1840s, but by 1850 the state had almost a million residents. Although there were many towns scattered across Indiana by mid-century, only a few of them were large enough to be called cities. Ninety-five percent of the total population lived in the country or in small towns. New Albany was the largest city with 8,181 residents, followed closely by Madison and Indianapolis which had just over 8,000 residents each. The greatest concentration of population was in the

Ohio River towns, but they reached the peak of their influence and prosperity during the early 1850s. By the time of the Civil War Indianapolis had emerged as the largest city in the state.

The constitution provided that the state capital remain in Corydon until 1825, but Corydon was so hard to reach and so far south that a new location was necessary. The New Purchase treaty of 1818 opened much of central Indiana for settlement, and two years later the legislature decided to locate the new capital, called Indianapolis, in the middle of the state, where Fall Creek flowed into the White River. The site was still wilderness, but the city plan provided for an ample population with a mile-square design, featuring wide streets at right angles, a circle in the center, and four diagonal avenues extending to the corners of the city. The governor's mansion was built in the circle, and large lots were set aside for the state capitol, the county courthouse, and the city market. State offices were moved to Indianapolis in 1825, but for years the "city" was a scene of vast open spaces and few dwellings. Despite its slow

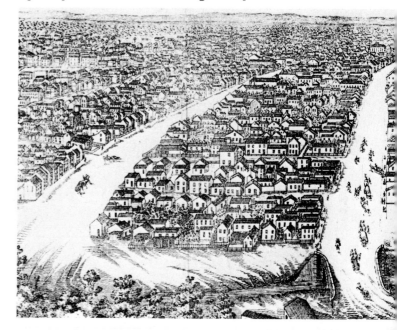

Artist C.M. Sonen's woodblock prints, done in the early 1930s under a Public Works of Art project, often captured landmarks now lost. The Old Ferry House near Vevay in Switzerland County, which was built between 1813 and 1826 by John David Dufour, marked a well-known Ohio River crossing point. The building was destroyed by fire in 1974. Courtesy, Indiana State Library, Indiana Division

Left, below: *This lithograph of the thriving town of New Albany boasts wide, smooth roads and a busy harbor. Courtesy, Amon Carter Museum, Fort Worth*

beginning Indianapolis was well located, and railroads and highways made it the state's leading transportation center. Early hopes for navigation on the shallow White River were disappointed and only one steamboat ever reached Indianapolis—and the *General Hannah* became stuck on a sandbar on her return voyage. The governor's mansion on the circle was the first major public building, but the builder forgot to include a kitchen, and the location was so public that no governor ever lived there.

Most of the people coming to make their homes in Indiana in the early years crossed the Ohio River from Kentucky and moved generally northward. Some had lived for a time in Kentucky and failed to secure firm title to land there,

PLAT
OF THE TOWN
OF
INDIANAPOLIS.

Engraved & Published by H. Platt, Columbus, Ohio, Dec.r 1821.

Notes.
Washington Street is 120 feet wide.
Circle — 80
North & South Carolina Streets are 60.
Alleys are 30 & 15 feet wide.
Regular lots abut on 30 feet alleys in
general, and have 67½ feet front by
195 feet depth, contain ¼ acre.
Irregular lots generally contain acre.

Notes.
The shaded squares No.s 12, 19 & 90,
are reserved for religious purposes.
Every lot numbered 1, 5 & 9, are reserved for some future sale.
Squares 45, 46, 55, 56, are called, together, "Governors Square."
White River is ½ a mile west of the west
line of the town.

This original plat of the city of Indianapolis was drawn in 1821. Virginia Avenue is the only street of the four diagonals that currently conforms to the original plan. In recent years, the other three diagonals have been truncated by new buildings built over their rights-of-way in the heart of the downtown area. Courtesy, Indiana State Library, Indiana Division

Facing page: New York architects Ithiel Town and A.J. Davis submitted this rendering of the new state capitol building in Indianapolis in 1834. The capitol was completed in December 1835. In 1877 it was demolished when construction of the present capitol was begun. Courtesy, Indiana State Library, Indiana Division

but many others simply passed through on their journey from backcountry Virginia or North Carolina. A lesser stream of immigrants came down the Ohio from Pittsburgh, some originating in Maryland or Virginia, others from Pennsylvania.

In the early 1830s when settlement increased in the northern part of the state, a new stream of population moving almost directly westward entered Indiana from Ohio, bringing people of different habits and ideas from Pennsylvania, New York, and southern New England. Ever since, the state has been divided by a cultural and political "line" which is located somewhere north of Kokomo, distinguishing the Yankees of the northern region from the larger regions of central and southern Indiana populated originally by people of upland southern origin. Politically this is known as the "spending line," and the people of northern Indiana have long been convinced that the state government spends more money on projects south of the line, although taxes are just as high in the north.

The early settlers of Indiana appeared to cultured visitors to be rough and crude. They dressed in deerskin or homespun fabric, in garments of no visible style. Their language was often embellished with profanity and they were fond of telling tall tales to credulous visitors. English visitors often noticed the widespread male habit of chewing tobacco and spitting the juice in every direction, while some farm women were fond of a pipe after the day's work.

Contrary to pious legends the pioneers were not particularly religious, and circuit-riding Methodists such as Peter Cartwright traveled many weary miles on horseback to preach for even a small group of worshipers. Next to the Methodists the Baptists were probably most numerous, but they were never as well organized. Many Quakers lived quietly in the Whitewater valley, but they did not actively seek converts. Catholic priests, often of French birth, continued their missionary work from Vincennes, which became the home of the first bishop of Indiana in 1834.

As soon as possible the pioneer clergymen would build a crude log church, and as circumstances permitted these were replaced by structures of increasing size and elegance. The clergy also struggled to raise money for colleges to teach the faith as well as traditional classical learning, and even at the tiny school at Bloomington which carried the imposing name of Indiana University, the presidents and, until after the Civil War, many

of the professors, were Presbyterian clergymen.

The Presbyterians established Hanover College in a log house in 1827, with the Reverend John Finley Crowe as the entire faculty. Wabash College at Crawfordsville opened in 1833 under strong Presbyterian influence. Methodists who feared the Presbyterian ascendancy established their own college at Greencastle in 1837. Named Asbury University after the pioneer bishop Francis Asbury, and later known as DePauw University, it was the most successful of the early colleges in Indiana. The Baptists opened Franklin College also in 1837, but it did not offer a degree program for many years. The pioneer Catholic college was the University of Notre Dame, which opened a few miles from South Bend in 1842, but it long remained small and obscure.

The most extraordinary pioneers in Indiana came not as individuals or families but in the religious community led by George Rapp. The Harmonists, sometimes called Rappites, had moved from Germany to Pennsylvania seeking religious freedom, and they came to Indiana in 1815 to es-

What Is A "Hoosier"?

Residents of Indiana have been referred to as "Hoosiers" since about 1830, but they have never agreed on the origin of this mysterious word. It first appeared in print in the *Indianapolis Journal* on January 1, 1833, in a poem by John Finley of Richmond:

I'm told, in riding somewhere West
A stranger found a Hoosier's nest —
In other words, a Buckeye cabin,
....
One side was lined with divers garments,
The other spread with skins of "varmints";
Dried pumpkins overhead were strung,
Where venison hams in Plenty hung;
Two rifles placed above the door;
Three dogs lay stretched upon the floor —
In short, the domicile was rife
With specimens of Hoosier life.

But what does "Hoosier" really mean? Originally it apparently signified rough country people, and only later was it applied to polite and educated city dwellers. One popular derivation is the pioneer's cry of "who's here?" as he

The derivation of the term "Hoosier" is subject to many interpretations, but it has been used commonly since the 1830s. "Good Old Hoosier Beer" was manufactured in South Bend, but it is a thing of the past. Courtesy, Discovery Hall Museum, South Bend

approached a cabin, an explanation popular by the late 1840s. Some say it is a corruption of "Hussar," a European cavalryman known for his boastfulness, a term which came to Indiana with Colonel Lehmanowski, a Polish veteran of the Napoleonic wars. Others trace Hoosier to "husher," a term describing men of great strength who would "hush" their rivals, but some who favor this version say that "husher" simply meant a bully, and was used to describe Indiana riverboat men.

Another story tells of a Louisville baker named Hoosier whose sweets were preferred by customers from the Indiana side of the river. Another learned version traces the word to "hoose," an English dialect term for a disease

in calves which caused a wild, staring look which reminded someone of the rough Indiana frontiersmen.

Supposedly one Samuel Hoosier was a contractor on the canal at Louisville who preferred hardworking men from Indiana who came to be called "Hoosier's men" and then simply "Hoosiers." Others prefer "hoozer" which means hill or people living in the hills in the Cumberland dialect of the north of England, but very few from that region ever migrated to America. James Whitcomb Riley invented the most interesting derivation, tracing "Hoosier" to the question asked by a stranger who came upon a brutal brawl in southern Indiana. Noticing a torn piece of flesh on the ground, the visitor asked "Whose ear?" Whatever the true source of the word, a mystery which Hoosiers will never solve, the people of Indiana have for a century and a half called themselves Hoosiers.

tablish a new community on the banks of the lower Wabash where they would have ample land to farm and build their own town called Harmonie. Father Rapp taught a doctrine of communal living, common property, celibacy, hard work, cheerful song, and the confidence that Christ would soon return to establish the millennium, a thousand-year period of peace and plenty on the earth. Rapp preached love above all, and the symbol of the Harmonie community was the Golden Rose which he carved in wood over the door of the church. The Rappites worked hard, wasted nothing, and within five years Harmonie was described as the most prosperous town in Indiana. The Rappites spoke German and had little contact with their neighbors. They were often disliked, both because they were different and because they were so successful as farmers, builders, and traders. Where other newcomers built only with logs the Rappites built with brick as well as carefully shaped logs, and many of their buildings still stand.

Harmonie was such a success in worldly terms that Father Rapp became concerned that there was not enough work to keep his people fully occupied, and he decided to return to Pennsylvania where there was greater opportunity for an industrial community. His adopted son Frederick Rapp acted as business agent for Harmonie, and his last assignment was to sell the entire town along with its 30,000 acres of land. He found a buyer, for the price of $150,000, far less than the value of the property. The buyer, Robert Owen, wanted a place to undertake his own vision of the ideal community, one which looked to human reason and science rather than toward heaven. He renamed the town New Harmony and in 1825 Owen attempted one of the most remarkable social experiments in America.

Owen believed that early education was essential for happiness and success, and so the first kindergarten in America appeared in New Harmony. He believed that in a true community labor would become a pleasure and that no one would have to work more than a few hours a day. Owen also believed in complete religious tolerance, rights for women, the elimination of private property, and larger associations in place of the traditional family. Blacks were excluded, however, except as servants. New Harmony attracted a remarkable group of talented people; among them William Maclure, geologist and educator, Thomas Say, the nation's most distinguished zoologist; Charles Lesueur, biologist and artist; Joseph Neef, educator; and Frances Wright, the controversial feminist and socialist.

Unfortunately the eccentric came along with the enlightened, all seeking to share Owen's dream of "Universal Happiness through Universal Education." Owen asked more than human nature could give, and within two years his glorious dream gave way to quarreling factions. Some of the brilliant people who had come to share Owen's vision remained in New Harmony, along with a tradition of free inquiry, scientific research, and education for all from kindergarten through the Workingmen's Institute and Library for adults.

Because it was the desire for land which inspired most of those who moved to the Indiana frontier, federal land policy was a matter of vital concern. In the Land Ordinance of 1785 Congress had established the basic principles of land management for the Northwest. In order to avoid the tangled disputes of the Virginia system of indiscriminate land grants and subsequent private surveys, Congress required an advance survey on a regular pattern. The land would be carefully mapped and the survey lines would be marked on the ground before lots were offered for sale. The territory would be divided into "townships" six miles square and each township would be further divided into thirty-six "sections," each one mile square. Townships were to be numbered in a regular pattern north and south from designated "base lines" and east and west from specified "principal meridians," while sections would be numbered within each township. In this way each section could easily be marked on a map and also found staked out on the ground. The success of the survey system is plainly visible today to anyone who flies over central Indiana on a clear day.

Originally the minimum lot size was one section

The Owen Family

Robert Dale Owen came to New Harmony with his father and later claimed a reputation in his own right as philosopher and social reformer. This portrait of him is attributed to his brother, David Dale Owen. Courtesy, Workingmen's Institute Library, New Harmony

Robert Owen spent only a few of his eighty-seven years in Indiana, but his utopian community at New Harmony had a wide ranging influence in education and science particularly. In addition, three of his sons played major roles in Indiana for many years after their father returned to Great Britain. Robert Owen was born in Wales in 1771 in modest circumstances, and made his reputation and his fortune in the textile business in England. He tried to put his reform principles into practice when he purchased the New Lanark cotton mill in Scotland, where he paid higher wages, provided improved housing for his workers and schools for their children, and still earned excellent profits. Owen won both wealth and fame, but despite all his efforts he could not put into practice his system of educational, economic, and non-religious views. He purchased New Harmony to give himself scope for a full-scale experiment of his ideal community, an enterprise which absorbed most of his money but only part of his energy. Owen traveled widely, and spoke and published at every opportunity, always seeking to make a better world, always without success.

Three of Owen's sons, all with the middle name of Dale in honor of their mother's family, inherited much of his enthusiasm tempered with greater practicality. Robert Dale Owen came to New Harmony and worked as a teacher and editor of the *New Harmony Gazette.* After the paper's failure he traveled for a time with Frances Wright, the famed women's rights advocate, but returned to New Harmony and served several terms in the state legislature and two in Congress, where he played an important part in the establishment of the Smithsonian Institution and its science programs. As a legislator and then as a member of the Constitutional Convention of 1850-1851 Robert Dale Owen advocated property rights for married women and more liberal divorce laws.

David Dale Owen reached New Harmony just as his father was leaving, but he remained to study geology with William Maclure and later took a degree in medicine at Cincinnati. In 1837 David Dale Owen became the first state geologist, although he soon left to work for the federal government in geological surveys west of the Mississippi. He was a skilled artist and before his early death in 1860 also served as state geologist in Arkansas, Kentucky, and again in Indiana.

Richard Dale Owen, the youngest brother, studied geology with David and did much of the Indiana field work for him. During the Civil War he commanded the Sixtieth Indiana Infantry through the western campaigns and returned to become professor of natural sciences at Indiana University. He served briefly as president of Purdue University before it opened, but gave up the position because he did not enjoy administrative work.

In recent years a combination of state and private funding has restored much of New Harmony. Jane Blaffer Owen, who married into the Owen family, has used her Texas oil fortune to revive much of historic New Harmony and to make the town attractive for visitors.

New Harmony in the late 1820s attracted notable individualists like Frances Wright, an early advocate of women's rights. A leader in the "free thought" movement, she and Robert Dale Owen coedited The Free Enquirer, a journal published in New York in the 1830s. In this engraving from a sketch made by her French friend Andre Hervieu, she is seen at age thirty-two, when she lived in New Harmony. Courtesy, Indiana State Library, Indiana Division

Left: *This circa 1855 engraving of the village of New Harmony was among many American landscapes included in a book titled* The United States Illustrated, *published in 1869 for European readership. Courtesy, Indiana Historical Society*

Below: *Frenchman Charles-Alexandre Lesueur lived in the house on the right while an intermittent resident of New Harmony. A natural scientist and a gifted draftsman, he made many study tours of the Ohio and Mississippi river valley areas between 1825 and 1837. He is perhaps best known today for his sketches of life on the midwestern American frontier. Courtesy, Indiana Historical Society*

or 640 acres, and the minimum price was one dollar an acre in cash. This was both too large and too expensive for pioneer farmers, and the entire system was loudly criticized by westerners. The Land Law of 1796 raised the basic price to two dollars an acre but extended payment to a year, still keeping government land beyond the reach of the pioneer. When William Henry Harrison was elected as the territorial delegate to Congress he gave full voice to the frontier demands for a more generous federal land policy, and the Harrison Land Law of 1800 marked the beginning of a significant change in federal land sale methods. The minimum purchase was reduced to 320 acres and four years were allowed to complete payment. In 1804 the minimum purchase was cut to 160 acres. This put enough land for a farm within the reach of the average citizen, for almost anyone with energy and ambition could hope to earn the down payment of eighty dollars.

Land offices opened at Vincennes in 1804 and at Jeffersonville three years later, making purchases more convenient for the new settlers in southern Indiana. Existing claims of the settlers near Vincennes and in the Clark grant at the Falls of the Ohio were settled by special legislation and separate surveys. The result can still be seen in the diagonal survey patterns in Knox and Clark counties. When new tracts of land became available the land offices were usually crowded with eager buyers, all hoping to acquire some favored piece of land at the minimum price. Although the law called for lots to be auctioned, secret arrangements and strong public opinion kept most sales at the minimum price of two dollars an acre. Land sales in the Northwest boomed under the 1800 law, and "doing a land office business" became part of the American language.

New land offices were opened as settlement spread northward during the peaceful years after 1815. The land offices enjoyed a steady stream of customers, and for a while there seemed to be no end to prosperity and expansion. The first setback came with the financial panic of 1819, when many pioneer farmers were unable to pay their debts to the government. Congress responded with the Land Law of 1820 which provided relief for those who could not pay and eliminated the troublesome credit system. The basic price was reduced to $1.25 an acre and the minimum lot to eighty acres, ample land to support a farm family in modest comfort.

For $100 cash a settler could buy a farm, free and clear of debt although most likely covered by thick forest. What seems cheap in modern terms was still beyond the means of some, and "squatters" simply occupied land without benefit of legal title. Shrewd purchasers tried to locate land partly cleared by squatters and buy it for themselves to take advantage of the improvements, while squatters replied with accusations that poor struggling pioneers were losing their land to the greedy rich. In political terms squatting became a demand for "preemption," a legal right to purchase illegally settled land at the minimum price whenever it was eventually offered for sale.

From 1834 to 1836 land sales boomed throughout the West, and the remaining public land in Indiana rapidly passed into private ownership, almost invariably in exchange for paper currency of doubtful value. The Fort Wayne land office had its best year in 1836, with sales reaching 1,300,000 acres. Disaster came in 1837 when the treasury announced that only gold and silver would be accepted at the land offices. The Panic of 1837 led to a prolonged depression but most of the land in Indiana had already been sold.

The public land system represented both a Jeffersonian ideal for a nation made up of small farmers securely established on their own land, and an opportunity for rich speculators and the politically favored to play the real estate market on a grand scale. Corruption and fraud were all too common, but there was land enough for every American citizen or European immigrant with white skin. Blacks and Indians were not included in the dream, although a few blacks did buy land in Indiana, and Indians formed their reserves until they were expelled.

Frontier Americans were sometimes fascinated by the Indians and they often traded with them, but they all wanted the government to move

Most of Indiana was covered by deciduous hardwood forests before 1800. In the early nineteenth century, pioneers cleared countless thousands of acres of trees to prepare the land for farming. In this early engraving published in a foreign publication about the United States, the foreground figures toil at felling trees and hauling away the trunks. Courtesy, Indiana Historical Society

them to some distant region. The original residents of Indiana offered no armed resistance to the advance of American settlers after 1815, but they tried in every peaceful way to keep some small portion of their ancestral lands. In 1830 President Andrew Jackson signed the Indian Removal Act and the federal government began the harsh task of moving the Indians to western lands which Americans then regarded as worthless desert. Several small bands of Potawatomi were persuaded or bribed into leaving peacefully for Kansas. The largest movement was the forced march under army escort by Menominee's band from Marshall County in 1838, on what was truly called the "Trail of Death." The Miami signed away their final reserve along the Wabash in 1840 and moved peacefully to Kansas six years later. Kokomo, according to tradition named for a Miami chief, was settled in 1844 in the midst of what had been the last Miami homeland in the state. Today only the Indian names on the landscape endure as reminders of their earlier presence in the state named for an exiled people.

The Indiana pioneer farmer selected land according to a variety of folk principles, judging fertility and healthful locations as best he could.

Once he had chosen his land and purchased it from the land office, or perhaps squatted illegally, he and his family faced years of hard work to turn the dense forest into farmland. Only in the 1830s did settlers in Elkhart, St. Joseph, and La Porte counties reach the rich open grassland of the scattered prairie openings.

The first requirement for a pioneer farm was a temporary shelter, at times a lean-to or a "half-faced camp" open to the weather on one side. Large trees were killed by "girdling," cutting a notch into the bark all around the trunk. Once the first small crop was planted it was time to build a cabin, using forty or fifty of the best logs nearby. If there were other families in the vicinity they might join to celebrate a "cabin raising" and build the cabin in a day or two with the help of perhaps a dozen men. The crude pioneer cabin was often enlarged and improved over the years, or else replaced with a log house built with carefully squared timbers which were often covered with clapboards.

Corn was the basic crop, but settlers usually planted potatoes, beans, cabbage, onions, peas, flax, and lettuce as well. As more land was cleared small grains such as wheat, oats, and rye were planted. Meat came from the wild game in the woods and from the tough razorback hogs which the pioneers often allowed to roam wild to eat whatever they could find until "hog killing time"

after the first frost in the fall. Fences had to be built to keep the livestock away from the crops, and boys spent their days splitting rails from logs too small to be of any other use. Boys also helped cut and haul firewood, a never-ending task. A farmer with the help of two or three sons and perhaps a hired hand might be able to clear four or five acres a year, so that clearing an entire farm was the work of twenty years or more. The farm wife and her daughters faced an exhausting round of work in food preservation and cooking, spinning wool and flax, weaving cloth and making clothing and household linens, as well as nursing the sick. Most families kept a cow or two, and farm women usually had the job of milking, making butter and cheese, feeding the chickens, and gathering the eggs. There was more than enough work for men, women, and children, but the land was rich and very few Indiana pioneers went to bed hungry.

Most of the corn crop was fed to hogs and cattle. Corn was heavy for its value and hard to get to market, while the livestock could be driven on the hoof to the river towns. Farmers along the customary routes provided strongly fenced lots and feed for overnight stops, and many farm boys first traveled to the "city" when they were old enough to accompany the hog drovers. Part of the corn crop was also converted into whiskey, a product of high value for its bulk and of great

This drawing illustrates a flatboat and two keelboats, one with a sail. Indiana farmers used these craft to transport their crops downstream to market. By the Civil War, steamboats and railroads replaced the flatboats and keelboats as the major freight carriers. Reprinted from The Keelboat Age on Western Waters *by Leland D. Baldwin by permission of the University of Pittsburgh Press*

comfort to its distillers.

As soon as Indiana farmers began raising crops and livestock beyond their immediate requirements at home, they faced the problem of getting their produce to market. The prime market for most Ohio valley produce was New Orleans, and the popular method of travel was to build a flatboat and drift downstream with the current. Those who lived some distance from the Ohio often built their flatboats on the banks of a small stream and sailed when the water was high in the spring. Travel was slow and often dangerous because of natural obstacles and river pirates along the lower Ohio. Going downstream was relatively easy, but moving northward against the current was slow and tedious work in narrow keelboats operated by the tough rivermen who boasted that they were half-horse and half-alligator. The first steamboat appeared on the Ohio in 1811, and by the late 1820s steam side-wheelers carried most of the passenger and upstream freight traffic, while the heavy produce continued to move down-

Steamboats travel a busy Wabash River in this lithograph. From Parker Gilmore, Prairie Farms and Prairie Folk, *1872*

stream on flatboats.

There were few roads worthy of the name, only trails through the wilderness. Pack animals could move well enough, but carts and wagons often became stuck in the mud, broke axles against tree stumps, had to wait for creeks to subside, and always moved at an exasperating crawl. Twelve miles a day was good progress, and that required heavy exertion by horses or oxen as well as drivers. Improved transportation was among the greatest needs of the frontier, but the new state government lacked the money to build improvements, and higher taxes were even less popular than bad roads.

The Indiana Territory authorized one major

transportation improvement, a short canal around the Falls of the Ohio at New Albany. Some dirt was moved and a good deal of money wasted, but nothing was accomplished. The first state legislature incorporated the Ohio Canal Company and authorized a $1,000,000 stock issue. The company had an elaborate ground breaking ceremony, but its lottery raised only $2,563 and the effort failed dismally. The canal was later built on the Kentucky side of the river with federal aid, and opened in 1830.

The federal government had far greater resources, and Indiana turned to Congress for help. The chief federal project was the National Road which began on the Potomac River at Cumberland, Maryland, and extended to Wheeling, Virginia, and on westward. A survey of the route across central Indiana was authorized in 1825, but construction did not reach the state until 1829. Even in the 1840s much of the road in Indiana was little more than a narrow clearing through the forest, with frequent obstructions to wreck the unwary teamster. The National Road entered Indiana at Richmond and stretched to Terre Haute by way of Indianapolis. It was the busiest highway in the state, and the same route was much later followed by U.S. Highway 40 and today by Interstate 70. Towns such as Centerville, East Germantown, and Cambridge City did a good business with travelers on the National Road until long-haul traffic was lost to the railroads in the 1850s.

The obvious need for a good road northward from the Ohio River was argued for several years before the legislature decided in 1830 that it should begin at Madison and extend to Indianapolis and then northward to Lake Michigan. South Bend representatives persuaded the legislature that the Kankakee Marsh was an impassable barrier, so the Michigan Road was built by way of Logansport, Rochester, Plymouth, and South Bend, and then westward to Michigan City.

There were other state roads throughout Indiana, financed in part by the 3 percent tax on federal land sales allowed the state for road building, but they were even more difficult to travel than the Michigan Road. The law generally required

that stumps be no more than twelve inches above the ground, although fifteen inches was sometimes allowed. Parts of the National Road were built with a crushed rock surface, but most roads were simply roughly scraped dirt, dusty in the summer, muddy in spring and fall, and often blocked during the winter. Many county roads existed only in legal descriptions in the courthouse records.

The ideal remedy for the transportation problems of the West seemed to be the canal. The obvious site for an Indiana canal was the old French portage from the forks of the Maumee at Fort Wayne to the Wabash, and then along the Wabash, which in many places was too shallow for boats. A route was surveyed in 1819, but as usual there was no money for construction. Governor William Hendricks proposed a modest canal from Fort Wayne to the Wabash in 1823, and the Indian merchant John Ewing soon expanded the governor's proposal into a canal system tying together the Ohio River and the Great Lakes by way of the Wabash. Congress agreed to provide a right-of-way across federal land as well as generous land grants to help finance construction. John Tipton came to play a leading part in canal development, combining canal building with his extensive real estate interests. He founded Logansport where the proposed canal would cross the proposed Michigan Road, a likely location for a prosperous commercial town.

Cash to pay construction workers was harder to find than speculative ambition, so in 1832 the legislature authorized the sale of bonds to raise money. Canal enthusiasts celebrated in Indianapolis in such rousing fashion that the floor in the governor's mansion collapsed beneath their feet, and an excited resident of Logansport blew himself forty feet by setting off a keg of gunpowder in place of more ordinary fireworks. Most of the digging was done by immigrant Irish laborers who quickly won a reputation for hard fighting and hard drinking. The canal commissioners employed a "jigger boss" on every construction crew to dispense whiskey to fainthearted workmen. As one old jigger boss recalled years afterward, "You wouldn't expect them to work on the canal if

2,000 LABORERS WANTED ON THE CENTRAL CANAL Of Indiana.

THE great Central Canal of Indiana is intended to connect the waters of Lake Erie and the Ohio river, and will be about 400 miles in length. In addition to that part already completed and under contract in the middle and northern part of the state, TWENTY miles commencing at Evansville, on the Ohio river, its southern termination, and extending into the interior, were put under contract in November last; since which time the work has been steadily progressing.

No section of country holds out greater inducements to the industrious laborer than the state of Indiana, and particularly that portion of it contiguous to the Central Canal, from the fact that there is much of the land belonging to the general government remaining unentered, which may be purchased at one dollar and twenty-five cents per acre; affording to those who are desirous of doing so, an opportunity of securing to themselves, with the avails of a few months' labor, a permanent home in this flourishing and rapidly growing state.

The contractors are now paying $20 per month, and the fare and lodgings furnished, is of the most comfortable character. It may not be amiss to say that the acting commissioner reserves, by an express provision in all contracts, the right to see that every laborer receives his just dues; therefore, no man need lose one dollar of his wages, if he pursues a proper course.

It is probable that more of this Canal will be put under contract during the coming fall or spring, when an opportunity will be offered to those who show themselves qualified of proposing for work.

Laborers coming from the south can take passage to Evansville, and find immediate employment upon their arrival. By order of JOHN A. GRAHAM, Act. Com.
Canal Office, Evansville, May 1, 1837.   C. G. VOORHIES, Res'dt Eng.

EVANSVILLE JOURNAL. PRINTER.

This broadside of 1837 was designed to attract the attention of laborers seeking work digging the canals. The lure of cheap land in the state was as great as the wages to be earned on the canals. Many Irish immigrants new to the country made their way to Indiana on the promise of "immediate employment upon arrival." Courtesy, Indiana State Library, Indiana Division, Broadside Collection

Facing page: *The Central Indiana Canal was never completed to its proposed length. Only a nine-mile stretch from north of Indianapolis to the White River was realized. This 1908 photograph shows the canal's course through Fairview Park in the Broad Ripple area of the city. Courtesy, Indiana State Library, Indiana Division*

they were sober, would you?"

The mid-1830s were the flush times of abundant credit, booming land sales, growing population, and great dreams for future prosperity. Canals would attract settlers, encourage towns, provide cheap transportation, and make Indiana so prosperous that only a slight tax increase would be needed to finance these wonderful dreams. Every section of the state demanded its proper share of the government's generosity, and Governor Noah Noble proposed a comprehensive internal improvements plan which the legislature approved early in 1836. The Mammoth Improvements Program offered something for everyone, and the var-

ious canals, roads, and railroads would all be built with borrowed money to be repaid from the tolls and increased tax revenues from land made more valuable by improved transportation. As Paul Fatout writes in *Indiana Canals*, "The mammoth Hoosier system of internal improvements was conceived in madness and nourished by delusion ... Yet in the 1830s the impossible seemed rational, for the paradox of the time was the normality of a lunatic climate." Interest alone on the bonds was more than five times the state government's yearly revenue.

The canal system employed a large number of well-paid officials, but there were few trained engineers, and design problems were common. The canals were supposed to be forty feet wide at water level and at least four feet deep, with a ten-foot-wide towpath along one bank and a five-foot berm on the other. Lock structures were numerous and almost all of the construction was with wood to save time and expense, although the maintenance costs were soon enormous.

The Panic of 1837 shattered the Mammoth Improvements dream. The Wabash and Erie Canal struggled on with its land grant and some additional borrowing, and a thirty-mile section of the Whitewater Canal was completed. A nine-mile portion of the Central Canal was built at Indianapolis, and this placid waterway still exists although it has never carried commercial traffic.

Some twenty-eight miles of railroad were completed from Madison toward Indianapolis, and forty-one miles of turnpike from New Albany to Paoli.

The state of Indiana officially defaulted on its debts, while contractors and canal workers were paid with $1,500,000 in treasury scrip which circulated at perhaps half its face value. The five-dollar notes were called "Blue Dogs" while the one-dollar notes became known as "Blue Pups." The Wabash and Erie Canal opened between Fort Wayne and Lafayette in 1840, and the canal towns of Huntington, Wabash, Peru, Logansport, and Delphi began to benefit from the improved low-cost transportation while farmers within a wagon haul of the canal found higher prices and much easier shipment for their meat and grain. British bondholders, meanwhile, blasted the state as the home of "the plundering vagabonds of India-Scampia" who refused to pay what they owed. By 1841 the state was fifteen million dollars in debt, with interest accumulating at $615,000 each year and only $50,000 in the treasury to meet its obligations. The state of Indiana was flat broke.

Legislators resisted demands from London and New York to raise taxes and proposed various plans to reduce the debt burden if only the bondholders would extend additional credit. Finally in 1847 a deal was arranged—amid cries of bribery and fraud—in which the bondholders agreed to accept a reduced sum in new bonds and to take over the Wabash and Erie Canal as compensation for their losses. The new canal trustees pushed ahead to complete the canal to the Ohio, paying workers eighty cents a day straight time and fifty cents a day with meals included.

Canal traffic flourished between Fort Wayne and Lafayette. In a good year the canal carried a million bushels of wheat and two million bushels of corn, seven million pounds of bacon and lard, as well as good cargoes of timber, tobacco, general merchandise, and many passengers. As many as 500 boats worked the canal at its peak, most of them hauling freight at about two miles per hour. One or two horses could pull a boat carrying eighty tons of freight, while a four-horse team on the road might be able to move one ton. Elegant fast packet boats up to 100 feet long and sixteen feet wide carried passengers and valuable merchandise. Three horses could pull the brightly painted packets, often white with red or other brightly colored trim, as fast as eight miles per hour, although the canal trustees posted an unenforceable four miles per hour speed limit to prevent washouts along the banks.

For a few years the Wabash and Erie Canal collected sufficient tolls to cover its operating expenses, but never enough to pay the interest on its debt. The canal finally reached Evansville in 1853, and at 468 miles it was the longest canal in the United States. By then the Hoosier enthusiasm for canals was exhausted and there was no celebration at all. Traffic was already suffering from

railroad competition, and the southern part of the canal was poorly built across difficult terrain. The canal leaked, it was often closed by washouts from spring rains or low water from summer droughts, and occasionally from malicious damage. Many of the residents of Clay County regarded the Birch Creek Reservoir as the cause of disease, so they destroyed the dam and drained the 1,000-acre lake which supplied the canal with water. The Clay County Regulators attacked the repair crew with rifles and pistols and the governor had to call out the militia to protect the canal. The reservoir was never rebuilt and the canal in that section depended entirely upon rainwater.

After 1857 the Wabash and Erie Canal failed to meet its direct operating costs, and prolonged closures further diminished its revenues. The full length of the canal was open for only two months in one eighteen-month period, and in 1858 all traffic was suspended for 113 days. The canal gradually fell into ruin because there was never enough money for needed repairs, and traffic south of Terre Haute ceased in 1860. The Wabash Railroad, completed across the state in 1856, paralleled the most successful section of the canal between Lafayette and Fort Wayne and gained more and more traffic. In 1873 the state adopted a constitutional amendment denying all liability for the canal's debt of more than sixteen million dollars and it is still in force. Official operation of the canal ended in 1874, although isolated sections carried some local traffic for an additional nine years until the canal decayed into ruin. For a few years the canal had indeed been a benefit for both farmers and towns between Fort Wayne and Lafayette, and those cities in particular were strong enough to flourish without it as the waterway decayed into ruin.

The horse-drawn canal boat could not meet the challenge of the steam-powered iron horse. Not only did the railroads devastate the canals, but they built over or alongside them, for a canal route meant a good level right-of-way. The canal's pathway through the bustling city of Fort Wayne was purchased by the Nickel Plate Railroad so it could lay its track in the city without having to

Above: *One of the small towns to develop as a result of the canal boom was Metamora in Franklin County, seen here in the 1920s in an evocative photograph by Frank Hohenberger. The state's Internal Improvement Act of 1836 spurred the construction of this canal. Later the tracks of the Whitewater Valley Railroad were laid along the towpath as seen at the right. Courtesy, Indiana State Library, Indiana Division*

Left: *In this drawing by Christian Schrader, a canal boat is being drawn under the bridge that once spanned the Central Canal at Washington Street. Courtesy, Indiana State Library, Indiana Division, Schrader Collection*

65

One of Madison's finest nineteenth-century residences is the Jeremiah Sullivan home, built in 1818. This photograph taken by Frank Hohenberger in 1925 focuses upon the entry's decorative iron railing. Ornamental ironwork manufactured in Madison was exported widely, often destined for buildings in New Orleans. Courtesy, Indiana State Library, Indiana Division

buy expensive developed real estate. The Whitewater Valley Railroad still operates in part over the towpath of the old Whitewater Canal, and in downtown Indianapolis a few railroad cars are still switched on a spur built on the towpath of the Central Canal.

Even as the canal advocates celebrated their political successes in the early 1830s other promoters persuaded the legislature to create more than thirty railroad corporations. Few of these efforts were able to raise enough money to build any track, but many citizens were convinced that the railroad with its greater speed and dependability was the real answer to Indiana's need for better transportation. Many of the early plans were for railroads to tap the hinterland of the larger river towns and bring additional farm produce for transfer to more efficient river transportation. The first significant railroad construction began at Madison in 1836 on the line to Indianapolis. The track reached Vernon in 1839, Columbus in 1844, and was completed to Indianapolis in 1847 for a

Facing page: *This five-dollar note of the Madison & Indianapolis Railroad was issued on May 2, 1843, in Columbus, a year before the track from Madison was laid to that city. The currency prominently features an oval inset of a train steaming its way across the countryside. However, the line was not completed to Indianapolis until 1847. Courtesy, Indiana State Library, Indiana Division, Manuscript Collection*

Above: *James Franklin Doughty (J.F.D.) Lanier was probably the richest man in Indiana in the mid-1800s. His house, shown here in 1876 when his son lived in it, was designed by Francis Costigan, who designed many of Madison's finest Greek Revival buildings. Although he moved to New York in 1848, Lanier was the chief financial support for Governor Oliver Morton's Civil War effort, lending Indiana over one million dollars without any security other than confidence the Republicans would win in 1864. Courtesy, Indiana State Library, Indiana Division*

total length of eighty-six miles. Eight-horse teams pulled single cars up the steep Madison cut until 1848, when a special steam engine took over the assignment. The line brought good traffic to Madison, which for a few years was the only river town in Indiana with railroad connections to the interior of the state. During the 1850s many competing lines were completed and Madison's economic position declined rapidly, but many of the elegant homes and public buildings of its brief period of glory survive to grace one of the state's most attractive small cities. The Ohio and Mississippi Railroad, later part of the Baltimore and Ohio system, crossed southern Indiana on its route from Cincinnati to St. Louis and the produce of farms along its line between Lawrenceburg to Vincennes began to move eastward by rail rather than by river to New Orleans.

Indianapolis emerged as the state's railroad hub, and it was the excellent railroad connections built during the 1850s which assured the capital's position as the state's largest city as well as its political heart. Between 1850 and 1852 the Indianapolis and Bellefontaine was rapidly extended from Indianapolis through Anderson and Muncie and eastward into Ohio where it connected with railroads leading to New York and Philadelphia. That same year Chauncey Rose's very successful Indianapolis and Terre Haute began service over high quality rails imported from England, and the following year the Indiana Central was built from Indianapolis to Richmond. Each railroad company had its own passenger station in Indianapolis, and people changing trains complained of the inconvenience. The Union Station which opened in 1853 was able to handle all of the passenger trains serving Indianapolis on its five tracks, and it set the example for union stations in many other cities.

The Michigan Central and its great rival the Michigan Southern raced across northern Indiana toward Chicago, arriving in a virtual tie in 1852. The only major north-south route was the New Albany and Salem, which began as a short line to bring more farm produce to the river at New Albany. It was financed by farmers and merchants along the route who were persuaded to buy stock in a railroad which would improve local business and give farmers a better outlet for their crops, as well as larger contributions from town and county governments. New Albany put up $100,000, and Bloomington soon matched the sum to guarantee construction beyond Salem. Work began in 1848 and in three years the line was completed to Salem, but it was quickly and cheaply built, with steep grades and sharp curves through the southern Indiana knobs, and rails made of bar iron laid over oak sills. Within five years everything had to be replaced with better materials, but the inefficient right-of-way is still in service. Money for expansion and improvements came from the well-financed Michigan Central which "merged" with the New Albany and Salem so that it could take advantage of the New Albany's generous charter to build its own line in the north, where lawyers of the rival Michigan Southern had tried to keep it from extending its tracks into the state. With proper financing and mergers with some earlier short lines the New Albany and Salem reached from Bedford to Bloomington in 1853, and then rushed to Crawfordsville, Lafayette, and straight across the Kankakee Marsh to Michigan City by 1854. Evansville also worked to enhance its position as a river port by increasing traffic from its hinterland. The Evansville and Crawfordsville began construction in 1852, and within two years had extended its track as far as Terre Haute.

Only thirty miles of railroad were operating in Indiana in 1845; by 1855 the railroad mileage had increased to 1,406 and every substantial city in Indiana could be reached by train. Getting from farm to town still meant slow and difficult travel over miserable roads, but once in town both people and freight could move quickly, easily, and at reasonable cost by rail. The Ohio River towns were still served by steamboats which were even cheaper than the trains, but the river offered a limited variety of destinations, while the growing railroad network offered shippers an almost unlimited choice. Indiana's commerce began to flow north to Chicago and east to the mid-Atlantic states, while the southern market declined in importance year by year.

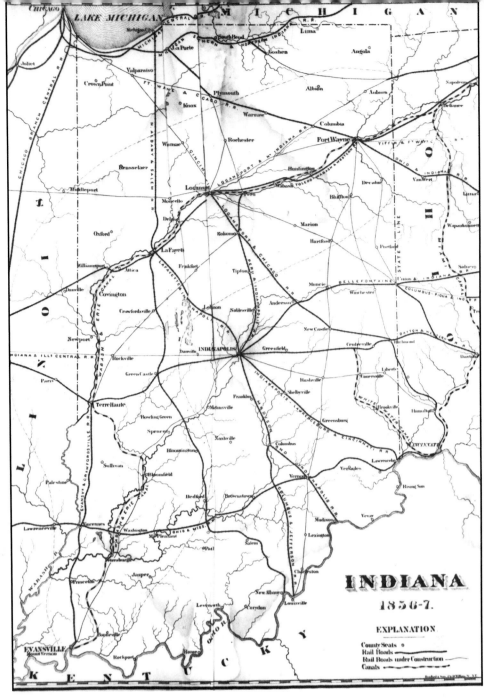

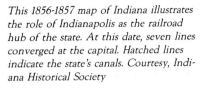

This 1856-1857 map of Indiana illustrates the role of Indianapolis as the railroad hub of the state. At this date, seven lines converged at the capital. Hatched lines indicate the state's canals. Courtesy, Indiana Historical Society

This woodcut of the first "union station" in the country appeared in an Indianapolis newspaper soon after the station's opening on September 20, 1853. The names of the five railroads jointly employing the shed have been inscribed in the arches of the west facade. Courtesy, Indiana State Library, Indiana Division

CHAPTER V

*The themes of the Presidential campaign
of 1840 are well illustrated in this lithograph. An American flag with "Harrison
& Tyler" flies from a frontier log cabin.
In front, a wounded war veteran, one of
General Harrison's comrades, shakes
hands with a Hoosier. Note the barrels of
hard cider at the side of the cabin, which
no doubt added to the spirit of amicabili-
ty. Courtesy, Indiana Historical Society*

Hoosier Politics In Peace And War

The citizens of the new state of Indiana did not expect much from their state government, and they were rarely disappointed. There were no political parties, and the politically ambitious all claimed to follow the principles of Jeffersonian Republicanism. Differences were personal and local, with the settlers of the Whitewater valley in the southeast matched against the residents of the lower Wabash valley in the southwest. Governor Jonathan Jennings was personally popular, but he did not establish a political organization. The general assembly met each year, but most of the laws it passed concerned strictly local matters. The state's annual revenue from taxes and other sources was less than $25,000, and most of this went to pay official salaries. The governor received $1,000 a year.

Despite the lack of great public issues, political campaigns were not without interest. Colorful figures such as Governor James B. Ray were lively orators who entertained the voters with florid speeches. Candidates were expected to travel throughout their districts, meet the voters, and speak wherever an audience could be gathered. Fourth of July celebrations and "court days" when the farmers came to the county seat for legal business and livestock trading were favored occasions for political talks. If no other platform were available the frontier politician might stand on a tree stump, hence the expression "stump oratory." As election time neared, the candidates offered refreshment to the voters and the liquor flowed freely.

The presidential election of 1824 marked the beginning of party politics in Indiana. There were electors pledged to three candidates on the ballot: Andrew Jackson, Henry Clay, and John Quincy Adams. Only Jackson's supporters held a convention to nominate their slate of electors. "Old Hickory" carried the state easily, but no candidate received a nationwide majority of the electoral vote and when the House of Representatives elected Adams, Jackson's many friends were furious. Jacksonians spent the next four years creating a true party organization, the Democratic party. Adams, Clay, and their supporters organized the National Republicans, later to become the Whig party, and the election of 1828 was a straightforward party contest. Both parties held state conventions in Indianapolis, nominated slates of electors, and campaigned actively. The newspapers were intensely political and the total vote in Indiana was more than double that at the last election. The Jacksonians carried Indiana, and did so again four years later, but the Whigs did not give up the struggle.

The two-party system flourished in Indiana, but the financial disaster of the Mammoth Improvements scheme undermined the popularity of the Whig party which had promoted the canals and railroads. The Democrats blamed the Whigs for bankrupting the state and for raising taxes. With the election of James Whitcomb as governor in 1843 the Democrats won total control of state government. The Whigs did not give in easily, and Hoosier elections were marked by intense partisan rivalry and a very high level of voter participation.

The Whig champion whose cause aroused such political enthusiasm was "Old Tippecanoe" himself, William Henry Harrison. He had left Indiana for Ohio in 1814, but distant memories of his victories combined with shrewd political publicity made Harrison more of a hero in his old age than he had ever been as a general.

The presidential campaign of 1840 set the new pattern for American politics. The Whigs were a party of respectability and support for business, while the Democrats boasted that they represented the common man. Harrison was born into a wealthy and prominent Virginia family, but Whig newspapers emphasized his frontier residence and his military record. When a Democrat snorted that a log cabin and a barrel of hard cider would be enough to satisfy "Old Tip," the Whigs had a perfect campaign theme. They adopted the log cabin, that most American of symbols, as their own, and provided ample supplies of hard cider to refresh the thirst of the voters. Their slogan was "Tippecanoe and Tyler Too," but that was all anyone heard of vice presidential candidate John Tyler.

Young Whigs tried to surpass young Democrats with such stunts as rolling large leather balls from village to village, and the torchlight parade became part of American political tradition. Both parties campaigned more actively than ever before, with strongly worded newspaper stories and stirring stump speeches, with banners and campaign badges, with barbecues and political songs. The result was an unprecedented voter turnout. Nationally almost four out of five white men over twenty-one voted, while in Indiana 86 percent of the eligible voters went to the polls. William Henry Harrison was seventy-six years old when he entered the White House and he died exactly one month after his inauguration. Hoosier Whigs would never again find a candidate with such strong appeal for so many voters.

The Democratic triumph of 1843 was symbolized by the editorial "crowing" of George and Jacob Chapman, whose *Indiana State Sentinel* carried the Democratic message from the capital in Indianapolis. The Democrats preached and practiced economy in government, and for years reminded the voters of Whig extravagance, Whig debts, and Whig taxes. The Democrats appealed successfully for the votes of the growing numbers of German and Irish immigrants, and after 1851 newcomers were permitted to vote simply upon

Lew Wallace

Lew Wallace was only thirty-five years old when this photo of him was taken in a New York City studio in 1862. He had risen to the rank of major general based upon his command of the Eleventh Indiana Regiment. Later he was to gain distinction for his service in the defense of Washington, D.C., in 1864. Courtesy, Indiana Historical Society

Lew Wallace is known today as the author of *Ben Hur,* but his varied occupations as a soldier, lawyer, politician, diplomat, and lecturer, as well as novelist, is typical of the careers of many nineteenth-century Hoosier gentlemen. Lew Wallace was born in Brookville in 1827, the son of a prosperous and successful Whig lawyer and politician who was elected governor in 1837. As a boy he was greatly interested in reading, drawing, and writing, and at the age of eighteen he worked as a political reporter for the *Indianapolis Journal.* After serving as a lieutenant during the Mexican War he settled in Crawfordsville as a lawyer and soon entered politics. In April of 1861 Wallace was appointed adjutant general of the state and quickly organized thousands of volunteers for war. He commanded the Eleventh Indiana with distinction and by early 1862 had advanced to major general. At the end of the war General Wallace served on the courts martial which tried the Lincoln "conspirators" and the cruel commandant of Andersonville prison camp.

After adventures among Mexican revolutionaries he returned to Crawfordsville to practice law and to write. He lost a race for Congress but won appointment as governor of the New Mexico Territory in 1876 and then as minister to Turkey in 1881. In 1873 Wallace published a successful novel about the Spanish conquest of Mexico called *The Fair God,* and in 1880 the bestseller *Ben Hur,* a tale of the Holy Land which became even more famous on the stage and later on the screen. Lew Wallace disliked the practice of law, but he was a fine amateur artist and a very popular lecturer as well as a prolific writer, among the earliest of many Hoosiers to achieve national renown as an author.

declaring their intention to become citizens.

The Democratic party nationally favored the westward expansion of America's boundaries, and Indiana Democrats enthusiastically supported war with Mexico in 1840. Thousands of volunteers were ready to rush to Texas to join the fight, but the militia system had decayed since the end of the Indian wars. Five regiments were eventually organized, all of them commanded by deserving Democratic politicians.

Only at Buena Vista did Hoosier troops meet the enemy in battle, and General Zachary Taylor's criticism of the Second Indiana's poor showing there cost him many votes when he ran for president on the Whig ticket in 1848. The Democrats won Indiana by 5,000 votes. In 1849 the Democrats consolidated their control of state offices by electing Joseph A. Wright as governor. Wright was an honest and popular figure, but as a political organizer he was always outclassed by his great rival, Jesse D. Bright, who was elected United States senator in 1845 but managed to retain his dominance of the party from Washington.

The original state constitution of 1816 was generally satisfactory, but many people came to believe that it allowed politicians to spend too much money. The failure of the Mammoth Improvements Program and the resulting public debt of more than fifteen million dollars shocked Hoosiers into altering their constitution. The general assembly was the chief target of objections, as many thought it met too often and spent too much money with its annual sessions, and it wasted time and money by passing hundreds of strictly local bills.

The constitutional convention met in Indianapolis in October 1850 and debated the new document for four months. In general the result showed the strong influence of Jacksonian Democracy, since Democrats outnumbered Whigs among the delegates by two-to-one. The Bill of Rights was unchanged, except to forbid state money for any religious school. The general assembly was limited to meeting no more than sixty-one days every other year and it lost the power of electing judges and state officials, while private and local bills

were sharply restricted. Governors were forbidden to succeed themselves.

More startling were the financial limitations. The state was forbidden to borrow money, except in cases of invasion or rebellion, and likewise forbidden to take over the debts of any county, town, township, or corporation. Counties were forbidden to use anything but cash to buy corporate stock, or to extend public credit to any corporation, while the state was forbidden to hold stock in any corporation at all.

The delegates were determined to keep the state out of business, and they were determined also to keep Indiana for white people only. Article XIII provided that "No negro or mulatto shall come into or settle in the State, after the adoption of this Constitution."

This time the constitution was submitted to the voters for approval, and Article XIII was voted

Facing page: *The Orange County Court-house in Paoli, built between 1847 and 1850, is one of the state's finest surviving examples of a public building in the Greek Revival style. The temple form structure features a portico of six fluted Doric columns supporting a classically correct entablature. This photograph was taken in the 1920s by Frank M. Hohen-berger. Courtesy, Indiana State Library, Indiana Division*

upon separately. Some Whigs opposed the consti-tution, and a few idealists objected to the exclu-sion of Negroes, but ratification was approved by an overwhelming majority of 80 percent, while Article XIII was even more popular, with 84 per-cent. Although much amended, including Article XIII, which was repealed in 1881, the constitution of 1851 is still in force, with all of its restrictions against state borrowing intact.

County governments functioned on similar low-cost principles. The justices of the peace lost their non-judicial responsibilities in 1832, and ad-ministrative and legislative duties passed to three elected county commissioners. There was no chief executive, and responsibility was widely dispersed. The voters elected a sheriff, a coroner, a treasurer, an auditor, a clerk, a recorder of deeds, and a sur-veyor in each county, as well as judges and a pros-ecuting attorney. The first public buildings in a county were usually the courthouse and the jail, and town promoters competed for the advantage of securing the county seat, which meant a steady flow of visitors for legal business. Aside from des-ignating roads and providing a minimum of law enforcement there was little activity within county government, and few citizens sought anything more. Township trustees were elected for more lo-cal concerns such as roads, schools, and poor re-lief, while city and town councils managed the business of the towns.

Beginning in 1852 Indiana at last made some ef-fort to provide tax support for public education, and each township maintained at least one and usually several one-room schools. The state's edu-cational spending and literacy rate, however, were the worst in the Old Northwest.

Party spirit and personal rivalries sustained a high level of voter participation. Two issues domi-nated political argument in the 1850s, liquor and slavery, and both frequently drew the churches into political controversy. Many Hoosiers objected to the Fugitive Slave Act of 1850 because it re-quired northerners, who objected to slavery, to cooperate in the return of runaway slaves. Both Methodist and Presbyterian bodies denounced the law, as they also denounced the easy sale of strong drink.

Abolitionists who wanted to destroy slavery were not strong in Indiana, although Quakers around Richmond and some Methodist and Pres-byterian groups elsewhere established a number of anti-slavery societies. George W. Julian of Center-ville was the only important politician who advo-cated the outright elimination of slavery, but many Hoosiers shared the growing free-soil senti-ment which opposed any extension of slave terri-tory in the West. In 1849 an angry crowd and a friendly judge in South Bend set free a slave fami-ly captured by a Kentucky slaveowner. An India-napolis case in 1853 attracted greater attention, when a long-time black resident was claimed as a fugitive and struggled for several months to prove that he was not the slave in question. Despite these occasional dramatic episodes there was never any organized effort to help escaping slaves reach freedom. The Underground Railroad existed only in myth, sustained by abolitionist propaganda in the 1850s and by embellished memories in later years.

The slavery issue erupted in 1854 when Con-gress passed the Kansas-Nebraska Act, opening the way for slavery in the western territories. There were furious objections throughout the North, particularly among members of the declin-ing Whig party. Hoosier Democrats were divided. Senator Bright supported the expansion of slav-ery, despite objections from Governor Wright and many party members, especially in the northern part of the state. The issue was not only slavery but also liquor, which Bright and his friends de-fended against the objections of many church-going Democrats. By no coincidence, Bright's party enemy, Governor Wright, was a prominent

MARION COUNTY, TEMPERANCE CONVENTION

WILL MEET ON

SATURDAY JUNE 10, AT THE COURT HOUSE IN INDIANAPOLIS.

The friends of temperance are requested to turn out en mass.   Several speeches will be made on the occasion.
INDIANAPOLIS. June 3. 1854.

Journal Steam Press.

Methodist and a friend of the temperance movement. The 1853 legislature had responded to many temperance petitions with a local option law which allowed townships to ban the sale of liquor, but the Supreme Court ruled the measure unconstitutional. Anti-liquor forces, with strong church leadership, moved for a statewide ban on the liquor trade, and won significant Whig support. The political struggle of 1854 was further confused by the rise of the Know-Nothing movement, an anti-foreign and anti-Catholic group which appealed to "true Americans" to resist the growing power of Irish and German immigrants. Both Irish and Germans resisted prohibition and they were not only largely Catholic but also largely Democratic.

In July of 1854 old Whigs, Free-Soilers who opposed any expansion of slavery, anti-Nebraska Democrats, and Know-Nothings all came together at Indianapolis and proclaimed themselves the

In 1854 temperance forces, with strong church leadership, moved for a statewide ban on the sale of liquor. The issue became important in the political campaigns of that year. This broadside advertising an anti-liquor rally in Indianapolis was found among the papers of Calvin Fletcher. Courtesy, Indiana Historical Society

People's party. They opposed the spread of slavery, the evils of whiskey, and above all they despised Jesse Bright's political principles. Their paper, the *Indiana State Journal,* blasted the Democrats as the party of "Slavery and Liquor, niggers and raw nips." The Democrats responded by calling the People's party candidates "mongrels over whom waves the black flag of abolitionism." It was a dirty and vicious campaign, despite the efforts of the anti-Democratic coalition to make it a moral crusade. When the votes were counted the coalition had won a great victory, carrying the state

Schuyler Colfax

Schuyler Colfax was in many respects a model mid-nineteenth-century politician. He was a devoted party man, an accomplished orator, moderately ambitious, and untroubled by any burning desire to change the world. He was born in New York and moved as a boy with his family to New Carlisle, not far from South Bend. When his stepfather was elected county auditor Colfax became his deputy, although not yet old enough to vote. He also showed an early interest in journalism, and contributed occasional articles to Horace Greeley's *New York Tribune*. After brief experience with the *Indiana State Journal* in Indianapolis he managed to raise enough money to buy a half-interest in the *St. Joseph Valley Register* in South Bend. The paper had a circulation of only 250 copies each week, but Colfax slowly improved its sales while preaching firm Whig principles. In 1851 he ran for Congress, touring the sprawling sixteen-county district with his rival. According to the *Register* report of the campaign, they "rode together—ate together—sometimes slept together—but attempted to slash each other on the stump most savagely." Colfax lost the election but not his interest in politics, and after a brief flirtation with the bigoted Know-Nothings he helped organize the Republican

Schuyler Colfax posed for this portrait in the famous studio known as Brady's National Portrait Gallery, probably during his term as vice president (1869-1873). Here he exhibits the facial expression that led to his nickname "Smiler." Courtesy, Indiana State Library, Indiana Division

party in Indiana. In 1854 he was elected to Congress where he was a faithful Republican, voting with his party on every issue and showing special interest only in improving postal service for mining towns in the far West.

Colfax was an effective speaker, both in Congress and in campaigning for fellow Republicans, and he became very popular. Some of his admirers suggested him for postmaster general in Lincoln's cabinet. In 1863 "Smiler" Colfax, as he was sometimes called, was elected speaker of the house and served for three terms to the complete satisfaction of his party. He was never a leader among the Republicans, but he did what was expected of him and did it well. In 1868 Colfax was rewarded with the nomination for vice president, the ideal position for a man of his talent. As Carl Schurz wrote at the time,

"Colfax is a very popular man. . . . His abilities are not distinguished but are just sufficient to make him acceptable to the masses. They are fond of happy mediocrity."

Vice President Colfax understood fully the honorific nature of his office, and made no effort to exercise influence on administration policies. His term would have ended in decent obscurity except for the Credit Mobilier scandal which exploded in 1872, when a corrupt congressman listed Colfax among those who had accepted bribes to favor the Union Pacific Railroad. He denied the charges and voluntarily appeared before the investigating committee, but his excuses were not entirely convincing.

Colfax spent his retirement years as a lecturer, addressing thousands on the beauties of the West or the greatness of Abraham Lincoln. Colfax had visited Lincoln on the morning of the fatal Friday, and declined the President's invitation to join him at Ford's Theatre that evening because he planned to leave early the next morning for California. The public lecture was a popular form of entertainment, and Colfax lived comfortably on his lecture fees. He died in a Minnesota railroad depot in 1885, while waiting for the train to take him to his next lecture.

offices and nine out of the eleven seats in Congress. Only in southern Indiana did the Democrats remain in the majority, a clear sectional division of lasting importance.

The new legislature quickly passed a strong prohibition law, forbidding the manufacture or sale of whiskey, but the Supreme Court struck it down as an infringement of property rights. The liquor issue faded away for many years, but the slavery question became more and more agitated. The People's party fought the state election of 1856 in Indiana, but it was clearly aligned with the national Republican party structure and soon adopted its name locally. Slavery was the chief issue in both national and state contests, and the election was fiercely fought. Both parties accused the other of stealing votes, but the Democrats won narrowly. There was a strongly sectional pattern to the vote, Republican in northern Indiana, Democratic in the south. The Democrats split in 1858 because many party members resented Bright's arrogant domination of the party and his support for slavery in Kansas. The Republicans campaigned hard against the extension of slavery and played down the anti-liquor and anti-foreign appeals of a few years earlier. The Republicans gained control of the general assembly by narrow margins in both houses, and overthrew a generation of Democratic domination.

Hoosier Republicans had high hopes for the 1860 elections because the Democrats were divided in both the state and the nation while the new Republican party was vigorous and united. Supporters of Stephen A. Douglas had managed to win control of the Democratic organization from Senator Bright, but Bright was so much in favor of slavery and so hated Douglas that he campaigned for the southern Democratic ticket. Hoosier Republicans generally supported the nomination of Abraham Lincoln as a moderate anti-slavery man and fellow westerner, and they eagerly worked for his election. The Republicans had some difficulty in arranging their state ticket, and compromised on Henry S. Lane for governor and Oliver P. Morton for lieutenant governor. The Republicans emphasized their economic program of free home-

steads, protective tariffs, and a railroad to California, and trimmed the slavery issue. They made a determined effort to win over the important German vote, using German-speaking orators like Carl Schurz and winning the endorsement of seven of the state's eight German language newspapers. Douglas and the northern Democrats struggled to save the Union, while Democrats accused Republicans of being "Negro-lovers" who favored "amalgamation" of the races.

Indiana was a critical state for both parties, and it was closely watched throughout the nation. In the state balloting in October the Republican ticket won decisively, and despite determined Democratic efforts before the presidential vote in November, Lincoln won 51 percent of the popular vote against 42 percent for Douglas. The strongest Republican vote came from the northern part of the state, while the southern counties remained Democratic.

When the newly elected legislature convened in January the Republicans were in firm control. After two days as governor Henry Lane was elected senator and sent off to Washington, and Oliver Morton became governor. He was firmly for the Union, and worried that President Lincoln was too weak to withstand the secessionists. Even be-

Facing page: *The determination of Governor Oliver Morton can be seen in this lithograph of him. No other northern governor did so much to support the Union in the Civil War. Those who failed to support Morton and the war effort with proper enthusiasm were called "Copperheads." Courtesy, Indiana State Library, Indiana Division*

fore the war began Morton offered 6,000 Hoosier soldiers to defend the Union. After the Confederate attack on Fort Sumter Lincoln called for 4,700 men from Indiana, and 12,000 volunteered within a week.

Governor Morton was arrogant, often brutal, and highly political in every action, but he was also amazingly vigorous and a master organizer. No other Northern governor did as much to support the war effort, and state action was essential at the beginning of the war because the federal government was so unprepared. There were enthusiastic volunteers in large numbers, but no organization, no training camps, and few weapons or uniforms. The militia had been neglected for years and everything had to be improvised. Morton pushed and prodded, showing no respect for generals or officials in Washington. He constructed a state arsenal to manufacture rifles and ammunition, and made a profit on sales to the federal government.

Morton spoke about all loyal men coming to the aid of their country, but in reality he put greater emphasis on party loyalty. As governor he appointed all volunteer officers from second lieutenant through colonel, and very few Democrats were named to positions of rank. Democrats were regularly condemned as rebels and traitors, and the *Plymouth Democrat* and the *St. Joseph County Forum* were censored into silence for opposing the war effort. By the time state elections were held in October of 1862 many Hoosiers had grown tired of the prolonged fighting and the ever-growing casualty lists. Enthusiasm had been undermined by conscription of unwilling recruits, new federal taxes, and finally by the preliminary Emancipation Proclamation issued a few weeks before the election. The Democrats blamed the Republicans for every hardship, but especially for

advocating equality between the races and Negro immigration into Indiana. The Democrats made gains throughout the Old Northwest in 1862, and in Indiana they narrowly won control of the legislature.

The political struggle reached a new level of ferocity in 1863, and Republican patriots boasted that Morton was fighting two rebellions, one in the South and the other at home. The label "Copperhead" was loosely used to describe anyone who failed to support Morton and the war effort with proper enthusiasm, and Republicans described uncooperative Democrats, no matter how loyal, as Confederate sympathizers. Morton himself became a leading issue, as Union clubs rallied to his aid while Democrats pictured him as a

In 1861 and 1862, Solomon Meredith was colonel of the Nineteenth Indiana Volunteer Infantry, a unit which achieved fame as part of the Iron Brigade of the Army of the Potomac. Meredith, a native of Wayne County, later rose to the rank of brigadier general. Courtesy, Indiana State Library, Indiana Division

power-hungry monster.

In this contentious atmosphere the 1864 elections were even more bitter than before. Democrats talked a lot about arbitrary arrests, economic hardships, and high taxes, but their most effective issue was racial prejudice. The Republicans now supported emancipation with greater enthusiasm as essential for winning the war, and condemned the Democrats as rebels at heart. Republicans were greatly worried about the elections, pressuring army commanders to allow Hoosier troops to return home on furlough so they could vote. Despite attacks on Democratic newspapers and publicity about the imagined traitors the election was closely contested, with Morton winning reelection by about 20,000 votes in October and Lincoln achieving the same margin in November.

The men of Indiana, whether as volunteers, conscripts, hired substitutes, or bounty-seekers, served in remarkable numbers. By one estimate nearly three-quarters of the men of military age were in uniform, at least briefly, at some period during the war. Altogether Indiana raised 169 regiments for a grand total of 196,363 men. Of these 1,537 were black, although they were not allowed to enlist within the state until late 1863. Over 1,000 Hoosiers sought greater adventure by enlisting in the navy or the marines.

Most Indiana regiments fought in the West, down the Mississippi to Vicksburg and then through Tennessee and Georgia, but the Nineteenth Indiana Infantry achieved fame as part of the Iron Brigade in the Army of the Potomac. Casualties were heavy and death from disease even more common. Through four years of bloody war 7,243 Hoosiers died in battle, while 17,785 died of disease and accident.

Only for a few days in July of 1863 did the war come directly to Indiana. The dashing Kentucky cavalryman John Hunt Morgan led 2,500 troopers across the Ohio River at Mauckport on July 8. Although under orders to remain in Kentucky, General Morgan wanted to carry the war into the Yankee homeland and he needed fresh horses and supplies. He also hoped to arouse the fabled Copperheads, but not a single Hoosier came for-

Frank Leslie's Illustrated Newspaper *of August 8, 1863, featured this engraving captioned "Morgan's Raid into Indiana— the Confederate Guerillas Destroying and Pillaging the Depot and Stores at Salem, Indiana, July 10." Courtesy, Indiana State Library, Indiana Division*

This poster of the Soldiers' and Sailors' Monument was used to solicit funds from subscribers for its erection. Of interest are the miniscule fountains at the base, which were later completely redesigned. One author has called this monument "the exclamation point of Indiana." Courtesy, Indiana Historical Society

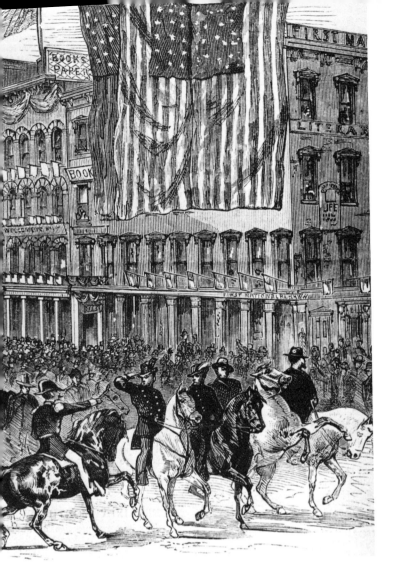

Above: *The October 14, 1876, issue of* Harper's Weekly *featured this engraving of a soldiers' reunion in Indianapolis with the obligatory parade down Washington Street.* Harper's *called the event "a magnificent Republican jubilee." Courtesy, Indiana State Library, Indiana Division*

Facing page: *This unknown young soldier undoubtedly had his photograph taken as a keepsake for his loved ones before he departed for war. Selfconsciously posed in his new uniform in front of a stage backdrop, he was photographed in J.W. Husher's Gallery, Greencastle, Indiana. Courtesy, Indiana State Library, Indiana Division*

found an abandoned farm house with the fire still warm on the hearth, fresh bread on the table, and "chickens strolling before the door with a confidence that was touching, but misplaced." Morgan captured Corydon on the 9th and Salem a day later, wrecking railroads at every opportunity while avoiding any organized militia resistance. The Confederates advanced quickly to Vernon, but skirted the town to avoid a fight and spent twenty-one hours that day on the move, resting only from midnight till three o'clock. Five days after he entered Indiana General Morgan rode into Ohio, leaving behind vivid memories of intermingled fear and bravery, and little damage except to the railroads.

Most Indiana soldiers were volunteers, although many were encouraged by the fear of being drafted after 1862. Local governments offered generous bounties to attract recruits who would meet the local quota, paying as much as $500 by the summer of 1864. For most of the new soldiers the army meant their first travel far from home and experiences vastly different from the familiar rounds of farm chores. They had photographs taken as keepsakes for their loved ones, and they recorded the excitement of battle and the boredom of camp life in their diaries and letters. All recognized that the war would be the great event of their lives, and those who survived renewed their wartime memories and kept friendships alive by establishing the Grand Army of the Republic.

The Grand Army of the Republic was a national association of Union veterans, closely allied in politics with the Republican party. It persuaded legislatures to establish Memorial Day as a legal holiday for the remembrance of the honored dead, and the inevitable parade in every town was led by the dwindling band of veterans year after year. The GAR had its national headquarters in Indianapolis, and its lasting symbol is the Soldiers' and Sailors' Monument in the center of the Circle. On the lawn of almost every courthouse in Indiana the veterans erected a statue honoring those who fought in the Civil War, with a heroic figure facing north to remind a younger generation of the great war which saved the Union.

ward to aid the Confederates, while 65,000 men turned out within two days to resist the invaders. Morgan's men found food in abundance, but they were greatly disappointed by the quality of Indiana horseflesh. Colonel Basil Duke fondly remembered his visit to Harrison County, where he

C H A P T E R VI

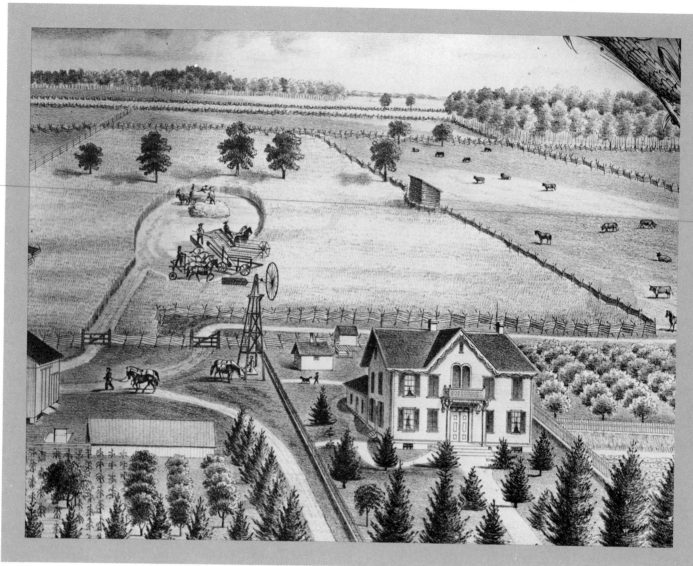

The farm residence of William Pinney
was chosen as an illustration in the
LaPorte County atlas of 1874. Advances
in farm machinery following the Civil
War greatly improved the farmer's life-
style. In the field behind the house, four
horses push a side-delivery hay rake,
while an adjacent wagon pulled by two
other horses receives the newly cut hay.
Courtesy, Indiana State Library, Indiana
Division

The Golden Years

any Hoosiers looked back to the period between the Civil War and the First World War as the best years for themselves and for Indiana. Most Hoosiers confidently believed that they were living in the heart of America, and that the people of the great midwestern heartland were the true Americans. Indiana did not have teeming cities crowded with immigrants, nor did it suffer from the hardships of a defeated South. Hoosiers lived on prosperous farms and in cities and towns of modest size, and Hoosier authors described this wonderfully American life in works which year after year ranked among the bestselling books in the country. Selective memory made this era seem golden, but Indiana did seem to be a land particularly blessed. "Ain't God good to Indiana, Ain't He fellers? Ain't He though?" wrote the Indianapolis journalist William Herschell.

By 1865 most parts of Indiana were well advanced from the hardships of the pioneer era. The struggle to establish farms in the wilderness and build up towns had been generally successful, and Hoosiers were able to enjoy the fruits of the labor of their parents and grandparents. Most farmers owned their own land—only 24 percent were tenants—and the average farm was ample for the support of a family. Few people thought of themselves as rich, but many regarded themselves as part of the middle class. Professional men, proprietors of stores and small factories, as well as many skilled tradesmen, lived comfortably in town, and it was the children of these prosperous farmers and businessmen who remembered "the good old days." Thousands of tenant farmers, factory workers, domestic servants, and unskilled laborers had harsher memories, but they and their children have left few written recollections. Most Hoosiers regarded hard work as the duty of the good Christian, and they looked forward with confidence to continued success for themselves and their children. It was a good time to be *Seventeen,* as the Indiana novelist Booth Tarkington remembered in his own middle years.

More than half of the people of Indiana still made their living by farming, but they were a steadily declining share of the population. Farming was hard physical work, but it was no longer as backbreaking or as lonely as it had been during the pioneer period. The seemingly endless forests had been largely cut and cleared for the plow, the soil was rich, and the climate generally favorable. Indiana farmers continued to grow corn and wheat and raise hogs and cattle, shipping their grain and livestock to market on the growing network of railroad lines. By the end of the century almost every county in the state had rail service, and few farmers were more than a day's wagon haul of ten or twelve miles from a railroad station except in the hill country of southern Indiana.

The telegraph came with the railroads, providing rapid transmission of news, market prices, and urgent personal messages. The trains also carried mail, and beginning in 1896 the post office extended regular deliveries to the farm gate along rural free delivery routes. Every small town of a thousand residents had its weekly newspaper, and the mail brought farm and religious magazines to subscribers with dependable regularity. Cities had daily newspapers, receiving news from distant places by telegraphic press services. Evansville, for example, supported five daily newspapers by 1880, four in English and one in German.

The population of Indiana continued to increase, but at a declining rate. The state's cities

and towns grew more rapidly than its rural areas, but not as fast as Ohio and Illinois. Not until 1920 was there an urban majority, with more than half the population living in cities and towns of more than 2,500 residents. Growth was concentrated in the cities and in the northern half of the state, with a significant decline of population in many of the rural counties of southern Indiana where the soil was thin and transportation poor. Indiana's many cities of moderate size experienced rapid growth of industry and population. The older towns along the Ohio River continued their long decline, except for Evansville which benefited from its excellent river and rail transportation and nearby coal deposits. Evansville became a major industrial center and the state's second largest city between 1860 and 1920. It was closely followed

Terre Haute hosted the Indiana State Fair in 1867, the year Terre Haute was incorporated as a city. Harper's Weekly ran a two-page illustration of the fair. Note the reputation of the Hoosier versus "real live Hoosiers." Courtesy, Indiana State Library, Indiana Division

By 1865 Indiana's towns had advanced considerably beyond their pioneer circumstances. This 1868 view of the north side of Main Street in Delphi shows the commercial block to be booming. Some buildings enjoy new board sidewalks, while several shops cater to their customers' comfort by constructing new awnings. Courtesy, Indiana State Library, Indiana Division

Following the Civil War more than half the people of Indiana still made their living by farming. The prosperity of this farm near Pipe Creek Falls in Cass County is evident in its large banked barn. Courtesy, Cass County Historical Society

by Fort Wayne, Terre Haute, and South Bend, all cities with good railroad connections and expanding industries. Other cities such as Lafayette, Muncie, Anderson, Marion, and Richmond exercised commercial influence over their surrounding counties, and by the turn of the century there were nineteen cities of 10,000 residents and competition among them was vigorous.

Indianapolis had more than 100,000 residents in 1890, three times the population of any other city in the state. Although the White River was useless for navigation, Indianapolis enjoyed excellent rail connections in all directions and the railroad yards and shops themselves made a substantial contribution to the local economy. Indianapolis was more than a commercial success and the political center of Indiana. It was also the cultural heart of the state. English's Opera House on the

Circle was the state's most noted theater, and many famous performers appeared on its stage. It was also the scene of rousing political meetings for both parties.

Ambitious young men from throughout the state made their way to Indianapolis seeking fame and fortune, some as writers and others as politicians, and they greatly enriched their adopted home. Good rail transportation made Indianapolis an important center for wholesale trade, supplying storekeepers in the smaller cities and towns with goods of every description. It had no significant rivals within the state, although there was strong competition from merchants in Chicago, Cincinnati, and Louisville.

The amount of farmland in Indiana increased gradually until the turn of the century, as the drainage of wetlands in the north opened additional acreage for farming, particularly in the Kankakee Marsh. At the beginning of the twentieth century more than 94 percent of Indiana's land was in farms, after which there was a slow decline. More than three-quarters of the farmland was "improved," meaning that it had been cleared of the original forest cover and developed as cropland or pasture. The average farm was ninety-seven acres in size and would soon begin to in-

county fairs where the value of new methods was demonstrated and promoted. Rural schools reached most children by the 1870s. The *Indiana Farmer* began publication in 1866 and kept farmers informed about improved seeds, better livestock, and more productive ways of doing farm work. Purdue University professors carried the message of scientific farming throughout the state. Farmers' Institutes brought farmers into town to hear experts from Purdue and elsewhere, and by the mid-1890s there was at least one institute a year in each county. The institutes included programs for farm women, covering such topics as food preparation and housekeeping. In 1905 Purdue began its popular "agricultural trains," using specially fitted railroad cars to carry exhibits and instructors

crease as the advances in farm machinery made it possible for fewer farmers to produce ever larger harvests.

The hilly land of southern Indiana could sustain farm families, but the rich level lands of central and northern Indiana, along with southern bottom lands, attracted the investments in machinery, drainage, and farming techniques which characterized up-to-date commercial agriculture. Farmers fenced in their increasingly valuable livestock rather than trying to protect crops by fencing animals out, and they used barbed wire rather than the split rails of frontier days. Better breeding stock improved cattle, swine, and sheep, and farmers proudly showed their prize animals at the

In the left foreground of this early 1890s harvest scene is a quaint-looking piece of steam-powered threshing equipment. Most farm implements continued to be pulled by horses until the 1920s. Courtesy, Cass County Historical Society

throughout Indiana. The first resident county agents were appointed in 1912, and within a few years expert farming advice was available in every county, supported by a combination of federal and state funds.

While farming techniques gradually improved, the basic agricultural pattern in Indiana remained remarkably stable. From the earliest days of settlement corn has been the most important crop, and this is still true. Wheat yielded second place in bushels harvested to oats after 1899, but remained second only to corn in value. The soft winter wheat was generally sold to commercial flour millers, but almost 80 percent of the corn and 70 percent of the oats were used on the farm to feed livestock, as was most of the large hay crop.

The greatest livestock market for central Indiana was Indianapolis, where the stockyards received more than 2,000,000 hogs in good years as well as 400,000 cattle. Livestock from northern Indiana often moved directly to the great Chicago stockyards, while Louisville and Cincinnati were major markets for southern Indiana farmers. Dairy cattle were widely kept by Indiana farmers, but only from the 1880s did commercial dairying become an important business. Vegetable crops were increasingly important, both for sale in nearby markets and for canning, and Indiana became well-known for its tomatoes and onions, as well as cantaloupes and watermelons which flourished in the fertile soil of the lower Wabash valley, particularly in Posey County.

The first local farm organizations in Indiana appeared in the 1820s, and the State Board of Agriculture was created in 1835. Its most visible activity was the state fair, which was first held in 1852. There were of course associations for those with special interests, whether Jersey cows or beekeeping, but the most vital farm organization was the Patrons of Husbandry, better known as the Grange, organized in Indiana in 1869.

During the difficult depression years after 1873 the Grange grew rapidly. Grangers were less political in Indiana than in Illinois or Iowa, but the 3,000 lodges offered social and educational opportunities for more than 60,000 members, as well as educational programs, buyer and producer cooperatives, and political support for such measures as better rural roads, tax reform, and free rural mail delivery. There were other political organizations for farmers, but most quickly disappeared, leaving the Grange for diminished social functions and the Farm Bureau organization for cooperatives and carrying the farm message to elected politicians.

The first Farm Bureaus appeared in 1912, often with the county agricultural agent playing an important role in their organization. A statewide association, eventually known as the Indiana Farm Bureau, was established in 1919 to voice the concerns of the state's larger and more prosperous farmers.

Despite the advances in agriculture the daily life of a farm family was still characterized by drudgery and isolation. Residents of the growing cities enjoyed many advantages and comforts. Major streets were usually paved with brick by the last years of the nineteenth century, and cities had abundant clean water from the water works rather than individual wells, water enough even for fire hydrants. The larger cities had gas lights on the streets and in stores and prosperous private homes, and by the early 1890s electricity was increasingly available. Telephones arrived in the late 1870s, all conveniences still unknown in rural areas. The larger cities had horse-drawn streetcars moving over steel rails set in the middle of major streets, replaced during the early 1890s by electric trolley cars which provided dependable and inexpensive public transportation.

Every town had its "downtown" section with stores, shops, and professional offices, often located around the courthouse square in the county seats. Many of the fashionable commercial buildings of the 1880s and 1890s still stand, and in a number of Indiana cities they are now being restored to their original beauty. Downtown also featured the bankers, lawyers, physicians, and dentists who made the towns both prosperous and comfortable. City police departments and well-equipped volunteer fire departments provided for the public safety, and every town of more than 1,000 or so residents boasted a high school, while farm boys and girls usually ended their formal education at the eighth grade.

Town life offered vastly greater opportunities for social life and for amusements. Farm families went to town once a week during good weather, usually on Saturday evening when the stores stayed open until midnight for the convenience of rural customers. In every town there were Ma-

Above: *Indiana's enthusiasm for politics in the late nineteenth century is illustrated in this photo taken during the campaign of 1868. Banners stretch across commercial buildings on the public square in Delphi. The top banner, "We stand by Congress, none but loyal men shall rule the nation," is a reference to the impeachment procedings against Andrew Johnson. Courtesy, Indiana State Library, Indiana Division, R.G. Bradshaw Collection*

Left: *Store proprietors, many of them sons of pioneers, found themselves living comfortably among the middle class in the "Golden Years" of Hoosier life. The store of Charles A. Hughes in Hagerstown, Wayne County, seen here in a turn-of-the-century photo, sold notions and dry goods. Courtesy, Indiana Historical Society*

sonic halls and Odd Fellows lodges for middle class men, as well as a great variety of other clubs for both men and women. Ordinary working men found food, drink, and friends in taverns and saloons. Churches of every denomination were convenient for townspeople, and most of them also sponsored clubs ranging from the Catholic Knights of Columbus to the Baptist Ladies Missionary Aid Society.

Every city had its "opera house," and if Wagner and Verdi were rarely heard there were frequent concerts, recitals, plays, and lectures to enrich and enliven the leisure hours. Farm families rarely enjoyed much leisure, and except for church on Sunday most pleasures were far away over miserable roads. Larger cities had public and private parks, and a Sunday afternoon outing during summer usually meant a band concert, perhaps following a spirited baseball game.

Many of the homes of late nineteenth-century Hoosiers are still occupied, with modernized kitchens and bathrooms but often little changed in exterior appearance. The mansions of the "richest family in town" have often been preserved, such as the Culbertson home in New Albany or the Barker mansion in Michigan City. The least fashionable houses still to be seen are the "shotgun houses" of the Ohio River towns, three rooms one behind the other, with doorways all in a row so a shotgun blast could carry clear through the house.

Almost as numerous as farmers in Indiana were the politicians, or so it appeared to visitors. The joke was often told of the two-year-old Hoosier boy whose first clear words were "I am not a candidate, but if my party needs me I am ready to accept nomination." Elective offices were many and elections were frequent, but most remarkable was the state's voter turnout. Since 1816 every white man twenty-one years of age or older was eligible to vote, and black men gained the vote in 1870. There was no requirement for advance registration, and statewide voting exceeded 96 percent of those eligible in the presidential elections of 1876 and 1896, while individual counties sometimes reported voter turnout greater than 100 percent. These high turnouts were the result of an intense

Thomas A. Hendricks, originally of Shelbyville, served as a U.S. senator in the 1860s and as Indiana governor from 1872 to 1876. In 1884 he was elected vice president on the Democratic ticket but died after only nine months in office. Courtesy, Indiana State Library, Indiana Division

Above: *Dapper Charles W. Fairbanks, at left, sits next to his running mate Charles Evans Hughes, the unsuccessful Republican candidate for President in 1916. Considered cold and conservative, Fairbanks was called "the Indiana Icicle." As Theodore Roosevelt's vice president he acquired the nickname "Cocktail Charlie" for serving cocktails when Roosevelt visited Indianapolis in 1907. Courtesy, Indiana State Library, Indiana Division*

Left: *When William English retired as a banker in 1877, he was said to be the richest man in the state. Although not a popular candidate or skilled orator, his personal fortune was not a handicap to his nomination as Democratic vice presidential candidate in 1880. He and the Democrats lost the election. Later in his life he was one of the chief promoters of the Soldiers' and Sailors' Monument. Courtesy, Indiana State Library, Indiana Division*

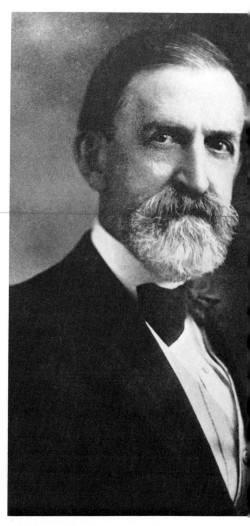

Thomas R. Marshall is perhaps best remembered for his remark about the country's need for "a really good five-cent cigar." He was elected vice president under Woodrow Wilson in 1912 and served two terms. Here he's seen seated in a wicker chair at a reception in 1915. A young FDR with cigar is seated below on the steps; he was then assistant secretary of the navy. Courtesy, Indiana State Library, Indiana Division

Above: John Worth Kern was another of Indiana's many vice presidential candidates; he ran on the ticket with William Jennings Bryan in 1908, which was Bryan's third unsuccessful bid. Kern later went on to a position of power as Senate majority leader and Progressive Democrat during the Woodrow Wilson administration. Courtesy, Indiana State Library, Indiana Division

Facing page, bottom: James D. "Blue Jeans" Williams, governor of Indiana from 1876 to 1880, earned his nickname from his fondness for wearing denim. A self-proclaimed "dirt farmer," he owned more than 3,000 acres of land by the time he was elected. As governor, Williams was honest and economical, true to the pioneer virtues of his youth. Courtesy, Indiana Historical Society

J. Frank Hanly served as governor of Indiana from 1905 to 1909. After a lifetime as a crusader against alcohol he was nominated as the presidential candidate of the Prohibition party in 1916. The Prohibition party won few votes and did little to secure nationwide prohibition. Courtesy, Indiana Historical Society

interest in politics, by all accounts the leading sport in Indiana during the latter part of the nineteenth century.

While Democrats and Republicans remained generally anti-black after the Civil War, Indiana Republicans gradually came to support the national party's program of voting rights for black men. Congressman George W. Julian was one of the few who favored civil and political rights for blacks as a matter of conscience. When blacks gained the vote in 1870 the Republicans immediately claimed to be the party of Lincoln and emancipation, and accused the Democrats of favoring slavery and white supremacy. The black vote was not large in statewide elections, but it was locally important in some cities and it remained firmly Republican until the New Deal.

Advocates of voting rights for women argued that white women were as qualified to vote as black men. In Congress Julian introduced a constitutional amendment to remove sexual as well as racial barriers to voting, but it received little support. The Indiana Women's Rights Convention of 1869 endorsed Julian's proposal and announced that women would soon destroy the deadly trade in liquor when they won the right to vote. The General Assembly debated the question of women's suffrage at great length and rejected the idea.

Women's organizations and church groups continued the fight against liquor, working through the State Temperance Alliance and later the Women's Christian Temperance Union. A law tightly regulating the liquor business passed in 1873, with strong Republican and weak Democratic support, and against the objections of many German societies. The temperance question was a major election issue in 1874, but a year later the law was replaced by a milder version allowing county commissioners to license liquor sales.

Left: *Generations of Indiana school-children learned to read and write in one-room schoolhouses like this one in Delaware County in 1879. From T.B. Helm,* History of Delaware County, Indiana, *1891*

Facing page: *Alumni of the Bear Creek School near Hagerstown in Wayne County gather for a reunion in 1911. Six years later, the school was destroyed by a cyclone. Courtesy, Indiana Historical Society*

Drinkers were able to prevent further regulation for many years, and women's groups carried on the anti-liquor crusade by persuading men to vote as they asked.

Both parties were divided on the complex questions of banking, greenback paper currency, and the gold standard, but after the financial Panic of 1873 these became the leading political issues. Bankruptcies were numerous, farmers could not pay their debts, and in 1877 Indianapolis and other railroad cities were the scenes of violent strikes. The *Indianapolis Journal* accused the strikers of "communistic sentiments."

In this era of general advance in wealth and comfort, schools also increased in number and improved in quality. Still, as late as 1900 nearly 2,000 one-room schools remained in use in the country-side. Teachers were miserably paid even by nineteenth-century standards, and many of them were still in their late teens, scarcely older than some of their pupils. Many county and township officials preferred male teachers despite their higher wages, and not until 1900 did women outnumber men as

teachers in Indiana. "Boarding round" was sometimes practiced, as rural teachers collected part of their wages in room and board from the parents of their pupils. Some teachers were trained in "normal institutes" which offered a few months of basic instruction in reading and arithmetic, teaching methods, and maintaining discipline. Most teachers relied more on good common sense and the lessons they learned in township or county institutes which offered a few days of instruction before schools opened in the fall.

Only twenty-three towns maintained high schools before 1870, but by the turn of the century every town had a high school, although enrollment was usually limited to pupils whose families planned to send them to college or into skilled clerical occupations. Only in the twentieth century did four-year high school programs become generally available for rural students or city boys and girls of working class families.

Indiana colleges grew in number and quality after the Civil War and some achieved a measure of national distinction. Wabash and DePauw were

the best-known before 1890, and many of their alumni won political and literary fame. The distinguished scientist David Starr Jordan greatly improved Indiana University during his presidency from 1885 to 1891.

By the turn of the century many colleges admitted women, but most Hoosiers were still not convinced that young women would benefit from higher education. The only colleges exclusively for women were opened by Catholic nuns on the foundations of older academies: St. Mary-of-the-Woods at Terre Haute and St. Mary's College at Notre Dame, just outside South Bend. Earlham, in

the Quaker tradition, was coeducational from its founding in 1858.

Rose Polytechnic Institute opened at Terre Haute in 1883, and though it was small it provided a high quality education in engineering. Purdue University was the state's land-grant college, supported in part by the proceeds from the sales of federal land in 1865.

Religion was of vital importance in the lives of many Hoosiers. Methodists remained the most numerous until about 1916, when they were overtaken by the rapidly growing Catholic population. The Disciples of Christ ranked third, followed by

Famed evangelist Billy Sunday was one of the single greatest forces in bringing about prohibition in Indiana. The former baseball player turned preacher held forth at Winona Lake, where he and his wife had a summer home. Courtesy, Bettman Archive

Baptists, the United Brethren, and Presbyterians. The Protestant predominance was still overwhelming, and this was of continuing social and political importance. The great dividing issue was temperance, as Methodists, Christians (Disciples), and Presbyterians generally agreed that the government should destroy the evil of drink. Catholics, whether German or Irish or Polish, argued that drinking was a private matter and no concern of the government except to punish drunkenness. The liquor question was bitterly fought, with many Baptists and most Episcopalians also in opposition to government regulation of private behavior.

Church building flourished among all denominations, although by the early years of the twentieth century many rural Protestant congregations could no longer support resident pastors. Some churches had always been served by part-time ministers. Revivals continued to flourish, with old-fashioned camp meetings giving way to summer assemblies, often modeled on the chautauqua meetings. The best known was the Winona Assembly on the shore of Winona Lake in Kosciusko County, where Billy Sunday often preached.

Until the 1870s the foreign population of Indiana was very largely German or Irish. The Germans were more numerous and formed a significant element of the population in most of the large cities, particularly Evansville, Fort Wayne, Hammond, and Indianapolis. Many Germans also continued their home country occupation of farming, and there were large numbers of Germans in the rural areas of Vanderburgh, Dubois, and Franklin counties. In such towns as Jasper and Oldenburg the German influence was pervasive. The growing industrial cities of South Bend, Hammond, and East Chicago attracted many thousands of immigrants from eastern and southern Europe: Poles, Hungarians, Czechs, Slovaks, Italians, and Greeks. This was a strange new element within the Indiana population, and it would be many years before the grandchildren of these newcomers would be called Hoosiers. Although powerful in the industrial cities of the Calumet Region, the influence of these new immigrants statewide was very slight. Blacks numbered only about 2 percent of the state's population, but concentrated in such cities as Jeffersonville, Evansville, and Indianapolis, the black minority was already a significant social and political influence.

Civic boosters claimed that Indiana had the highest proportion of native-born white residents of any state in the Union (92 percent in 1920), as well as the lowest proportion of foreign-born of any northern state (5.2 percent). The typical Hoosier was indeed of old American stock, and very likely Protestant as well as white and "Anglo-Saxon."

Indiana's cultural life flourished in this more

James Whitcomb Riley

Hoosier poet James Whitcomb Riley is seen surrounded by children in a 1916 photo, taken one month before his death. His little poodle Lockerbie sits on his lap. Courtesy, Indiana State Library, Indiana Division

No Hoosier has ever been more admired or more widely read than James Whitcomb Riley. For two generations he represented Indiana in the minds of many Americans, and no American poet except perhaps Longfellow was more widely read. Riley's verse is out of fashion today, but his name remains famous as the author of charming rhymes for children.

Riley was born in Greenfield in 1849, and drifted through a variety of odd jobs before settling down as a newspaperman. He moved to Indianapolis in 1877 and gradually came to publish more verse than news stories. His first collection of poems was published in 1883 as *The Old Swimmin'-Hole*, and *'Leven More Poems*, and in succeeding years he brought out many collections of verse, usually timed for the Christmas market. Riley has been called a "natural poet," and he never attended college.

Riley wrote often about the natural scene of rural Indiana, sometimes in a "Hoosier dialect" which owed more to his imagination than to his ear for conversation. His most popular poems are still recognized by title: "Little Orphant Annie," "When the Frost is on the Punkin," and "The Raggedy Man." Riley toured the nation reciting his poetry, and he was noted for his ability to make an audience laugh or cry as he chose. His verse was sentimental and remained fixed in the rural and small town world of his youth. He always appeared elegantly dressed, to the surprise of urban audiences who expected him to resemble the shabby figures of his verse. Despite his famed love for children he never married. Riley died in 1916, universally mourned, and for years Indiana schoolchildren celebrated Riley Day in his memory. As Edgar Lee Masters wrote of Riley, "He put Indiana as a place and a people in the memory of America...."

EF YOU DON'T WATCH OUT

BY JAMES WHITCOMB RILEY

Facing page: *The line "the Gobble-uns'll git ye—Ef you don't watch out!" is from Riley's popular poem "Little Orphant Annie." Illustrator Ethel Franklin Betts here depicts Annie on the cover of a 1908 publication of the poem as a child's picture book. Courtesy, Indiana State Library, Indiana Division*

settled age. Although a few musicians and a larger number of landscape painters achieved distinction, Hoosier talent was typically expressed in literature. From the 1870s until the 1920s an astonishing number of Indiana writers achieved national fame, many of them writing about their home state and its people.

The Golden Age of Indiana literature began in 1871 with the publication of Edward Eggleston's novel *The Hoosier School-Master*. Eggleston described with fascinating detail the backwoods life of his native southeastern Indiana during the 1830s, with close attention to dialect and folk traditions. Eggleston sought to show that the West deserved a place in American literature along with New England, and *The Hoosier School-Master* was an immediate success throughout the country. *The Circuit Rider* was the story of a heroic young Methodist missionary who died in his effort to bring the gospel to the reluctant pioneers, and it too was a bestseller. Eggleston was in New York, far from his birthplace in Vevay when he achieved fame, but he made the Indiana frontier come alive for millions of readers.

Maurice Thompson's historical romances lacked the realistic touch of Eggleston's work, but his *Alice of Old Vincennes* is still read. It is a story of tangled love and loyalties set at the time of George Rogers Clark's capture of Vincennes. Thompson lived in Crawfordsville, and for a time was a law partner of Lew Wallace.

Other Hoosier authors wrote of more exotic worlds, whether ancient Rome and Palestine for Lew Wallace in *Ben Hur* or the England of Henry VIII for Charles Major in *When Knighthood Was in Flower*. Both were bestsellers as novels and achieved even wider renown on stage and later as films. Wallace never set a story in Indiana, but Major's *Bears of Blue River* was a great success.

George Barr McCutcheon wrote romantic novels also, but his exotic locale existed only in his mind, the mythical Balkan kingdom of *Graustark*. McCutcheon also attempted a historical novel set in his native Lafayette, but *Viola Gwyn* was not among his bestsellers. *Brewster's Millions* was a success, although McCutcheon published it under an assumed name to see if the book could succeed on its own.

Meredith Nicholson, often called the "dean of Hoosier writers," featured Indiana in all of his works. Born in Crawfordsville and a resident of Indianapolis in his maturity, Nicholson was a journalist, lecturer, poet, and diplomat as well as a novelist and essayist. As a young man he talked often with Lew Wallace, who encouraged his writing. Nicholson's most enduring work is *The Hoosiers*, a study of Indiana literature and culture with shrewd observations on the state and its writers. His most popular novel was the romantic *House of a Thousand Candles*, a highly successful effort to apply the Graustark theme in an Indiana setting, in this case Lake Maxinkuckee in Marshall County. His *Hoosier Chronicle* drew upon his experiences as a student at Wabash College.

In *The Hoosiers* Nicholson identified James Whitcomb Riley as the foremost poet in Indiana, and there was no one to challenge his judgment. For most Americans Riley typified the Hoosier, and if few read his poetry today except in children's anthologies, he nevertheless had a great impact upon the public's idea of what "Hoosier" signified. Many critics say that Riley's version of "Hoosier dialect" was largely his own invention, but there are still New Yorkers who imagine that residents of Greenfield say "I hain't no hand at tellin' tales," or "the little Town o' Tailholt is big enough fer me!"

Gene Stratton Porter did not write in dialect, nor did she publish historical romances. Her stories all involve ordinary people combined with an extraordinary concern for nature. For years she explored the Limberlost Swamp adjacent to her home in Geneva, and she became an expert amateur naturalist and nature photographer. Her first success was *The Song of the Cardinal*, but her

best-known novels were *Freckles* and its sequel *A Girl of the Limberlost,* sentimental stories of young people who struggled to earn enough money to support and educate themselves. When Limberlost Swamp disappeared as a result of drainage and timber-cutting Mrs. Porter built a new home on the shores of Sylvan Lake near Rome City. She continued to write nature tales until she moved to California in 1923, where she helped make a number of her books into successful films.

Booth Tarkington's long career extended into the harsher age of industrial Indiana, but two of his early novels rank with the major works of the Golden Age. *Monsieur Beaucaire* was a historical romance set in eighteenth-century England. It was an immediate success and Tarkington soon made it into a popular play. *The Gentleman from Indiana* featured vicious night-riding "white caps" and Tarkington was accused by some sensitive Hoosiers of maligning the state, but vigilante bands

were indeed a serious problem in a number of southern Indiana counties during the late 1880s and early 1890s.

Indiana's Golden Age was not really golden, but it was a dream not entirely divorced from reality, a dream of selective memory more than any intended distortion. Although it describes a land that never was, it is still possible to enter this golden vision of Hoosier bliss by admiring the idyllic landscapes of T.C. Steele, William Forsyth, or Clarence Ball, reading the verse of James Whitcomb Riley, or the prose of Meredith Nicholson. They all imagined a world too good to be true, but so happy that the modern reader can only wish that it might have been. As Riley wrote:

There's a ghostly music haunting
Still the heart of every guest
And a voiceless chorus chanting
That the Old Times were the best.

CHAPTER VII

Early industry in the state was closely tied to agriculture. Beck's Mill in Washington County, just southwest of Salem, was built in the early 1860s on the site of two earlier log structures. The flour mill operated daily until 1943. Courtesy, Indiana State Library, Indiana Division

The Rise Of Industry

While pioneer Indiana was known chiefly for its agricultural riches, manufacturing appeared early on a small scale. Farmers needed millers to grind their grain into flour, and hundreds of mills were built as corn and wheat production expanded. It was slow and expensive to haul grain for more than twelve or fifteen miles, so millers followed the farmers into new lands and built their mills where they could dam a stream and secure an adequate supply of water to turn the millstones. A few mills still grind grain in this time-tested fashion, such as Spring Mill south of Bedford and Bonneyville Mill in Elkhart County, which has been in use since 1840.

Sawmills were another early feature of the industrial landscape. Pioneers had to fashion logs into planks with ax, adz, and hand saw, but water-powered sawmills saved labor, time, and expense. Sawmills were essential for the new method of "balloon frame" construction which spread from Chicago in the mid-1830s, a technique of building which depended upon lighter and easier-to-handle timbers fastened together with cheap machine-made nails. Many sawmills also shaped part of their timber into furniture, and a number of these early furniture centers are still active, such as Jasper and Nappanee. Wood was also widely used in the manufacture of farm implements, notably by

Gaar and Company at Richmond and two South Bend firms, James Oliver's plow works and the Studebaker Brothers' wagon factory. Cutting veneer from fine hardwoods, particularly walnut, emerged as an important industry in the later years of the nineteenth century. The finest walnut trees brought more than $100 by 1880, and a single large tree was worth more than an acre of prime farmland. Today New Albany remains a major producer of walnut veneers.

Meat packing was important from the early days of settlement, as most of Indiana's enormous corn crop was converted into beef or pork on the farm. For distant markets the animals were driven to the Ohio River towns and slaughtered, and the meat was packed in heavily salted water or smoked, in the case of hams and bacon, and then shipped downriver to New Orleans. In mid-century, as the rail network expanded, meat packing appeared in inland towns as well. Farmers generally butchered their own meat, and every town had its own butchers for local needs.

Much of the grain which was not used for an-

imal feed was converted into other valuable forms. Small-scale brewing of beer was widespread, but when large numbers of Germans began to reach Indiana in the 1840s brewing became a major business in such cities as Evansville, Terre Haute, Indianapolis, and Fort Wayne. Many other residents preferred their liquid refreshment in the form of corn whiskey, and Lawrenceburg and Terre Haute became major distillery centers. Whiskey production in Terre Haute was destroyed by Prohibition in 1920, but distilling survives as the largest industry in Lawrenceburg.

Most of these early manufactures were closely tied to the farmers who made up most of the state's population, whether as suppliers or customers, or often both. Most of them also relied upon a dependable supply of water, whether for power, transportation, or as an essential ingredient for quality beer and whiskey.

Boat-building yards at Madison, New Albany, and especially Jeffersonville were successful. The Howard Ship Yards of Jeffersonville became the foremost boat builders on the western waters during the 1850s. By the early twentieth century Howard shifted successfully from wooden hulls to steel, and then from paddle wheels to propellers. Although Howard survived the railroads it succumbed to the Depression, closing in 1941 after ninety years at the same location under three generations of family ownership.

Indianapolis was the largest city in Indiana by 1860, but its industries were dependent upon agriculture. Meat packing was the leading industry, both pork and beef. Flour milling came second, until overtaken by iron foundries late in the century. The National Starch Manufacturing Company, using Indiana's abundant corn as its raw material, was one of the largest starch producers in the country by 1890. Baking and vegetable canning were also important, with Frank Van Camp's pork and beans in tomato sauce becoming a household name throughout the nation, often called "Boston-baked beans" despite their Hoosier origin.

The city's best known manufacturer opened in 1876 when Colonel Eli Lilly, a Civil War veteran

Above: *The Eagle Brewery in Vincennes was one of the numerous breweries in Indiana founded by German immigrants. It claimed to be "the only brewery in the country that manufactures absolutely pure beer, having no equal as a beverage or for medicinal uses." Courtesy, Indiana State Library, Indiana Divsion*

Right: *Boat building in the Ohio River communities of Madison, New Albany, and Jeffersonville was an important industry during the nineteenth century. By the early twentieth century, the shift was made from wooden hulls to steel and then from paddle wheels to propellers. This aerial view of the Jeffersonville Boat and Machine Company, taken during the 1940s, shows both old and new technologies. Courtesy, Indiana State Library, Indiana Division*

Facing page: *This piece of Indiana-made furniture was generically known as a Hoosier kitchen cabinet. It features drawer bins for flour and other staples, a pullout cutting board beneath the counter work space, and convenient small drawers and glass-doored cabinets above. This catalog photo illustrates a 1912-1913 model for the modern kitchen. Courtesy, Indiana State Library, Indiana Division*

who had already failed in several businesses, began making drugs. From the start Lilly emphasized ethical drugs which were sold to physicians, rather than the more popular home remedies. By 1898, when Colonel Lilly died, his company produced some 2,000 pharmaceutical preparations, most of them made from plant extracts. Lilly remained under family management for three generations and became one of the nation's leading pharmaceutical companies. Its most notable advance came with the first commercial production of insulin in 1923. Insulin was made from animal pancreas glands which Lilly purchased by the ton from stockyards around the Midwest. Almost overnight diabetes was changed from a deadly illness to a controllable condition, and within a year insulin sales exceeded one million dollars.

Miles Laboratories of Elkhart is a pharmaceutical company which developed from the patent medicine era. Dr. Franklin L. Miles began in 1882 with Dr. Miles' Restorative Nervine, a calmative for nervousness which remained in production until 1979. Nervine was followed by Dr. Miles' Restorative Blood Purifier, Dr. Miles' Anti-Pain Pills, and a variety of similar products. Miles was an energetic promoter, and proudly advertised that his medicines were entirely free of dangerous ingredients such as opium and cocaine, which were widely used by his competitors. In later years Miles Laboratories became a major producer of ethical drugs and medical tests, best known to the public as the maker of Alka-Seltzer.

Although there was neither gold nor silver, mineral wealth abounded in the hills of southern Indiana. Bricks were made from local clays throughout the state by the 1840s, but gradually the industry developed into a few large-scale operations, notably around Evansville and Terre Haute. Two well-known firms were the Indiana Paving Brick Company of Brazil, which opened in 1891 for the production of hard-surface bricks used for paving city streets, and the Burns and Hancock Company of Vermillion County, a manufacturer of firebricks for steelmakers and other industries.

Coal was mined in Perry County during the

The Van Camp Packing Company, established in 1861, pioneered both in advertising and in the canned foods industry. This was one of the first full-page advertisements for canned foods in a national magazine. The exclusive Van Camp product—pork and beans with tomato sauce—originated in Indianapolis, not Boston. Courtesy, Indiana State Library, Indiana Division

1830s, but widespread coal mining could not develop until railroads reached the coal fields near Brazil in Clay County during the early 1850s. Coal production increased rapidly thereafter, at first from surface mines and later from deep shafts sunk into the earth with little regard for engineering or safety. A miner's working life was dark, dangerous, and often ended in serious injury or death. By 1860 coal production reached 100,000 tons, and by 1872 it had increased to one million tons, chiefly from Clay, Fountain, and Daviess counties.

Just to the south and east of the coal mining

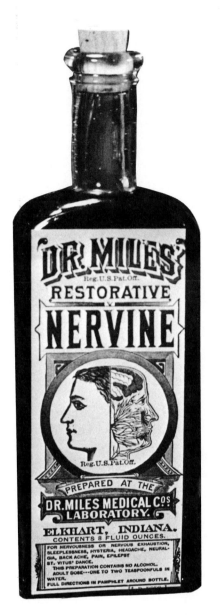

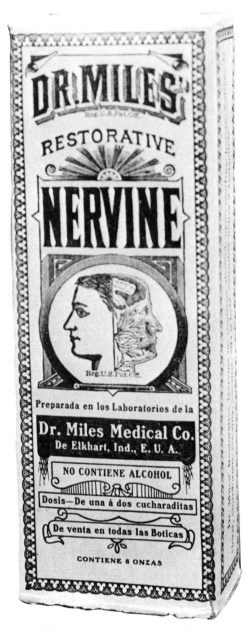

In the early 1880s Dr. Franklin L. Miles of Elkhart began bottling a patent medicine designed to cure various forms of nervousness, from hysteria to St. Vitus' Dance. The product remained in production by Miles Laboratory through 1979. Courtesy, Miles Laboratories

The coal deposits of southern Indiana were mined as early as the 1830s. In this coal mine near Brazil in Clay County, coal is being screened at the tipple. Courtesy, Indiana State Library, Indiana Division, photo by Chicago Architectural Photographing Company

Right: *Indiana once produced 65 percent of the finished cut stone in the United States. This scene in a limestone quarry near Bedford contains some interesting steam-operated cutting machinery. Courtesy, Indiana State Library, Indiana Division*

Facing page: *Ball jars for canning, manufactured in Muncie, are known throughout the country. Here a newly formed fruit jar is shown at the moment it was removed from the blow mold and transferred to a conveyor that would carry it along to a tempering oven. Courtesy, Indiana State Library, Indiana Division*

districts another mineral was brought into production as the railroads opened the hill country for commerce. Limestone from Owen County was used commercially as early as 1853 and the high quality of Indiana limestone gradually acquired a national reputation. New York builders took note in 1879 when William K. Vanderbilt used Indiana limestone for his elegant Fifth Avenue mansion.

The discovery of natural gas in Jay County in 1886 came as a profitable surprise. Many other wells followed quickly in east central Indiana, and for a few years the Indiana natural gas field was the world's most productive. The "Gas Boom" meant quick prosperity for Muncie, Kokomo, Anderson, New Castle, Marion, and the new town of Gas City. Pipelines were laid to Indianapolis, Fort Wayne, Richmond, and even Chicago, and some Hoosiers dreamed of easy wealth that would endure forever.

Industry rushed in to take advantage of the cheap fuel, particularly glassmaking for which clean-burning fuel was especially important. The

five Ball brothers settled in Muncie in 1887 when the city offered them free gas for their glass-making enterprise. The chief Ball product was a patented glass jar for home canning, known usually as a Ball jar. By 1899 there were 110 glass works in Indiana, most of them in the gas belt, and the state ranked second nationally in glass production. The Indiana Tumbler and Goblet Company, located at Greentown in Howard County, was a leading producer of ornamental colored glass from 1894 until 1903. Its "Greentown glass" is highly prized by collectors today.

Unfortunately the boom mentality led to excessive production and wasteful consumption. By the mid-1890s gas production dropped sharply and the boom collapsed, although some of the industry remained, particularly the Ball factory at Muncie. In 1890 oil was discovered just north of the gas field, but it was a sour crude with high sulfur content that could be processed only by the new Standard Oil refinery at Whiting. The oil field was also a shallow formation, and its output declined sharply after 1907.

Indiana workingmen who labored in mills and factories earned about $2.00 to $2.50 a day for skilled labor around 1870, but many could not depend upon working every day. Layoffs were common because of weather or business conditions. Unskilled men usually earned no more than one dollar a day, and women and children workers made even less. Many women were employed as domestic servants, and middle class families generally had at least one servant to do the cooking and housework.

As wages were cut after the Panic of 1873 some workers began to organize unions to secure higher pay and better working conditions, as printers

and railroad workers had done earlier. Successes were few, but the legislature did begin to regulate child labor and to require minimum safety precautions in coal mines by 1879. Strikes among coal miners were not uncommon, and frequently the company response was to hire black strike breakers, often leading to violence. Four black miners were murdered in Fountain County in 1878, and militia troops were sent from Indianapolis to restore peace.

While the rest of the state filled up with farmers and small towns, the northwestern corner of Indiana remained almost untouched. The Calumet Region was a land of swamps and sand dunes and few people chose to settle there until after the

Civil War. Between 1852 and 1865 four mainline railroads built across Lake County, but only in their rush to reach Chicago. Easy transportation brought some progress, with a few farmers growing hay and berries and producing dairy products for the nearby Chicago market. Another thriving trade in the 1870s and 1880s was cutting ice from ponds during the winter for sale to the Chicago meat packers. The ice was stored in warehouses insulated with sawdust or cork and used through the summer to cool the railroad cars which carried meat to market.

The first city of the Calumet Region was Hammond, established in 1869 by George H. Hammond, a developer of the railroad refrigerator car. Hammond and his partner Marcus M. Towle chose the location because it was convenient both to the Chicago stockyards and to the ice ponds. Hammond disliked the city he named for himself and preferred to live in Detroit, but Towle lived

THOMAS E. KNOTTS
POZOR SLOVACI
A Polaci dobre vam znamo je že stari mayor našeho mesta je naj lepši prijatel našeho naroda.

Ne za pomňice na ňeho. Na 7ho November 1916. Na Election Den. On je jeden prijatel nas vo Lake County. Hlasujte na neho
Za SHERIFFA

in Hammond and served for years as the city's mayor. Much of the population was German, and at the peak of operations G.H. Hammond & Company employed 1,800 workers who butchered 400,000 cattle, 500,000 sheep, and 850,000 hogs a year. The plant burned in 1901 and was never rebuilt, and since then Hammond has relied upon petroleum, chemical, and soap plants.

John D. Rockefeller's Standard Oil Company established the lakefront town of Whiting in 1889 as a location for the world's largest refinery. The Standard Oil Company of Indiana was organized to operate the refinery, but its executives have always maintained their offices in Chicago. Standard Oil built Whiting on bare sand to provide housing for its skilled workers, but the unskilled had to shift for themselves elsewhere. The compa-

ny dominated the town's government, and more than 43 percent of its residents in 1910 were foreign-born, largely German, Polish, Hungarian, and Slovak. Blacks were excluded completely. Standard Oil no longer owns Whiting, but its refinery is still virtually the only business in town.

Gary was conceived in 1905 by the newly merged United States Steel Corporation because it wished to expand in the booming Chicago market. It intended to build the world's greatest steel complex and it needed ample space, good lake and rail transportation, and an ample water supply. Its agents quietly bought 9,000 acres of virtually uninhabited sand dune and swamp, including seven miles of lakeshore. The steel mill came first, and the town followed to provide homes for the workers. Gary was named for Judge Elbert H.

Madame C.J. Walker

Madame C.J. Walker's line of cosmetics established her as one of the most important woman entrepreneurs in the history of Indiana. She has been called the first black woman millionaire in the United States. Courtesy, Indiana Historical Society

Of all the talented entrepreneurs who created the new industrial Indiana, none was more extraordinary than Madame Walker. Sarah McWilliams was born in Louisiana in 1867, the daughter of former slaves. Married at fourteen and widowed at twenty, she endured a life of poverty and desperate effort. With $1.50 saved from her earnings as a laundress

she began to make small batches of cosmetics specially formulated for black women. Her first success was a hair dressing, and a full line of hair and skin care products followed.

She married a newspaperman named Charles J. Walker and was known thereafter as Madame Walker, even after their divorce. She settled in Indianapolis in 1910 and built a thriving business, winning the respect of white businessmen through her shrewd management. Madame Walker's line of cosmetics was sold by a large and enthusiastic sales force of black women, many of whom

later established themselves as independent businesswomen.

Entirely self-educated, Madame Walker generously supported local charities and black schools throughout the country. She always refused, however, to give away any of her products. Her cosmetics were for sale, and women who wanted them would have to pay. Company publicity proudly identified Madame Walker as the first black woman millionaire in the United States. She died in 1919, but The Madame C.J. Walker Manufacturing Company continues to manufacture cosmetics.

Madame Walker's only child, A'Lelia Walker, used her mother's fortune to aid black artists, writers, and musicians of the Harlem Renaissance of the 1920s.

The company erected the Walker Building at the corner of Michigan Street and Indiana Avenue in Indianapolis in 1927. It housed company offices, a beauty salon and a beauty school, offices for black lawyers and physicians, as well as a movie theater on the ground floor and a ballroom at the top level. In the largely segregated Indianapolis of the 1920s and 1930s, the Walker Building was a social as well as business center for black residents. It has recently been restored and continues to house the company's offices.

Gary, chairman of the board of U.S. Steel, but he never had any personal connection with the town. Construction began in 1906 on a grand scale: three mainline railroads were relocated, fifty-one miles of new track was laid, and a two-mile stretch of the Great Calumet River was shifted to a new channel. Eight blast furnaces produced molten iron which fifty-six open hearth furnaces made into steel, and the rolling and fabricating mills were on a similar scale.

The Gary Land Company was the town-building subsidiary, and U.S. Steel did try to avoid the usual problems of the company town. Gary was carefully planned and lots were sold rather than rented. Armanis F. Knotts was the first president of the Gary Land Company, but he was discharged when his superiors at U.S. Steel discovered him selling his own lots instead of the company's. Armanis Knotts and his brother Tom dominated Gary for years, despite frequent clashes with U.S. Steel. "North Side" Gary was a neatly planned city with comfortable homes for supervisors and skilled workmen. The "South Side," also known as "The Patch," was a ramshackle of tents and shacks, inhabited by unskilled workers and a generally unruly population. There were at least 217 saloons, one for every seventy-seven residents. During his first two years in office Mayor Tom Knotts was arrested fourteen times, and acquitted each time. When the city was legally dry in 1909, Mayor Knotts as city judge simply fined saloonkeepers fifty dollars every month.

The business and political leaders of Gary were native-born Americans, but 49 percent of the rapidly-growing population was foreign-born, while another 22 percent was of foreign parentage. Men outnumbered women by two to one. Gary had a population of 16,800 by the time the town was four years old in 1910. The First World War brought an even greater boom to the steel mills and a serious labor shortage as European immigrants could no longer reach America. By 1920 Gary had a population of 55,400, with 22 percent of the residents foreign-born and 9 percent black.

Everything in Gary depended upon steel, and U.S. Steel was even more hostile to labor unions than most large corporations. During the First World War labor received some protection from the federal government, but Judge Gary viewed the steelworkers' union as a communist conspiracy. The inevitable strike began on September 22, 1919, and feelings were tense on both sides. Many of the strikers were European immigrants, but the company hired blacks and Mexicans as strikebreakers and kept the mills operating. On October 4 there was widespread rioting as veterans' organizations such as the Loyal American League attacked the strikers and tore away their red scarves. There were many injuries but no fatalities, and both national guard and federal troops occupied the city to preserve order. Many of the "Gary Reds" and the "Wobblies," members of the radical Industrial Workers of the World, were arrested or run out of town. The strike was abandoned early in January and the army left town a few days later, without having fired a shot.

East Chicago, located between Hammond and Gary, was also a steel town, dominated by Inland Steel, which erected a large integrated steel mill in 1901. Nearly 80 percent of the residents were of foreign or mixed parentage, and when many of the workers joined the strike in 1919 Inland Steel responded by recruiting hundreds of Mexican workers. Mexican labor was welcome even after the strike and by 1926 almost one-third of Inland Steel's employees were Mexican, making the firm the nation's largest employer of Mexican workers. During the Depression there was an organized campaign by the residents of East Chicago to force Mexican workers to return to Mexico.

The Calumet Region, often called simply "The Region," differed greatly from the traditional Hoosier culture. It was a land of overwhelming foreign presence and giant steel mills spewing flame, smoke, and ash into the air. More than a few Hoosiers expressed the wish that the northern part of Lake County would break off and float away into Lake Michigan. Yet at the same time Gary was a fascinating example of the new urban America. Under the direction of William A. Wirt from 1907 until 1938 the Gary schools were a model of progressive community education from

kindergarten through adult programs, and the "Gary plan" attracted national attention. Wirt stressed study, work, and play, and he set new standards in school design as well. Schools would have parks and athletic fields nearby, and gymnasiums and auditoriums for community as well as school use.

Steel was limited to northwest Indiana, but the automobile industry had a much wider impact. Although Kokomo's claim to be the home of the first successful automobile in the United States is fervently disputed by several other cities, the automobile certainly came early to Indiana. The state had thousands of workers skilled in machine operation, metal working, and carriage building, as well as ample supplies of hardwood and steel, and a financial and cultural tradition which encouraged the entrepreneur, the individual with fresh ideas for new products and new businesses.

Elwood Haynes grew up in Portland, Indiana, and studied science at Worcester Polytechnic Institute and Johns Hopkins University. He was one of the few automobile pioneers with a college educa-

U.S. Army troops were mustered in front of the Gary Public Library during the 1919 steel strike. U.S. Steel was even more hostile to labor unions than most large corporations, and Judge Gary viewed the steelworkers' union as a communist conspiracy. The troops tried to preserve order in the clash between the red-scarved strikers and veterans' organizations. Courtesy, Calumet Regional Archives, Indiana University Northwest

tion. Haynes was a gas company executive and got his idea for a gasoline-powered vehicle while driving his horse and buggy many weary miles over unpaved country roads as he supervised the construction of a gas pipeline. Haynes designed the car and its power transmission, purchased its gasoline engine, and hired Elmer and Edgar Apperson to build the machine. On July 4, 1894, Haynes made his first test drive on the Pumpkinvine Pike just a few miles from Kokomo. It required several years of development before Haynes and the Apperson brothers had a reliable and practical model, but by 1900 they were able to build some 200 Haynes-Apperson cars a year. In 1906 Haynes and the Appersons went their separate ways, with

Above: *These children at the Bailey Branch of the Gary Public Library demonstrate the ethnic diversity of the city's large foreign-born population. Courtesy, Calumet Regional Archives, Indiana University Northwest, Gary Public Library Collection*

Left: *On July 4, 1922, a commemorative marker was placed on the spot where Elwood Haynes test-ran America's first car. Here Haynes stands next to his invention, which leaves no question as to the derivation of the term "horseless carriage." Over 7,000 people attended the event that day near Kokomo. Courtesy, Indiana State Library, Indiana Division*

Haynes reaching peak production at Kokomo in 1916 when 7,100 cars were built. Haynes was a man of wide engineering interests, and he also invented a vastly improved tool steel known as "Stellite" and played an important part in the development of stainless steel as well.

More than 200 firms manufactured automobiles in Indiana, many of them closing after a few years. Several of the more successful manufacturers were located in Indianapolis, which for a few years around 1910 rivaled Detroit as America's automotive capital. Howard Marmon built his first car in 1903 and for many years the Marmon was among the most elegant of American motor cars. David Parry and Joseph Cole built cars carrying their names at Indianapolis, combining in 1909 as the Cole Motor Car Company which flourished until the early 1920s. Carl G. Fisher established the Prest-O-Lite Company in 1904 to manufacture acetylene gas lamps for night driving and soon shifted to batteries and electric lights.

In 1909 Fisher joined with James Allison and other local businessmen in an ambitious plan to promote the rapidly expanding automotive industry. Their Indianapolis Motor Speedway provided an opportunity to test new cars and equipment

under competitive conditions, and to attract additional attention they sponsored a 500-mile Memorial Day race in 1911. The winning car was a Marmon "Wasp" which completed the distance at an average speed of seventy-four miles per hour, and the "Indy 500" was soon established as Indiana's foremost sporting event. Two years later James Allison established the Allison Engineering Company to build racing cars and experiment with improved automobile design and equipment. Allison was purchased by General Motors in 1929 and later specialized in the production of airplane engines.

Two other Indianapolis auto makers eclipsed Marmon as producers of large, fast, and very expensive luxury cars. The Stutz Company built many fine cars between 1912 and 1936, but none more famous than the "Bearcat" model of the late 1920s. Fred and August Duesenberg built their first car in 1920, and the Duesenberg straight-eights were the quintessence of American automotive achievement. Like Stutz the Duesenberg was also a victim of the Depression, but both are fondly remembered while the Maxwell, the Elcar, the Auburn, and the Hoosier Limited are almost forgotten.

The most enduring automobile manufacturer in the state was Studebaker, established as a blacksmith shop and wagon builder in South Bend in 1852. By the end of the nineteenth century Studebaker claimed to be the largest wagon and carriage manufacturer in the world, and it was certainly the largest of the more than 400 wagon builders in Indiana. Early automobiles were in truth "horseless carriages," but Studebaker was the only firm in the carriage industry to survive into the automotive age. Among the Hoosier auto makers only Studebaker ever became a true mass production operation.

The pattern for the industry's future was set by Henry Ford and the other Detroit automakers, and Indiana became primarily a producer of automobile parts. Frank and Perry Remy of Anderson

This Studebaker Special raced in the 1933
Indy 500. It represented the height of
technological achievement for an Indiana
company founded in South Bend in 1852
as a blacksmith shop and wagon builder.
Studebaker was the only firm in the
carriage industry to survive into the
automotive age. Courtesy, Bass Photo
Company

Booth Tarkington

This portrait of Booth Tarkington was taken when he was thirty, for publication in the magazine Indiana Woman *in February 1899. That same year Tarkington's book* The Gentleman from Indiana *was published. Courtesy, Indiana State Library, Indiana Division*

Booth Tarkington is best remembered for his cheerful stories of boyish mischief and young love, but *Penrod* and *Seventeen* are only part of his achievement. Tarkington was also an acute observer of changing Hoosier society and many of his novels can be read as extended commentary in social history.

Tarkington was born in India-napolis in 1869 and spent most of his life there, and whether by name or in slight disguise his native city was the scene of most of his stories. He was educated at Purdue and Princeton, and achieved fame with his first novel, *The Gentleman from Indiana,* in 1899. Most of his earlier works chronicle the happy life of the prosperous middle class residents of the north side of Indianapolis. By 1915 in *The Turmoil* he began to express a darker view of the way in which industry was changing the American way of life.

This was the explicit theme of his two novels which were awarded Pulitzer Prizes, *The Magnificent Ambersons* (1918) and *Alice Adams* (1921). The Ambersons were the leading family of an un-named city which is obviously Indianapolis, but their wealth was based upon property and as the fashionable areas moved to the suburbs their position declined rapidly. More than anything else it was the automobile which changed the city. George Amberson Minifer, a grandson of the Amberson family, soon discovers that his familiar surrounding had become a strange city, where "the streets were thunderous; a vast energy heaved under the universal coating of dinginess."

Similarly, in *Alice Adams*, a dream of genteel aristocracy is shattered by the onrush of industrialism. Alice Adams is the beautiful daughter of an ambitious mother, and their dream is to win acceptance by high society. Her father, however, is a small businessman who meets his ruin in an effort to compete with big business. Alice is compelled to give up any hope of country club dances and enroll instead in a secretarial school so she can support herself as a working girl.

In these two novels of frustrated dreams and devastated pretense Tarkington described the reality of a new, harsh, and grimy Indianapolis.

Three Sons Of Terre Haute

The smoky city of Terre Haute was the birthplace and boyhood home for three extraordinary men whose careers show diverse responses to the growth of modern industrial society. Eugene V. Debs was born in 1855 when Terre Haute was still a small town, but during his youth it grew rapidly as a manufacturing and railroad center closely tied to the nearby coal mines. His father was a successful small businessman, but Debs dropped out of high school at fourteen and went to work as a paint scraper in the shops of the Vandalia Railroad. He quickly advanced to fireman and in 1875 became a charter member of the local Brotherhood of Locomotive Firemen. From the beginning of his union career Debs sought harmony between workers and owners, and he strictly opposed any kind of violence. He was a leader in organizing the American Railway Union, but the new union was destroyed when the 1894 Pullman strike in Chicago was broken by federal troops, and Debs was jailed on a contrived contempt charge.

After two years of soul-searching Debs concluded that a new effort was needed to achieve a more just society. "I am for humanity," Debs said, as he announced his adherence to socialism. Already famous as a labor leader and renowned for his pow-

Socialist Eugene V. Debs, born in Terre Haute in 1855, was another Hoosier who attained national political fame . He ran as the presidential candidate of the Socialist party of America in five national elections: 1900, 1904, 1908, 1912, and 1920. Courtesy, Indiana State Library, Indiana Division

erful oratory, he immediately played a major role in the socialist movement. Debs differed with many of his comrades in holding to a strong belief in individualism and in rejecting Karl Marx's class interpretation of industrial society. As the Socialist party candidate for president in every election from 1900 to 1912 Debs carried his appeal for reform throughout the country. In his fourth campaign he received 900,000 votes, at 6 percent the highest share of the vote ever won by the Socialist party. As much a prophet as a politician, Debs struggled to rouse

the working men and women of America rather than win elections.

During World War I Debs continued to proclaim his nonviolent principles, and he was eventually convicted of violating the Sedition Act. When the Socialist party again named him as its candidate for president in 1920 he accepted the nomination in the warden's office at the federal penitentiary in Atlanta. American socialism had been torn apart by internal disputes and government persecution, but Debs still received 919,000 votes. He was released late in 1921, called to Washington to visit President Warren Harding, and then returned to a hero's welcome from 25,000 of his friends in Terre Haute.

The Dreiser family lived in such desperate poverty that the children gathered coal from along the railroad tracks to heat their home. Paul escaped at the age of fourteen, briefly as a student at St. Meinrad's Seminary and then by joining a minstrel show. He Americanized his name to Dresser and became a successful actor and composer while living in Evansville with the city's leading madam, remembered today as *My Gal Sal* in the song he wrote for her. Terre Haute later placed a marker in front of Paul Dresser's boyhood home, but his more famous brother Theodore Dreiser was not mentioned in polite Hoosier society. Dreiser's novels were considered scandalous because of their harshly realistic view of poverty, greed, and corruption, and even more for their sexual frankness, although modern readers wonder what anyone found offensive.

Theodore Dreiser left home at the age of sixteen and made his way to Chicago. His first novel, *Sister Carrie*, was the harsh story of a small-town midwestern girl who survived in the city by destroying the men who loved her. Now regarded as a classic, it was a dismal failure in 1900. After several miserable years of poverty, heavy drinking, and unhappy relationships with women, Dreiser found success as a magazine editor, working for a time with his brother in New York. Although Paul Dresser received the credit, the beloved chorus and opening verse of *On the Banks of the Wabash* were actually written by Theodore Dreiser.

Several of his later novels exposed the evils of corrupt businessmen and their political friends, but his greatest success was *An American Tragedy*. For the remainder of his life Dreiser wrote articles in support of labor and social causes. A few months before his death in 1945 he joined the Communist party, a symbolic gesture of his support for the po-

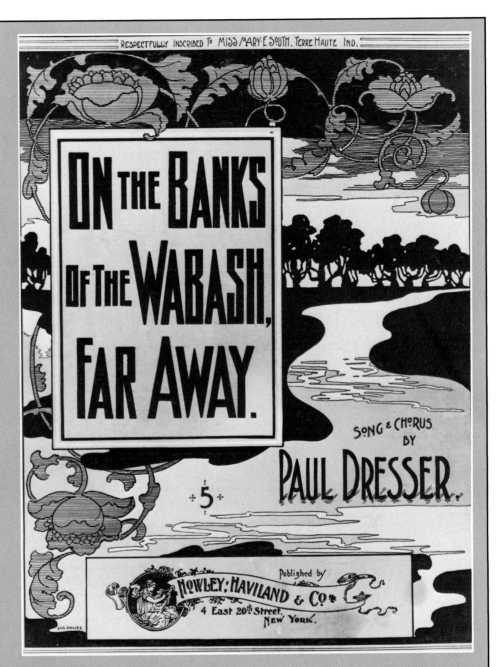

litical left. Although Dreiser and Debs both spent most of their lives trying to improve conditions for working men and women, they apparently never met, although Dreiser sent an admiring letter to Debs. Gene Debs always went home to Terre Haute, while Theodore Dreiser avoided his hometown throughout his adult life.

The Dreiser brothers of Terre Haute both had a hand in the official state song, "On the Banks of the Wabash, Far Away," copywritten in 1897. Although Paul Dresser (Americanized spelling) received the credit for both music and lyrics, the chorus and opening verse were actually written by Theodore Dreiser, author of An American Tragedy *and* Sister Carrie. *Courtesy, Lilly Library, Indiana University, Bloomington*

developed an improved electric dynamo in 1895 and used their profits to establish the Remy Electric Company in 1901, building magnetos and later generators and other automotive electrical items. Remy became a division of General Motors in 1918, and while the last Madison car was built in Anderson that same year the city remains an essential part of the American automotive industry. Every GM car today contains Delco-Remy and Guide Lamp parts manufactured in Anderson.

The expansion of large-scale industry by the early years of the twentieth century furthered the growth of Indiana's cities. Indianapolis remained the leader and by 1920 boasted 314,000 residents. Fort Wayne and Evansville were far behind with about 85,000 each, followed by South Bend, Terre Haute, and Gary. All had become industrial cities, and except for Gary they enjoyed a diversity of industry. Terre Haute, however, did not share fully in the prosperity of the 1920s as Prohibition destroyed its distilleries and richer coal fields in Kentucky captured customers from Indiana coal mines. South Bend had Studebaker and the new Bendix Corporation which manufactured a variety of automotive parts, especially brakes and ignition systems. Fort Wayne attracted a large International Harvester truck plant in 1923, and was also the home of several large General Electric plants which developed from the local firm established by James and Charles Jenney in the early 1880s. Evansville shared in the automobile industry with a Plymouth assembly plant, but more important for its economy was Mead Johnson, which made a variety of food products and vitamins.

Automobiles were not the only new means of transportation at the end of the nineteenth century, and indeed for many years more people traveled by trolley cars. Lafayette set the example in 1888, and by the turn of the century all of Indiana's major cities enjoyed electric streetcar systems which provided safe, clean, and inexpensive transportation. Many city streets were paved with brick or concrete and all of the larger cities developed prosperous downtown shopping and entertainment districts, with the trolley cars giving

easy access to department stores, theaters, restaurants, and specialty shops.

The electric streetcar was so convenient and the city streetcar companies so profitable that energetic builders soon extended the rails into the countryside. These interurban lines used larger cars and often carried packages and light freight as well as passengers, and frequently picked up milk cans at rural stops. The first interurbans went into service at Brazil and Marion in 1893, and within the next twenty years Indiana developed the nation's most comprehensive system of interurban lines. With many changes of cars and companies it was possible to travel entirely by interurbans from New Albany to South Bend or from Fort Wayne to Terre Haute. Most interurban trips were short, and the steam railroads remained faster and more

Indianapolis was served by a dozen interurban lines which radiated in all directions from the Union Traction Terminal downtown on Market Street. From this station approximately 400 cars departed on a daily basis. In 1920 there were 2,600 miles of interurban lines in the state. Courtesy, Bass Photo Company

Indiana developed the nation's most comprehensive system of interurban lines, whereby electric cars provided transportation beyond the cities. The first interurbans went into service at Brazil and Marion in 1893. This photo of the Marion, Bluffton & Eastern Traction Company's car was taken in 1906. Courtesy, Bass Photo Company

Thomas Taggart

Irish immigrant Thomas Taggart was as close as Indiana ever came to the classic "city boss." He served three terms as mayor, was state chairman of the Democratic party in 1892, and was national chairman from 1904 to 1908. The large and elegant resort hotel he built at French Lick offered the best-equipped gambling casino in the Midwest. Courtesy, Indiana State Library, Indiana Division

Tom Taggart was the Democratic "boss" of Indianapolis for a generation as well as the proprietor of Indiana's most elegant resort hotel. Taggart was born in Ireland in 1856 and came to America as a child. He moved to Indianapolis at the age of twenty-one when he was hired as manager of the Union Station eating room. His genial personality and business ef-

ficiency soon brought success as a restaurant manager. In 1886 this popular young man about town was elected county auditor in a campaign where he showed exceptional talent for political organization. Two years later Taggart became the Democratic county chairman, beginning a career as a party official which would lead to the state chairmanship in 1892 and the national chairmanship from 1904 to 1908. Taggart was as close as Indiana ever came to the classic "city boss," and he remained chief of the local Democratic organization until the mid-1920s.

After three terms as mayor of Indianapolis Taggart built a large and elegant resort hotel at French Lick, a southern Indiana spring long renowned for its odorous water which was reputed to have curative properties. Taggart advertised luxury, fine food, and the healthful spa, but visitors flocked to his fashionable French Lick Springs Hotel because it offered the best-equipped gambling casino in the Midwest. Taggart often denied ownership of the casino, but it was located on his hotel grounds and Hoosier politicians never doubted that he was always in control. Although this "Monte Carlo of America" was open for men, women, and even children, local residents were not

allowed to gamble and Orange County prosecutors generally ignored the gambling for forty years.

Tom Taggart looked upon politics as winning elections and putting his friends into government jobs, and he showed little interest in the grandiose arguments about party principles. He played an important part at the Democratic national convention of 1912, throwing Indiana's vote to Woodrow Wilson at a critical moment, and then winning the vice presidential nomination for Governor Thomas R. Marshall. Marshall had helped prevent Taggart's nomination for the Senate a few years earlier, but politics came before mere personal disputes.

Taggart was known as an "easy boss." His political machine was corrupt but never vicious or grasping. His success was entirely personal, for as an immigrant he was an outsider among old-stock Americans, and as an Episcopalian he was an outsider among the largely Catholic Irish.

French Lick and neighboring West Baden have never been as exciting as they were in the days when Tom Taggart entertained the "swells" at his hotel, and the nearby casinos offered roulette, poker, and slot machines through the night.

The French Lick Springs Hotel was a
fashionable gambling resort in the early
twentieth century. The springhouse for
the famous Pluto water, another attrac-
tion of the resort, is seen here at the
right in the midst of the beautifully land-
scaped grounds. Courtesy, Indiana State
Library, Indiana Division

comfortable for long journeys. Indianapolis was served by twelve interurban lines radiating in all directions from the Union Traction Terminal downtown on Market Street, with about 400 scheduled departures daily. In 1920 there were 2,600 miles of interurban lines in Indiana, but the interurban system could not withstand the increasing popularity of the automobile. Most of the interurban track was abandoned by 1940, and the only surviving line in the United States is the Chicago, South Shore and South Bend Railroad, which still operates through the streets of Michigan City in traditional interurban fashion.

The first demands for improved highways came from bicycling enthusiasts of the 1890s and they were soon followed by growing numbers of automobile owners. Although Indiana was a pioneer in the manufacture of automobiles, few early car owners ventured far from town except in favorable weather. Roads were used for little more than local hauling, and maintenance was the reluctant responsibility of township trustees who summoned farmers for a few days of work on the roads each year. Private toll road companies had improved some highways, but most of these were taken over by county governments after 1889. Farmers suffered more than any other element of society from the miserable rural roads, but generally they were more afraid of higher taxes than of being stuck in the mud.

Carl Fisher of Indianapolis played an active part in organizing auto manufacturers and dealers to campaign for improved highways. Fisher's efforts led eventually to construction of the Lincoln Highway from coast to coast and the Dixie Highway from Chicago to Miami, both with Indianapolis as an intermediate point. The Indiana Good Roads Association was formed in 1910 to lobby for improved highways, but the struggle was long and difficult and Indiana did not establish a state highway commission until 1917. The basic highway network was designated and routes were numbered by the mid-1920s, but not until the early 1930s were most of the major state roads paved with hard all-weather surfaces. Most county roads were gravel, at best, for many years longer.

Hesitant as it was, the beginning of the state highway system soon changed rural life forever. The familiar pattern of limited and difficult travel to the nearest small town and virtual isolation during the winter gave way to widespread car ownership, easy travel over much greater distances, and ready access to cities for shopping and recreation. As a result many small towns lost their trade with nearby farmers, and their businesses closed except for a gas station and perhaps a grocery.

Automobiles also made it possible for growing numbers of Hoosiers to travel into the countryside seeking places of natural beauty to enjoy. In connection with the state's celebration of its centennial in 1916, Richard Lieber of Indianapolis led a drive to preserve a valuable tract of virgin timber at Turkey Run in Parke County from the Hoosier Veneer Company. Lieber succeeded by a narrow margin, and along with McCormick's Creek in Owen County Indiana had the beginning of a state park system, a conscious effort to preserve at least a few reminders of an earlier age for the benefit of future generations.

The great conflict which began in Europe in August of 1914 was of little personal concern to residents of Indiana, except for those whose homelands were at war. Most Hoosiers of British ancestry sympathized with the allies, but many thousands of German and Irish descent strongly favored Germany. The Indiana German-American Alliance, led by Joseph H. Keller of Indianapolis, supported the old fatherland while firmly proclaiming its loyalty to the United States. Irish-Americans, most notably Joseph Patrick O'Mahony, editor of the *Indiana Catholic,* favored the Germans because they were fighting the hated British. Most of Indiana's residents of German ancestry loyally supported their adopted homeland, and Governor James Goodrich wisely appointed Richard Lieber as a colonel on his staff to mobilize German opinion in support of the war effort.

Even so there were devastating blows to the many German-American societies, as churches were pressured to use English instead of German for services, German language instruction was

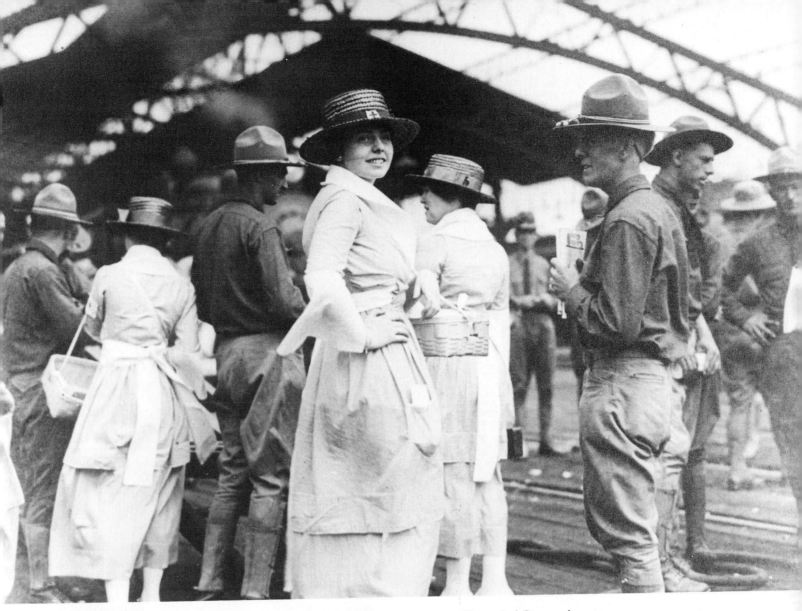

Above: *Women Red Cross workers are seen here in Union Station in Indianapolis "greeting the boys on their way through." Because the capital city was still an important rail hub, many doughboys of World War I passed through the city on their way to training camps and to Europe. Courtesy, Indiana Historical Society, Bretzman Collection*

Left: *Richard Lieber has been called the father of Indiana's state parks. A native of Germany, he came to the United States in 1891. While the director of Indiana's Department of Conservation he gained a national reputation in his field. Here he is seen at Turkey Run State Park. Courtesy, Bass Photo Company*

Above: *Hoosiers purchased $500 million in Liberty bonds, spurred on by patriotic manifestations such as this parade down Meridian Street in Indianapolis in April 1918. Courtesy, Bass Photo Company*

Above left: *The Allied War Exhibit, held in Indianapolis in September 1918, was held to gain public support for the war effort. This soldier was on hand to explain this mortar. Courtesy, Bass Photo Company*

Left: *Four months after war was declared against Germany in April 1917, this group of soldiers was in training at Fort Benjamin Harrison near Indianapolis. Courtesy, Bass Photo Company*

Facing page: *"Welcome Home Day" was celebrated in Military Park on May 7, 1919. Here soldier Charles Robinson of Madison is greeted by a small boy sporting the unusual combination of American flag, Liberty Loan armband, and German martial helmet. Courtesy, Bass Photo Company*

halted in the schools, and many names were changed in response to hostile public opinion. The gymnasts of the Turnverein became Turners, Das Deutsche Haus in Indianapolis became the Athenaeum, and the Wayne County town of East Germantown became officially known as Pershing, renamed in honor of General John J. Pershing. In Evansville popular pressure forced the *Taeglicher Demokrat* to stop publication in 1918, not because the newspaper opposed the war but simply because it was printed in German. Enthusiastic patriots ate "liberty cabbage" instead of sauerkraut, while everyone was expected to observe "Wheatless Monday" and "Meatless Tuesday" every week.

War meant conscription and particular hardship for young men from the Mennonite and Amish communities of Elkhart and Lagrange counties. Religious opposition to military service in any form had led their ancestors to flee from Europe, and adherence to this principle led to prison for a few and abuse for many Hoosier pacifists.

For Indiana's farmers the war meant unprecedented efforts to increase food production as America undertook to feed much of Europe. The result was an additional million acres planted in corn and wheat, enormous harvests, and prosperity which remained a fond memory through many difficult years to come. Factory production benefitted greatly from war orders as well, particularly the steel mills of the Calumet Region. Hoosiers bought $500 million in Liberty bonds, despite rapidly rising prices for almost everything.

More than 130,000 Hoosiers served in the armed forces during the First World War, and when they returned home in 1919 most of them found a society which seemed little changed since their departure. Only those of German ancestry discovered immediate differences, but for all Hoosiers the once-familiar pattern of farm and small town life was indeed changing beyond recognition. Steel mills, new factories, mechanized farming, bustling cities, and above all the automobile were altering traditional social and economic patterns, and the twenties would mean a new way of life for almost everyone.

CHAPTER VIII

A horse-drawn wagonload of suffragettes
pulls for Indiana's ratification of the
Nineteenth Amendment. The general assembly gave its assent to women's right
to vote in 1919. Courtesy, Indiana Historical Society

Prosperity, Depression, War

While the 1920s brought great and often troubling change to the people of Indiana, they remained confident that they still represented America's heartland. The literary culture of the Midwest was as yet little troubled by strange voices from Greenwich Village or the mysterious South. Sinclair Lewis might ridicule the people of Main Street, but he remained a midwesterner at heart. Indiana doughboys had helped save Europe, and most of them returned home and resumed their ordinary lives, despite the song about how difficult it was to stay down on the farm after seeing "gay Paree." Whatever their dreams, the returning veterans quickly discovered that the way of life they had left in 1917 could never be quite the same again.

One important change concerned the population itself. New federal immigration laws cut off the movement of peoples from eastern and southern Europe to the bustling industrial cities of northern Indiana. Gradually the cities became less foreign, although in Gary and East Chicago there was a new ethnic group to be noticed. The wartime demand for factory workers had attracted thousands of southern blacks to northern cities, and many of them remained after the war. Nevertheless, 97 percent of the residents of Indiana in 1920 were native-born whites, the highest proportion of any state in the Union. This was a subject of widespread boasting during the 1920s, as civic boosters gloried in the "purity" of Indiana's people. Irvin S. Cobb wrote in 1924 that Indiana was "the most typically American state" of the Union, and most Hoosiers happily agreed. When Robert and Helen Lynd sought a "typical American city" for their pioneering sociological study they selected Muncie, and in 1929 described it for the world as *Middletown*.

The single most effective agent of change was the motor vehicle: cars, trucks, and tractors. By the mid-1920s Indiana cities began noticing a downtown parking problem, and traffic congestion often clogged the streets and delayed trolley cars. Middle class residents were able to enjoy the advantages of new suburban housing developments which were no longer limited to streetcar routes, and driveways and garages became common sights in the better neighborhoods.

In the countryside farmers were converted to the idea of highway improvement and purchased cars for themselves, most often Model T Fords. State highway officials noted in 1925 that horse-drawn traffic had almost vanished from the major roads, where only a few years earlier the automobile had been a rare sight. Farmers were not so quick to give up horses for working their fields, but the pattern of change was clear. Only 4 percent of Indiana farms had tractors in 1920, but by 1930 the figure was 22 percent and the number of horses declined rapidly as the larger and more prosperous farmers turned to mechanization. Oat production dropped along with the horse population, but dairying increased rapidly as better transportation made it easy to carry fresh milk into town. Improved rural roads also brought great changes in education, as it was no longer necessary to have a schoolhouse within walking distance of every farm home. School buses and consolidated schools meant greater educational opportunities for many rural students. There were 4,500 one-room schools in 1922, and less than 10 percent of their underpaid teachers met minimum qualifications, although many of those who began their studies in such schools remember still how

well they were taught. Township trustees and their rural constituents struggled to maintain their traditional control of country schools, and every effort at county-wide consolidation was defeated. Larger schools were built, but pupils came only from districts no larger than a single township, and in 1945 there were still more than 600 one-room schools in Indiana.

As a growing proportion of teenagers attended high school in both city and rural districts there were significant changes in the educational program as well. No longer did most students leave for full-time jobs before graduating, and the curriculum came to include more "practical" courses such as shop and home economics. The dream of steady educational progress was countered by bitter disputes in some of the larger cities. As the number of black students increased, white parents often demanded segregated schools to insure separation of the races even in cities not traditionally segregated. Racial segregation became official school board policy in Indianapolis and Gary by 1927, but South Bend and Fort Wayne, with smaller black populations, remained integrated. Separate and unequal schools for black and white children were the rule throughout southern Indiana, and not until 1949 did the legislature outlaw racial segregation in Indiana's public schools.

At the turn of the century, when high school attendance was still the exception, oratorical contests attracted wide attention. Boys like Albert J. Beveridge won such acclaim that they could move easily into politics as a career. By the 1920s, when a much greater proportion of young people attended high school, boy's basketball won public favor and "Hoosier hysteria" or "Indiana madness" became what some critics worried was almost a religion for many fans. School districts which could not find the money for science laboratories or libraries often erected gymnasiums with room to seat the entire population of the town. Martinsville, for example, built a gym large enough for all 5,000 residents. The state basketball tournament began in 1911, and during the 1920s as many as 700 teams participated. Small town and rural schools were often victorious, and Franklin High

Above: *Shortridge High School in Indianapolis was one of the state's most progressive schools in the 1930s. Here members of the class of 1932 study in the school's library. Courtesy, Indiana Historical Society, Shortridge Collection*

Left: *Members of the Lebanon High School basketball team pose for a photo in 1911, the year of the first high school basketball championship. Although these boys lost to Crawfordsville that year, the team went on to win the championship the following year, defeating Franklin. Courtesy, Indiana High School Athletic Association*

School achieved fame by winning for three consecutive years. Teams from private, religious, and black high schools were excluded until 1943, and girls' basketball was virtually ignored until the late 1970s.

The 1920s also meant Prohibition, that hopeless effort to prevent the drinking public from enjoying a glass of beer. Indiana adopted statewide Prohibition in 1917, and the Anti-Saloon League and its supporters in many evangelical Protestant churches urged rigorous enforcement of the law. Under the "bone dry law" of 1925 simple possession of even an empty liquor bottle carried a penalty of thirty days in jail and a fine of $100. In some places law enforcement agents made determined efforts to destroy all forms of liquor, but particularly in the cities of northern Indiana the Prohibition laws were often ignored while bootleggers became popular heroes. By 1932 the Democrats were overwhelmingly in favor of repealing Prohibition, but Republicans argued bitterly over the issue before deciding to support repeal. At a special election in 1933 a strong majority of the voters favored the return of legal liquor.

Efforts to legislate morality were by no means limited to the destruction of "demon rum." Evangelists preached against the "evils" of modern life, particularly movies and sabbath-breaking, as more and more people sought Sunday amusements which often involved automobile travel. Fire and brimstone preachers such as Billy Sunday attracted thousands to revivals. In the town of Winona Lake, near Warsaw, location of the 7,500-seat Billy Sunday Tabernacle, local ordinances were so strict that smoking on the street was a crime. Methodists, Baptists, and Disciples of Christ in particular suffered from bitter internal disputes between fundamentalists and modernists, and churchmen of every denomination were troubled by the decline of rural churches as farm families moved to town and rural congregations often became so small they could no longer keep the church in repair or support a minister.

Without a doubt the most disturbing organization to fight against troubling change in society was the Ku Klux Klan. The Klan of the 1920s was

D.C. Stephenson led the Ku Klux Klan in Indiana, which at one time boasted a membership of 400,000. Many successful Republican politicians owed their victories in the 1924 election to Klan support. The secret Klan empire crashed into ruin when Stephenson, the self-proclaimed champion of morality, was convicted of rape and murder. Courtesy, Indianapolis Star-News

as much midwestern as southern, and white-robed Klansmen objected not only to blacks, Catholics, and Jews, but also to such evidence of social decay as women who smoked cigarettes in public. The Klan in Indiana was lead by David C. Stephenson, who proclaimed a doctrine of 100 percent Americanism which excluded all who were not white and Protestant. The Indiana Klan claimed a membership of 400,000, and while this was probably exaggerated the great Klan rally at Kokomo on the Fourth of July in 1923 drew a crowd estimated at 300,000 by the Klan, although others said only 10,000 attended. Stephenson arrived in a gold-painted airplane and stepped out in his brightly colored Grand Dragon's robe to address his followers.

The Indiana Klan relied on intimidation and boycotts to show its power, and rarely resorted to violence. Masked and robed Klansmen paraded openly in many cities, and only in heavily Catholic South Bend were they challenged on the streets. The Klan was deeply involved in both parties, although its greatest strength was among Republicans. Many successful politicians owed their victories in the 1924 elections to Klan support.

Governor Ed Jackson was a Klan favorite, and Stephenson sought to be his most powerful backroom adviser. Just at the moment of the Klan's triumph the whole secret empire crashed into ruin when Stephenson, the self-proclaimed champion of morality and the protector of innocent women, was accused of rape and murder. The Grand Dragon had drugged Madge Oberholtzer of Indianapolis and assaulted her in a Pullman sleeping compartment on the train to Chicago. After they left the train at Hammond she bought poison at a drug store and swallowed it as soon as she re-

turned to their hotel room. Stephenson refused to take her to a hospital and instead drove her back to Indianapolis. Before her death a few weeks later Madge Oberholtzer gave a full statement of Stephenson's crimes and he was tried and convicted of murder in a sensational trial. The Grand Dragon spent nearly thirty years in prison despite numerous appeals, and the Indiana Klan was shattered by his disgrace and the accompanying disputes over its finances.

Despite its threatening activities, the Ku Klux Klan was never entirely successful in Indiana politics, and it failed dismally to persuade the legislature to pass laws against Catholic schools. The Klan had also campaigned against corruption in high places, and the Grand Dragon was not the only Klan hero to find himself in legal trouble.

During the 1920s, the Ku Klux Klan attained popularity in many small towns in Indiana. Here officers of the Klan in Hartford City pose for their photo in their official robes. Courtesy, Indiana Historical Society, Cecil Beeson Collection

Governor Jackson was indicted in 1927 for joining with Stephenson to bribe his predecessor, Governor Warren McCray, to appoint a Klan favorite as prosecutor in Marion County in 1923. The evidence was overwhelmingly against Jackson, but he escaped on a technicality because the charge was not filed within two years of the offense. Ed Jackson served out his term as governor in disgrace, but Warren McCray was not as lucky. He was convicted on a federal mail fraud charge in 1924 and forced to resign as governor before beginning his prison sentence.

Despite the Ku Klux Klan and the scandal of one governor in prison and another who should have been, the 1920s were good years for most Hoosiers. Something of the new spirit of the period can be seen in the more active social role played by women's organizations. Not only were increasing numbers of women working in stores and offices, thousands of middle class women joined organizations which took them far beyond the traditional concerns for home and church. Women gained the right to vote in Indiana in 1920, but despite the dreams of women's rights crusaders and the fears of male politicians the women's vote made no significant difference. The League of Women Voters was the institutional successor to the Woman's Franchise League, but it concerned itself with such issues as efficiency in government and child welfare and rarely attracted the attention of political leaders.

The League is a national organization, but no other state has an organization quite like Tri Kappa, a sorority for adult women which has no connection with college campuses. Tri Kappa is both social and charitable in spirit, and it flourishes particularly in smaller cities and towns. In many cities women's clubs came to outnumber those for men, although men also established new organizations, notably the American Legion which located its national headquarters in Indianapolis. Civic clubs for men, usually meeting once a week for lunch, became a regular feature of Indiana urban life, and names such as Rotary and Kiwanis began to appear regularly in the newspapers.

Throughout the 1920s and 1930s gradually increasing numbers of youth entered colleges and universities. Although few in number, they attracted wide attention, for these were typically the children of the prosperous middle class and they often set the standards which those of lesser means tried follow. Women students enrolled in growing numbers, and the "coed" was a popular figure in films and novels.

The two major state universities, Indiana and Purdue, grew in both size and academic programs. Most private colleges held their own, but the state teachers colleges at Terre Haute and Muncie were of such low standard that both were refused accreditation in 1928. None of Indiana's larger colleges reached academic distinction before World War II, and the Bloomington campus of IU was better known as the home of the distinguished composer Hoagy Carmichael than for any intellectual achievement.

Students of the 1920s certainly studied, but

The national headquarters of the American Legion, the world's largest veterans' organization, was built in Indianapolis in the 1920s. This photo dates to March 1930. Courtesy, Indiana State Library, Indiana Division

These bathing beauties adorned the cover of a 1928 promotional brochure extolling the recreational virtues of Michigan City. The claim to "America's cleanest, finest sand beach" was questionable even fifty years ago, although Michigan City was a very popular summertime resort then. Courtesy, Indiana State Library, Indiana Division

many of them showed greater enthusiasm for football. College football in the Midwest came of age during the 1920s, attracting large crowds on Saturday afternoons. Indiana and Purdue fought for the "Old Oaken Bucket" while Wabash and DePauw battled for the "Monon Bell," but no one could challenge the national reputation of Knute Rockne at Notre Dame.

One notable response to the modernization of Hoosier life was a growing nostalgia for a simpler and happier era. The artists who gathered in the hills of Brown County during the 1920s built upon a long-standing tradition of landscape painting. The finest painter of the group was T. C. Steele who settled there in 1907, but the popularity of the Brown County artists came only when Hoosier collectors began to appreciate scenic works which celebrated the bygone era of their own youth.

Disruptive change was a frequent theme of Booth Tarkington's later novels, but Indiana wri-

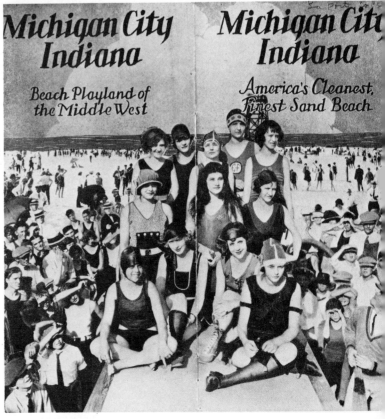

The football rivalry between DePauw University and Wabash College heightened in 1932, when the Monon Railroad Company donated one of its old bells to be held by the winner of the annual game. At the end of this game at Wabash in 1939, the bell went to DePauw. Courtesy, The Archives of DePauw University

A native of Bloomington, Hoagy Carmichael became one of the most popular songwriters of his day. He is perhaps best remembered for "Stardust," which he wrote in 1931. Courtesy, Indiana State Library, Indiana Division

ters no longer won a great national audience, except for Theodore Dreiser, whose bleak view of modern American life clashed sharply with the more cheerful tradition of Indiana's Golden Age. Three of the most popular literary Hoosiers of the early twentieth century developed the themes of nostalgia and the virtues of rural life to a high level. Kin Hubbard's stories featuring the salty dialect sayings of "Abe Martin" of Brown County were widely syndicated, and his tales still delight readers. George Ade published dozens of plays, books, and stories, most of them humorous efforts to explain the Midwest to the rest of the nation. Some of Ade's early stories were illustrated by his friend John T. McCutcheon who became the staff cartoonist for the *Chicago Tribune* and often used rural midwestern themes in his most popular drawings. Ade, Hubbard, and McCutcheon were all famous before 1920, but their later work had a particular appeal for many thousands of midwesterners who had grown up on the farm or in small towns, but found themselves mature adults living in bustling cities where they cherished fond memories of an idealized world of their youth.

The Great Depression hit Indiana with a devastating impact. Few Hoosiers were active in the stock market and for many people the excitement of the "Roaring Twenties" or the "Jazz Age" was something to read about in magazines or watch at

Above: *Norwegian immigrant Knute Rockne was head coach of the Notre Dame football team for thirteen years between 1918 and 1931. He led the Fighting Irish to five undefeated seasons. His most famous team was that of 1924, featuring "The Four Horsemen." He immortalized the line "Do it for the Gipper." Courtesy, University of Notre Dame*

duce their payrolls and thousands of workers lost their jobs. There are no precise unemployment statistics, but when business hit bottom in the winter of 1932-1933 the jobless rate was at least 25 percent. In the steel towns of Lake County unemployment was even higher. The steel mills worked at only 15 percent of capacity in 1932, and those still working saw their wages cut by 25 percent.

Until 1933 relief was strictly a local responsibility, and the unemployed looked to their township trustees to meet their most desperate needs. Vol-

Below: *The character Abe Martin was the creation of cartoonist Frank McKinney (Kin) Hubbard. A regular feature of the* Indianapolis News, *the cartoon was nationally syndicated in 1910. Courtesy, Indiana State Library, Indiana Division*

the movies, rather than part of their own lives. Even so the Wall Street crash of October 1929 marked the end of an era of general prosperity and widespread optimism, and the beginning of a decade of depression.

Troubles were nothing new for midwestern farmers, and agricultural problems elsewhere caused serious difficulty for Indiana implement manufacturers such as the Oliver plow works in South Bend. The Great Crash shattered the exuberant and shaky boom of the late 1920s and within a few months manufacturers began to re-

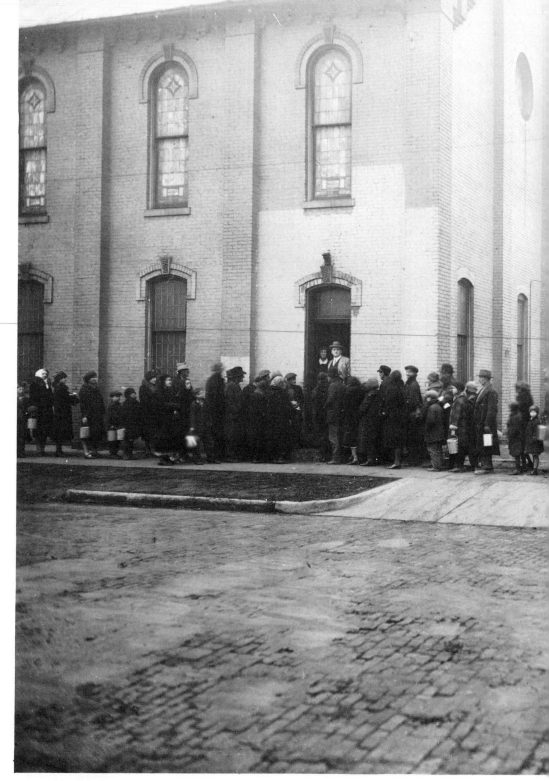

Right: *During the early years of the Great Depression, relief to the needy was usually given through a local charity rather than a federal program. Here Terre Haute residents line up for a meal at a church in the city. Courtesy, Indiana Historical Society, Martin Collection*

Facing page: *John Dillinger poses outside his home in Mooresville, holding a machine gun and the famous wooden pistol he used to break out of prison. This photo was taken in April 1934 at the height of the manhunt; a few weeks later he was gunned down in Chicago at age thirty-one. Courtesy, Indiana State Library, Indiana Division*

unteer agencies, often church-sponsored, provided what help they could, but after three or four years of the Depression there were few people still able to contribute. Many who still had families in the countryside returned to the farms where they could grow enough to feed themselves, and the number of small farms increased significantly. Small-town residents helped one another in the traditional fashion, and by sharing resources and postponing payments managed to get through the most difficult years. But private and local efforts were in no way adequate to meet the needs of the many thousands of unemployed, particularly in

the industrial cities. The traditional American faith in economic success and a better life in the future was devastated, as hard-working men and women found that there were no jobs of any kind, and those lucky enough to be working usually had to accept shorter hours and reduced wages.

At first the victims of the Depression tended to be the factory workers, laborers, or clerks, those who had never been particularly well-off financially. But as the Depression deepened year by year the middle class suffered as well, as managerial and professional jobs disappeared, incomes declined,

and home mortgages could not be paid. Even for those without a dollar on deposit the failure of so many banks came as shock. Amid distress bankers were never popular, because banks which remained open greatly reduced their loans to businessmen while continuing their efforts to collect from unfortunate customers who had no hope of repaying what they had borrowed in happier days. Some Hoosiers even glamorized the gangs of bank robbers who sped through northern and central Indiana in their sleek automobiles. John Dillinger was a hero of many stories which told how he gave stolen money to the poor or out-

witted simpleminded policemen and jail guards.

Federal agents shot Dillinger in Chicago in 1933, but his criminal career pointed up the need for something more efficient than separate small and untrained police departments for every county and town. In 1933 and 1935 the legislature changed the Highway Patrol into a state police force with general criminal jurisdiction and a fleet of modern radio-equipped patrol cars. This provided the first professional law enforcement in many counties, where only an elected sheriff and his political deputies had patrolled before.

As if the Depression were not trouble enough,

in 1937 the Ohio River towns were inundated by the greatest flood on record. New Albany and Evansville were hard hit by water levels more than forty feet above normal, and the disaster was so great that the federal government undertook a massive construction program to build flood walls to protect the larger river towns from future floods.

Indiana Republicans cannot fairly be blamed for the Depression, but they were in office when it began and the voters turned against them by a decisive margin. The new hero for Hoosier Democrats was Paul V. McNutt, who led his party to a sweeping victory in 1932. Local governments could no longer carry the burden of relief for the jobless, and many voters looked to state government for help. Governor McNutt took office in January 1933, three months before Franklin D. Roosevelt's inauguration as President, and Indiana achieved notable reforms before the New Deal was underway at the federal level.

McNutt was the most dynamic and powerful governor in Indiana since Oliver P. Morton dur-

The Ohio River flood of 1937 caused extensive damage in many Indiana communities along the river. A car swept under the porch of this grocery store/gas station in Clark County provides refuge for a small dog lying on its roof. Courtesy, Bass Photo Company

ing the Civil War, and he moved quickly to reshape state government and to fight the problems of the Depression. Desperate people everywhere looked to the government for direct assistance in their needs and for action against abuses by certain businessmen who had been heroes during the prosperous 1920s. With overwhelming majorities in both houses of the legislature, and a united party supporting him, McNutt had the votes to pass virtually any measure he wished. He promised an active government, working as "a great instrument of human progress," in place of the old belief that the state should leave the citizens alone as much as possible. The state assumed much of the burden of relief, and the unfair property tax was partly replaced by corporate and personal gross income taxes which provided revenue for the new

Paul V. McNutt

Governor Paul V. McNutt stands between microphones in a 1935 radio broadcast. A law professor at Indiana University, he was elected national president of the American Legion. Courtesy, Bass Photo Company

Paul V. McNutt was born in Franklin in 1891 and raised in Martinsville. His father was active in politics, and Paul showed an early inclination in the same direction. At Indiana University he was editor of the student newspaper, student union president, and a leading figure in the dramatic club. He went on to Harvard Law School and soon after his graduation joined the IU law faculty. After service with the field artillery McNutt returned to Bloomington as a law professor, but he was also prominent in organizing the American Legion for veterans of the World War. He

was elected state commander in 1927 and national commander the following year, while also rising to dean of the law school. His drive for high office was obvious to everyone who knew him.

The Democrats had excellent prospects for winning Indiana in 1932. McNutt pushed aside the established party leaders, made a few essential concessions to win nomination for governor and then trounced the Republicans in a landslide victory. His only serious mistake was his hesitation in supporting Franklin D. Roosevelt's nomination, a slight which FDR did not forget.

With his handsome appearance, forceful oratory, and American Legion background, combined with a record of achievement as governor, McNutt aimed for the Democratic presidential nomination in 1940. He had difficulty in finding an appropriate office when his term expired, however, for there was no election for senator in 1936 and FDR was not likely to give him an important job in Washington. Instead the crafty FDR sent McNutt across the Pacific as American high commissioner to the Philippines, which were then an American possession. In July 1939 McNutt was called to Washington as

chairman of the new Federal Security Agency, which supervised a myriad of New Deal relief programs. In addition to his many political enemies, McNutt was troubled by several financial and tax investigations which left him legally clean but politically tainted. His presidential dreams were fading even before FDR announced that he would break tradition and accept a third term.

McNutt loyally supported the Democratic ticket in 1940, and during the war headed the War Manpower Commission as well as the Federal Security Agency. The WMC appeared to be a powerful office, but McNutt clashed repeatedly with the Labor Department and with the military, and suffered from his own administrative weaknesses as well. At the end of the war he returned to the Philippines for two years and then left public life for a New York law practice until his death in 1955.

Often charming, McNutt had such a high opinion of himself and such ruthless ambition to become president that he made too many enemies among his fellow Democrats. Roosevelt used McNutt but never trusted him, and the most ambitious Hoosier politician of the twentieth century faded into obscurity.

programs by taxing those with money to pay. At the same time county and city power was lessened because local government depended upon the property tax, and the new revenue went to the state instead.

Governor McNutt also attacked the notorious inefficiency of the state administration, reorganizing more than a hundred separate agencies into eight departments. The reorganization law also had the effect of greatly increasing the governor's powers of appointment and supervision, and McNutt used his power ruthlessly to build a political machine which led some critics to call him a state dictator, even a "Hoosier Hitler." This was an exaggeration, but no governor except Morton ever wielded such power in Indianapolis, or had such opportunities for patronage appointments.

Built shortly after the turn of the century at the northwest corner of Washington and Illinois streets in Indianapolis, the Claypool Hotel is seen here in October 1935. Only a block from the statehouse, it was a favorite meeting place for state politicians and those who wished to influence them. Courtesy, Indiana State Library, Indiana Division

When legal liquor returned later in 1933 there were even greater opportunities for political favoritism, and wholesale liquor and beer licenses went entirely to Democrats. All state employees were expected to contribute 2 percent of their pay to the party, and this "Two Percent Club" proved so useful that the Republicans continued it after they regained the governorship in 1945.

Despite all of the efforts of the McNutt administration, state resources were far from adequate to

146

meet the unprecedented demands imposed by the Great Depression. Fortunately by mid-1933 the torrent of federal money from the New Deal in Washington began to carry much of the burden.

Many federal programs in Indiana, particularly under the Works Progress Administration (WPA) between 1936 and 1938, were accused of doing more for Democrats than Republicans, but none of the charges could be proven. Indiana governors were not allowed to seek reelection until 1976, but McNutt controlled the party organization and his ticket won decisively in 1936. Within a year, however, the Democrats were feuding bitterly, and the McNutt machine suffered from internal disputes as well as a revived Republican party. By 1940 the Republicans were able to win control of the legislature and came within 4,000 votes of electing a governor. In the presidential contest Indiana turned against FDR and favored Wendell Willkie, the surprise Republican candidate who spoke often of his Hoosier origin although he had left the state twenty years before for a career as a Wall Street lawyer.

Small town and rural Indiana returned to their Republican traditions, but the Democrats won significant support from the growing number of black voters and from the new industrial unions. Blacks certainly never received a fair share from either state or federal relief programs, but they did win important benefits symbolized by the Lockfield Gardens public housing project in Indianapolis, and they voted largely Democratic from 1936 onward.

Although small unions of skilled workers had existed in Indiana since the 1860s, labor had only occasionally played an important part in public affairs. Through the National Recovery Administration and then the Wagner Act in 1935 the New Deal encouraged and supported union organizing efforts. The old-line unionists of the American Federation of Labor (AFL) were unable to cope with the needs of large numbers of industrial workers, and the new Committee for Industrial Organizations (CIO) led the way with unions for large numbers of workers on a basis of industries rather than particular skills. In South Bend the

United Automobile Workers attracted national attention with a successful sit-down strike against the Bendix Corporation in 1936. The UAW also won bargaining rights at Studebaker in South Bend and at General Motors plants in Anderson, New Castle, and Indianapolis. Local officials in Muncie were able to keep the union out of town for months, and the national guard was called out to maintain order in Anderson.

Terre Haute was the scene of Indiana's most dramatic labor dispute. The city had a strong union tradition, but since about 1920 its industries had declined and local business leaders were firmly anti-union. Employers resisted the rising union efforts under the New Deal and a bitter strike at Columbia Enamel in 1935 caused even greater tension.

Other unions generally supported the strikers, and when the firm prepared to reopen with strikebreakers there was a large demonstration. Some of the crowd forced their way into the plant and wrecked several offices, but they left the production machinery unharmed. The company brought in fifty armed guards from Chicago and local labor leaders responded with a call for a general strike of all workers in Terre Haute. The strike began on July 22, 1935, and Terre Haute was almost entirely closed except for public utilities and the drugstores. Although some 20,000 men and women answered the strike call there was no violence. Businessmen put pressure on city officials to call for troops, and Governor McNutt declared martial law and ordered 1,100 national guardsmen to Terre Haute on the following day.

There was only minor violence and about 100 arrests, but national commentators described the strike as a communist-inspired insurrection. The general strike lasted only two days and most of the troops were soon withdrawn, but McNutt kept Terre Haute under martial law for nearly seven months. Columbia Enamel reopened with nonunion labor and eventually defeated the union before the federal courts.

In the Calumet Region the Steel Workers Organizing Committee (SWOC), an arm of the CIO, worked quietly for months to establish the union.

During
women
pecially
operates
Norris
manufac
Historic

jobs
diana

Th
high-
new
produ
by a
tion
thoug
two
Harb
shock
force
no ch
terne
acteri
absen
state
Th
arme
10,00
air co
Wayr
India
milit
large
India
Mad
pot i

English's Opera House on Monument Circle often served as the background for political rallies. Here Wendell Wilkie, the Republican candidate for president in 1940, campaigns in his home state. Courtesy, Indiana Historical Society, Bass Photo Collection

U.S. Steel agreed peacefully in 1937 to recognize the United Steelworkers as the bargaining agent for its employees, but the smaller steel companies held out against the union for five bitter years. By 1940 about 22 percent of Indiana's urban work force belonged to unions, but opposition to organized labor remained strong, especially in smaller towns and among small firms.

The efforts of the McNutt administration in Indianapolis and FDR's New Deal in Washington eased the pains of the Depression and provided relief and work for millions of jobless Americans, but after eleven years the nation was still suffering from massive unemployment. The only effective remedy for the economic problems of the Depression era was the defense program which began in 1940 as the United States felt increasingly threatened by Hitler. Few Hoosiers showed much concern for European politics until Hitler's expansive ambitions compelled attention in 1938, and fewer still wanted to see American troops once again involved in a European war.

This spirit of isolationism, a desire to keep America clear of European troubles, was particularly strong in the Midwest. A few years earlier Congressman Louis Ludlow of Indianapolis had led an unsuccessful effort to require a national referendum before the United States could declare war. A public opinion poll in the spring of 1941 showed that only 15 percent of those questioned in Indiana favored American participation in the war, marking the state as one of the strongholds of isolationist sentiment.

Even most of those who opposed fighting on the other side of the Atlantic were ready to support Roosevelt's policy of building up America's military power to protect the Western Hemisphere from possible German attack. Only determined pacifists rejected the hundreds of thousands of

149

Err

Thous
lives v
ing th
Indiar
war w
front
diers.
on a f
lived
left In
senior
be a jo
tion w
Porte
years
where
cal sto
tion a
throug
Amer
ple an

Wit
in Eu
eign a
was se
the G
vivid
often
British
can tr
North
Pyle w
corresp
rear an
stayed
ing pa
life an
death
man. (
told th

A new Studebaker Lark (manufactured in South Bend) and a ranch house in the suburbs were symbols of prosperity in the 1950s. The GI Bill financed an amazing construction boom in housing, and thousands of acres of Indiana cornfields were turned into suburbs. Courtesy, Discovery Hall Museum, South Bend

Still The American Heartland?

Indiana joined with all of America in celebrating the war's end in 1945. Workers in the industrial heartland had made an enormous material contribution to the war effort, and they shared in the military victory. Government officials and grateful relief administrators also praised midwestern farmers for their outstanding contribution to feeding hungry millions around the globe.

The end of the fighting meant the immediate shutdown of war industry, however, and hundreds of thousands of highly paid factory workers lost their jobs within a few weeks of the Japanese surrender. Unlike so much of the wartime industrial expansion in the South and West, there was little peacetime carryover for most of Indiana's new wartime factories. The great ammunition plants at Clarksville and Kingsbury were quickly closed, and the new production facilities for airplanes, aircraft engines, and parts in Fort Wayne, Indianapolis, South Bend, and Evansville closed as well. The airliners of the postwar world would be built in Southern California or Seattle, not in the Midwest.

Established Hoosier industries, so far as possible, shifted from defense work to their normal peacetime output, and employment returned as soon as production lines could be "reconverted" to the familiar products. A large proportion of the women who entered the industrial labor force during the war returned to full-time housekeeping.

The war had brought such sweeping changes that it was impossible to return completely to life as it was before the war. Hundreds of thousands of Hoosier men had served overseas, traveled parts of the world only dreamed of before the war, and survived dangers and hardships which they had never before imagined. Women had gone to war themselves, or waited and watched as sons, husbands, and brothers had gone to war. Women had taken to offices and factories in unprecedented numbers, and their lives would never be the same. No matter how earnestly anyone hoped to return to normal patterns of life, normal patterns had changed irrevocably.

The GI Bill of Rights was one of the most powerful forces for change. This 1944 law provided educational benefits which allowed millions of veterans nationwide to attend college. Indiana, Purdue, and Notre Dame in particular struggled to find housing for the veterans and their families, as the married student became a familiar sight on campuses once the preserve of carefree youth. The opportunity for higher education was open for many men who had never dreamed of attending college before the war, and to the surprise of worried deans and professors the veterans were often outstanding students.

The GI Bill also provided generous federal loans for buying homes, with low down payments and long-term mortgages which made homeownership a reality for the average American. During the Depression few people could afford to build a house, and during the war labor and lumber were unavailable, so after 1945 the nation faced a serious housing shortage. Veterans and their new brides were often forced to live in crowded apartments or with relatives. The GI Bill financed an amazing construction boom which changed the image of the American city. New houses were built with incredible speed on the fringes of almost every city, and thousands of acres of Indiana cornfields were turned into suburbs.

Despite all of the high hopes for a future of peace and prosperity, for a college education and

Facing page: *Actor James Byron Dean returned to his boyhood home of Fairmount in 1954 with photographer Dennis Stock for a series of photos for* Life *magazine. Although his career spanned only three films before his 1955 death in a car accident, Dean became a Hollywood icon, and fans still visit his grave in Fairmount. Courtesy, Magnum Photos, Inc., photo by Dennis Stock*

a home of their own, many Hoosiers were troubled by serious doubts in 1945. They worried along with many Americans that depression might return without the exceptional economic stimulus of defense spending, and they hesitated to invest in new businesses. Perhaps even more than most other Americans they worried about a vague menace of communism which threatened to undermine their cherished social and political institutions.

Every year there were a few more Hoosiers, but the population of the state increased more slowly than the nation as a whole. Those who left Indiana generally moved west or southwest, with California as their favored destination. During and after the war there was also a movement into Indiana as thousands of whites from Kentucky and Tennessee were lured northward by higher wages in Hoosier factories. Still more noticeable was the influx of blacks from Kentucky, Tennessee, Alabama, Mississippi, and Arkansas, as displaced farmworkers sought both economic opportunity and at least partial recognition of their basic civil rights. The white newcomers came to most of the industrial cities of central and northern Indiana, while the blacks were concentrated in the larger cities, particularly Gary and Indianapolis.

Meanwhile the Indiana countryside continued its long population decline, as fewer farmers produced larger crops by using improved seeds, fertilizers, and pesticides, along with larger and more efficient tractors and implements. The average farm grew from just over 100 acres in 1940 to 200 acres by 1984.

For a decade or so after the war the larger cities appeared to flourish in a familiar pattern, but by 1960 it became painfully clear that the principal growth among the prosperous middle class was in the spreading suburbs, and soon retailers followed their customers away from downtown to new sub-

Following World War II, many railroads invested heavily in new passenger coaches. The Monon Railroad's new parlor car on the well-known "Hoosier" line between Indianapolis and Chicago is seen here in a September 1947 photo. Courtesy, Indiana Historical Society

urban shopping centers. Older neighborhoods, often abandoned by the children of the European immigrants of an earlier generation, were now occupied by people who had little money to maintain homes or to support downtown department stores. The heart of the city was dying, deserted by shoppers and yet still choked with traffic.

Transportation change was not limited to the cities, and the entire state experienced rapid and unexpected shifts in movement of people and freight. For several generations Indiana shippers and travelers had enjoyed an excellent network of railroad services, which flourished for a few years after World War II. Steam power gave way to diesel locomotives. The Monon Railroad continued as a proud symbol of Hoosier railroading, particularly its elegant trains between Indianapolis and

Chicago. Although the last of the electric interurbans serving central Indiana ceased running by about 1941, the South Shore Line has maintained its service between Chicago and South Bend and remains as the last electric interurban in the nation.

Almost unnoticed at first, business travelers began to fly on longer trips, rather than take overnight Pullman sleepers on the rails, and more of the short haul passengers chose to drive their own cars. The railroads cut back sharply on local passenger service while trying to keep up their main line traffic, but their customers continued to desert the rails for airplanes and automobiles. In similar fashion short haul and package freight shifted to motor trucks and the railroads lost their entire less-than-carload freight traffic. Indiana's total rail-

early 1950s was the construction of a toll road. Here travelers and especially truckers from other states would pay the full cost and Hoosier taxpayers would not be troubled. The Indiana Toll Road, opened for traffic in 1956, was intended to speed traffic between Chicago and the East, and local usage was discouraged by long intervals between interchanges.

With the passage of the federal Interstate Highway Act in 1956 Indiana occupied a central position in a new transportation system. Indianapolis, served by seven interstate highway routes as well as an interstate beltway, came to occupy a leading position in highway transportation just as it had earlier served to link converging railroad lines.

In the new age of air transportation the state's place was less distinctive. Bendix in South Bend and Allison in Indianapolis were major producers of aircraft components, and those cities along with Fort Wayne and Evansville built airports which were served by major airlines beginning in the late 1930s. The only airline based in Indiana was Lake Central Airlines, a local service carrier established at Indianapolis in 1949 by the barnstormer and aviation pioneer Roscoe Turner. Lake Central served much of the Midwest for two decades but was forced to merge into a larger airline as interstate highways took passengers from its shorter flights and the cost of new jet aircraft was beyond its resources.

In Hoosier politics Democrats and Republicans exchanged control of the governor's office or the general assembly from time to time, but with rare exceptions a conservative spirit prevailed in both parties. The Republicans recovered from the burden of the Depression by 1940 and gradually came to predominate at both the state and local level, although Democrats have never conceded defeat. In national politics William E. Jenner and Homer Capehart offered a strongly conservative program which carried them into the Senate soon after World War II. Capehart was a businessman and gentleman farmer who helped revive the Republican organization in Indiana, beginning with his highly publicized "Cornfield Conference" in 1938. Jenner was a lawyer who achieved notice as a

road mileage declined as branch lines became unprofitable and were abandoned, but total rail traffic remained heavy, particularly in bulk commodities such as coal and grain.

The increasing reliance on automobiles and trucks placed an impossible load on the state's highway system. Although all of Indiana's principal highways had been hard surfaced by the mid-1930s, they were still largely two-lane roads. Congestion, delays, and increasing accidents led to four-lane construction for a few major routes. Progress was slow and expensive, and motorists stalled behind a line of heavy trucks often cursed the incompetence of the state highway department. The state's problem, of course, was finding the money to complete needed improvements, and a partial solution for northern Indiana in the

young state legislator before the war. Both were outspokenly anti-communist and furthered the investigations of suspected subversives which became so common in Washington during the late 1940s and early 1950s. Back in Indiana Henry F. Schricker was twice elected governor, in 1940 and 1948, but his popularity was largely personal and his victories gave little help to his fellow Democrats. Schricker was noted for always wearing a large white hat, and his administrations attempted few new programs.

The conservative Hoosier view of politics was symbolized by the explicit rejection of federal aid voted by the general assembly in 1947 and reaffirmed four years later. "We want government to come home," the legislators told Washington, while *The South Bend Tribune* denounced the "octopus on the Potomac." This philosophy of states' rights and self-reliance led Indiana to reject most federal aid programs, except for highway construction money, and this policy was not overturned until 1961. Even then the issue was so sensitive that the resolution authorizing acceptance of federal aid passed in a deal between party leaders so quietly managed that few legislators understood for what they were voting. Indianapolis newspa-

This crowd gathered at Weir Cook Airport on September 9, 1952, for a "We Like Ike" rally. Courtesy, Bass Photo Company

pers also failed to notice that their pet anti-"socialist" measure was no longer in effect. For years money intended for Indiana had been spent elsewhere, and Hoosiers had done without many education, welfare, health, and conservation programs. Into the mid-1980s Indiana still suffered from one of the lowest return ratios of federal expenditures for tax dollars paid of any state in the Union.

While Hoosier voters sometimes send moderate liberals such as Senator Birch Bayh or Congressman John Brademas to Washington, state politics continues to be dominated by conservatives in both parties. The chief exception was Governor Matthew Welsh, a Democrat who was narrowly elected in 1960 and undertook a program considered rather liberal by Hoosier standards. Welsh

campaigned on the theme that Indiana had shamefully neglected the needs of its residents, and that energetic action was needed to improve schools, repair highways, and reform state government generally.

Welsh was an efficient administrator, combining fresh ideas with the political skill needed to win approval for most of his suggestions from an often hostile legislature. Welsh was an organization

*Two well-known Hoosier politicians of
the 1960s, Senator Birch Bayh (left), and
Governor Matthew Welsh (right), stride
alongside President John F. Kennedy in
October 1962. Courtesy, Indiana State
Library, Indiana Division*

During the civil rights movement of the 1960s these members of the NAACP Rights March Committee assisted in preparing 300 signboards for a march in Gary in September 1963. Courtesy, Calumet Regional Archives, Indiana University Northwest, Gary Collection

Democrat and he worked within Indiana's traditional system of filling many state jobs with patronage appointments. He did reform state administration for the first time since McNutt in 1933, regained control of the budget for the governor, improved educational funding, established an effective civil rights agency, and somehow managed in 1963 to push through a tax reform package including a sales tax to remedy the state's desperate financial condition. "Matt's Tax" was severely criticized, but the new revenue was essential to finance Indiana's unprecedented effort to attack so many problems at the same time. Among Welsh's more visible efforts was the renewal and expansion of the state park system.

In 1964 Alabama's segregationist governor, George Wallace, entered the Democratic presidential primary in Indiana as part of his effort to show that northern voters opposed federal civil rights programs. Governor Welsh decided to run against Wallace to show that Hoosiers were not bigots. Despite the handicap of his unpopular tax increase program, Welsh campaigned with great energy, and championed state and federal efforts to advance civil rights for blacks. "I was determined to prevent his making a good showing in the Hoosier state," Welsh said of Wallace. "Frankly, I was furious—and I guess it showed." Wallace carried Lake County with its heavy "white blacklash" vote, but statewide he won just under 30 percent of the vote, far less than the opinion polls had predicted.

State politics returned to its traditional pattern after 1964, with little effort by either party to change the system in any significant way. It was politics as usual: rough personal disputes to see who would enjoy the rewards of office. As an anonymous Hoosier politician supposedly told a national reporter, "Hell, we play it rough in Indiana. There's always blood on the floor, and the guy whose blood it isn't just happens to be on top—temporarily."

The election of Dr. Otis Bowen in 1972 marked the triumph of a small-town family physician and veteran state legislator who became one of the state's most popular governors. He had been

pushed aside by the Republican state convention four years earlier, an insult which opened the way for restoration of the direct primary to select candidates for governor and senator, and a constitutional amendment allowing a governor to serve two consecutive terms. Bowen brought quiet respectability to the governor's office and his program to restrain property tax increases was a major achievement which never received the national attention given to similar measures in California and other states.

More fundamental political change came to the state's two largest cities, where dynamic mayors symbolized contrasting patterns of change. By the early 1960s the steel town of Gary had come to symbolize the problems of urban industrial America. It was shabby, dirty, and corrupt, with its air and water polluted, its school system in decay, and its white residents rapidly moving to the suburbs to escape the growing numbers of blacks. Yet when the distinguished Indiana University folklorist Richard Dorson studied Gary in 1975 he discovered an unsuspected success story. The crime, the pollution, and the abandoned buildings were real enough, and white residents told stories of a better life in years past. The surprise came from the black residents, who explained how Gary represented an improvement for them, just as it had for thousands of European immigrants sixty years earlier. Racial prejudice had obscured the once familiar pattern of a more recently arrived ethnic group moving in at a lower level of society as older immigrants advanced to better jobs and more comfortable homes. Gary still suffered from many problems, but its new black majority did not look upon the city as hopeless because for many of them it offered an opportunity to improve their lives.

Political changes in Gary were marked by efforts to mobilize black voters to elect black candidates. When Richard G. Hatcher was elected mayor in 1967 it became clear that black citizens had won control of the city, and many whites predicted that city services would collapse. Mayor Hatcher has been reelected four times, city departments function effectively, and Gary has survived.

Sculptor Robert Indiana here supervises the temporary installation of his famous LOVE piece on the plaza outside Indiana National Bank in February 1972. The artist joked: "I would like to see it on top of the Soldiers' and Sailors' Monument on a revolving pedestal. That would put Indiana back on the map." Courtesy, Indianapolis News, *photo by Tim Halcomb*

The blizzard of 1978 will long be remembered in Indiana. This aerial view of a farmstead in the northern part of the state, taken several days after the snowfall, dramatizes the isolation that occurs in rural areas during bad winter storms. *Courtesy, South Bend Tribune*

letters. Robert Indiana first won attention as part of the "Pop Art" movement during the early 1960s, but he became famous for his *LOVE* sculpture, first shown at the Indianapolis Museum of Art in 1971. *LOVE* in its many variations has been widely exhibited and frequently copied, and in 1973 the artist himself incorporated it in the design of a highly popular postage stamp.

Changes in the Indiana pattern of life in recent years mirror those elsewhere in the Midwest and Northeast. Long-established cities and mature industries have declined as new cities and new industries have grown to prosperity, often in warmer regions of the South and West.

By 1970 the precarious position of Indiana's cities was too obvious to ignore. Traditional downtown shopping districts had lost so many customers to the shopping centers and enclosed malls of the suburbs that vacant storefronts were a common sight. Efforts to promote downtown business with street closings, parking schemes, and "urban renewal" meant the destruction of many buildings, the closing of still more retail stores, and some-

times the construction of new office buildings. No matter what downtown retailers tried, too many of their customers had moved away from the heart of town and into the sprawling suburbs, and they refused to drive through city traffic and pay to park in order to shop downtown. Foresighted businesses opened suburban stores of their own, and those that stayed downtown watched in dismay as their profits disappeared.

Across the country the young families of the post-World War II era preferred homes of their own, with large yards and garage space for one car and then two. With mortgage financing from the GI Bill and other federal programs the cost of home-ownership came within reach of most Americans, and for a generation the cities expanded rapidly into the countryside, and retail shops and professional services followed. The smaller families, apartment complexes, and condominium developments of the 1970s set a new pattern, but by then many older neighborhoods had fallen into decay, and the new multiple-family dwellings were largely built in the suburbs.

This 1985 overview of Indianapolis, with the domed stadium in the foreground, emphasizes the revitalized downtown. Photo by D. Todd Moore

No city in Indiana shows this new pattern more clearly than Indianapolis. Although the metropolitan area is large enough so that downtown has not disappeared, it is no longer the shopping district of choice for affluent consumers. L.S. Ayres still dominates the intersection of Washington Street and South Meridian, but it does better business at its suburban stores in the malls, where it now competes with stores from other cities which came to the outskirts of Indianapolis with no interest in the old heart of the city. The new fashion can be seen most easily along Interstate 465, a multi-lane bypass which encircles Indianapolis with a ring of heavy traffic day and night. Shopping malls, apartment complexes, discount stores, and office towers mark the interchange where bypass traffic mixes with that on highways radiating from the city in a dozen directions.

The downtown skyline is now dominated by office skyscrapers, elegant hotels, a convention center, and the sports dome which has become the mark of civic pride for the modern city. Except for sports fans and convention delegates downtown Indianapolis of the late 1970s was largely empty of people soon after five o'clock, for the residents of the city went home to their suburbs or to the restaurants, theaters, and shops in the malls. Now, once more, new restaurants, shops, and theaters are beginning to attract customers downtown.

On a smaller scale the same pattern can be seen in Evansville, Fort Wayne, South Bend, and the lesser cities, while most of the stores which used to serve Gary have shifted well southward to an area loosely known as Merrillville, whose precise limits cannot be determined by casual visitors. City boundaries still matter for tax collectors, but customers heading for a shopping mall often have no idea of its legal address. "Downtown" is only a shadow of its former excitement and prosperity. Traditional midwestern cities have lost their commercial hearts.

For many smaller towns untroubled by shopping centers, the most startling changes have come in the reorganization of the schools. For more than a century after the school law of 1852

Rochester was devastated in an April 1974 tornado. Courtesy, South Bend Tribune

the township was the basis for Indiana's public schools. Each township constituted a separate school district, while towns and cities maintained their own distinct school systems. There was some voluntary consolidation as the school bus appeared in the 1920s and made it possible for rural children to travel to more distant schools, but the usual pattern was a shift from scattered one-room schools to a single high school and several grade schools in each township. As farm mechanization led to lower rural populations many farming townships had too few children for an effective school system, and often too small a tax base as well. Rural high schools in particular were often so small that students had no opportunity to study sciences or foreign languages, but reform

was blocked because small communities identified themselves so closely with their own school and their own basketball team.

When the legislature finally passed a school reorganization law in 1959, education officials classified 801 of the state's 966 school districts as "too small" because they had fewer than 1,000 pupils in all twelve grades. There were thirty-seven school districts which had fewer than 100 pupils, yet they attempted to sustain a separate school system.

The legislature wisely avoided the political turmoil of devising a uniform reorganization plan, and committees in each county devised programs to meet local requirements. Some small districts continue to resist consolidation, but within a few years the number of districts was cut by half, leading to the elimination of hundreds of proud but sadly inadequate high schools and thousands of elementary schools. Many school districts straddle county lines, as several rural townships have come together to form districts which are large enough for modern needs but still safe from control by nearby cities.

In certain cities, most notably Gary and Indianapolis, district boundaries remained the same but great changes resulted from another state law, the 1949 measure outlawing racial segregation in Indiana schools. The strict separation of white and black pupils which had prevailed for many years was eliminated, but neighborhood patterns and the white movement to the suburbs left many inner city schools almost entirely black.

During these same years Indiana's higher education system also experienced great change. Indiana and Purdue both expanded rapidly after 1945, as the veterans crowded in to catch up with their civilian dreams. Large enrollments remained after the veterans graduated, as attending college became the expectation of the new and expanded American middle class. As the children of the postwar "baby boom" reached school age there was an unprecedented demand for teachers, and Indiana State in Terre Haute and Ball State in Muncie grew from sleepy teachers' colleges into state universities. Indiana, Purdue, and Notre Dame grew into major research universities, but traditional liberal arts colleges such as DePauw, Earlham, and Wabash still attract good numbers of high quality students.

Rapidly growing numbers of students placed higher education under increasing strain because so many of the state's larger cities lacked a convenient state college campus. The need was met in the early 1960s by the creation of "regional campuses" developed from extension centers which for years had operated late afternoon and evening classes in high school buildings. Both Indiana and Purdue extended themselves throughout the state, and after a period of competition their various branches in Indianapolis were combined with the IU medical center and several specialized programs in law, art, and physical education to form Indiana University-Purdue University-Indianapolis. Both the name and the abbreviation IUPUI are somewhat awkward, but the concept is highly successful and after a century of argument the state's capital city at last has a state university campus of its own.

How should Indiana be characterized in the mid-1980s? To pretend that every part of the state is flourishing would be inaccurate, but at the same time it is foolish to join with those who say that Indiana and the Midwest are finished, and that the future of this nation lies elsewhere. The Midwest is not dying, although certain industries are dying. Steel, automobiles, and machine tools do face serious foreign competition, but at the same time midwestern farmers remain among the world's most productive, and exports of grain and soybeans help balance the nation's imports of cars and cameras.

Perhaps a few residents of Indiana believe that their state is a dull place to live, lacking towering mountains or ocean beaches or plastic and neon resorts. Many others, however, have learned to appreciate its quiet rural beauty, its lakes and streams, its comfortable and settled cities and towns. With more and more Americans living in traffic-packed metropolitan areas Indiana remains a place of more human scale. Indianapolis, expanded by Unigov, ranks as the nation's thirteenth largest city, but it has not yet become so overwhelming that it intimidates its residents or dominates the state.

Hoosiers enjoy a wide variety of cities, towns, and countryside, moderately large to very small, flat as a pancake or picturesque as the wooded hills from Brown County southward to the Ohio. For years many Hoosiers gave only slight attention to their own heritage, but this too is changing and the people of Indiana once again take proper pride in their own rich history. At Conner Prairie near Noblesville an entire community of pioneer structures has been assembled, and a skilled staff convinces visitors they have stepped back into central Indiana as it was in 1836. In the river towns of Madison and Evansville entire "historic districts" of elegant nineteenth-century homes have been revived and restored, as have James Whitcomb Riley's Lockerbie Square neighborhood in Indianapolis and the West Washington district of South Bend. Fort Wayne has recreated its fort, New Harmony once again attracts fascinated visitors from near and far, and Columbus has become a mecca for students of modern architecture.

The story of Columbus is a fine combination of industry and art, of preservation of historic structures and the construction of wonderfully imaginative public buildings by world-famed architects, including such "ordinary" structures as public schools and a fire station. Columbus was a typical county seat town, with a few small factories, one of which happened to be run by a self-educated inventive genius with the unusual name of Clessie L. Cummins. Cummins Engine began in 1919, building diesel engines for marine use, but the Depression destroyed the market for yacht engines and Cummins managed to do the impossible, to make a diesel engine light enough for automotive use. By the mid-1930s Cummins diesels helped create a practical long-haul trucking industry, and Cummins became the nation's largest producer of engines for large trucks. Cummins Engine went eighteen years before it made its first profit, and the business was financed by a local banker who had once employed Clessie Cummins as his chauffeur. William G. Irwin became wealthy by backing Cummins, and his great-nephew and heir, J. Irwin Miller, has used his fortune to make Columbus one of the most attractive small cities in the nation. The Cummins Engine factory itself is an architectural showpiece, and downtown Columbus, a combination of restored older buildings and a strikingly modern civic center filled with shops, remains the retail heart of the community.

What else does Indiana have in its favor? From the earliest days of American settlement it was the land itself which lured men and women through the forests to make their homes in Indiana. While there are fewer farmers every year the soil remains rich and productive. With ever-increasing management skill and improved machinery and techniques, Hoosier farmers produce more than four billion dollars worth of crops and livestock every year. As has been true since the mid-Mississippian period of Indian farmers, the chief crop in Indiana is still corn, with soybeans second in acreage and value, followed by hogs, cattle, and wheat. While only 5 percent of Indiana's residents are farmers today, Indiana ranks tenth among the states in the total value of its agricultural production.

The steel mills and oil refineries of the Calumet Region remain the greatest concentration of industry in Indiana, and automotive components are of major importance in Kokomo, Anderson, Columbus, South Bend, and many other cities. Everywhere, however, heavy industry continues its gradual decline, with employment dropping faster than output as automated machinery replaces manpower. But Indiana has never depended upon only a few industries, and in cities and towns throughout the state a wide variety of products are loaded from factory shipping docks, from the pharmaceutical products of Eli Lilly in Indianapolis to compact disc recordings from CBS Records in Terre Haute to caskets in Batesville or baby formula and diet foods from Mead Johnson in Evansville.

A wide variety of financial and service companies now employ as many workers as the factories, although they are often less noticed by the public than plants which manufacture some highly visible consumer product. These service industries range in size from giant banks such as American Fletcher in Indianapolis and insurance firms such as Lincoln National in Fort Wayne to personal computer centers in virtually every town in Indiana.

Now that many Hoosiers in prominent positions in government, labor, and industry have recognized a need for new efforts in education, transportation, and resource development, Indiana is regaining its confidence in itself and its hope for the future. A century ago Indiana was entering upon what many Hoosiers came to regard as a "Golden Age" of prosperity and cultural achievement. That era was in truth a period of struggle and worry, for no real place could ever be quite as cheerful as James Whitcomb Riley, Booth Tarkington, or T.C. Steele envisioned. Today in the mid-1980s, despite its problems, Indiana remains what it has always been for ambitious men and women, a land of rich resources where honest effort offers real opportunity for success.

Facing page: *This picturesque barn stands in Martinsville. Photo by Bill Thomas*

Preceding page: *The setting sun creates a dramatic silhouette in southern Indiana. Photo by Bill Thomas*

Above: *Conner Prairie, a working pioneer village in Noblesville, preserves pioneer life for visitors. Photo by Bill Thomas*

Left: *Susannah Zimmerman sweeps the pantry at Golden Eagle Inn, a recreated 1836 inn at Conner Prairie. Photo by R. Hatchett*

179

Above: *Built between 1852 and 1856 for Thomas Gaff, this home in Aurora, Dearborn County, is known as "Hill-forest." From the circular belvedere above the semicircular portico, Gaff could enjoy views of the Ohio River. The house was restored in 1969. Photo by Darryl D. Jones*

Facing page: *The formal parlor of the Culbertson home in New Albany opulently expresses the wealth of its owner, William S. Culbertson, considered one of the richest men in the state during the nineteenth century. Built in 1869 overlooking the Ohio River, the house's woodwork was crafted by skilled boat builders. The spectacular hand-painted ceiling is the focus of the room. Photo by Darryl D. Jones*

Facing page: *Large Amish and Mennonite communities in Indiana live lives largely unchanging through the years. This horse-drawn sleigh passes through a covered bridge in a timeless scene. Photo by Ruth Chin*

Right: *These Amish children play with a patient pet. Photo by Bill Thomas*

Above: *This Amish family drives along the Wabash near Berne. Photo by Bill Thomas*

Above: *This prosperous farm, with its bright red barns and white fences, is in Morgantown. Photo by Bill Thomas*

Left: *This old farm near Muncie stands open to the onset of winter on a cold December day. Photo by Bill Thomas*

Left: *Squire Boone Caverns, near Corydon, features this mill. The caverns were discovered by Daniel Boone's brother escaping from Indians. Photo by Bill Thomas*

Below: *This wagon is a remnant of an earlier era in a Brown County field. Photo by Bill Thomas*

Left: *This young farmer and his wiggling friend pose on a bright fall day. Photo by Bill Thomas*

Facing page, top: *A fisherman enjoys the early morning solitude on Ogle Lake. The lake was built by the Civilian Conservation Corps in 1934-1935. Photo by Bill Thomas*

Left: *Cattle graze under a full moon near Madison. Photo by R. Hatchett*

Facing page, right: *Softly rolling hills unfold in this vista near Bloomington in southern Indiana. Photo by Bill Thomas*

Facing page, far right: *The mist forms a lacy cloud over Ogle Lake in Brown County State Park. Photo by Bill Thomas*

Facing page, top: *Pioneer artist T.C. Steele's home and studio is preserved near Belmont. Many of his noted landscapes are displayed there. Photo by Bill Thomas*

Facing page, bottom: *Clifty Falls cools the woods in Clifty Falls State Park. Photo by R. Hatchett*

Right: *Built in 1870 to the design of architect G.P. Randall, the Marshall County Courthouse in Plymouth features a central clocktower and classical pavilions at its east and west facades. Photo by Darryl D. Jones*

Below: *This road leads to a country church near Hartford in far southeastern Indiana. Photo by R. Hatchett*

Facing page: *The Cole Motor Car Company advertises its new 1920 model in the stylish form of a Vogue magazine cover of the period. This Indianapolis-based company was one of many automobile manufacturers in the state before Detroit dominated the automotive industry. Courtesy, Indiana Historical Society*

Right: *DePauw University was established in Greencastle in 1837, and has retained its fine reputation. Photo by Ruth Chin*

Below: *The Pyramids in Indianapolis provide a dramatic contrast to traditional architecture. They were designed by Kevin Roche, John Dinkeloo Associates, a nationally prominent architectural firm. The Pyramids are among the many office buildings on Interstate 465 circling Indianapolis. Photo by Bill Thomas*

Above: *The striking First Baptist Church, designed by architect Harry Weese of Chicago, is among the notable modern architecture in Columbus. Photo by Balthazar Korab, Ltd.*

Indiana Dunes in the north is a unique and beautiful state park. Photo by Bill Thomas

Alfred C. Kinsey

Alfred C. Kinsey was born in New Jersey in 1894, educated at Bowdoin College and Harvard University, and arrived at Indiana University in 1920 as an assistant professor of zoology. Kinsey was a fine lecturer and a popular teacher, but his reputation beyond Bloomington depended upon his exhaustive field study of the gall wasp, for which he collected more than four million specimens.

Kinsey was asked to teach a new course on marriage in 1938, and he quickly discovered that there was no scientific research on human sexuality. Kinsey naturally applied his customary approach of collecting a massive quantity of data for analysis, setting out to gather 100,000 individual sex histories.

Kinsey realized that his work would be controversial, and from the start he was supported by the young president of the university, Herman B Wells, who sustained him against federal and state investigators, worried politicians, and an outraged public for eighteen years. On one occasion when an angry Governor Schricker telephoned, Wells advised his old friend to cool down and call him again later.

From 1940 Kinsey devoted most of his enormous energy to his new topic. Thousands of men and women from all walks of life

Professor Alfred Kinsey (left) and President Herman Wells (right) enjoy a lighter moment in their years at Indiana University. Wells often defended Kinsey's controversial research and helped to dissuade federal and state investigators and outraged politicians who sought to stop the professor's work. Kinsey's books on human sexuality were pioneering works in their field. Courtesy, Kinsey Institute, photo by Dellenback

were interviewed, and in 1948 Kinsey published his *Sexual Behavior in the Human Male*. The book was a sensation despite its deliberately dull prose, and became an unexpected bestseller for its respected medical publisher. Kinsey estimated that half of the husbands in America were unfaithful to their wives and that homosexuality was more common than anyone suspected.

The university went to court when a customs agent tried to stop delivery of allegedly obscene books and art objects and after seven years of legal argument won a decision that legitimate re-

search material could not be seized as pornography. By that time Kinsey's collection of erotic writings and illustrations was said to be the largest in the world outside the Vatican Library.

When *Sexual Behavior in the Human Female* was published in 1953 it attracted even greater attention than its companion volume. Kinsey was condemned as immoral, communistic, and subversive, but throughout the dispute Herman Wells resolutely defended him. The Kinsey affair proved, as Wells proudly said later, "that the university had an integrity that could not be bought, pressured, or subverted." Kinsey died in 1956 and in many respects his work has been supplanted by more sophisticated research, much of it by the Alfred C. Kinsey Institute for Research in Sex, Gender and Reproduction at Indiana University. Few people read the "Kinsey Reports" today, and those who do find it difficult to understand what people found so objectionable thirty years ago. Better understanding of the role of sex in human behavior is based soundly on the pioneering studies by Alfred Kinsey, and Indiana University remembers him as a classic case for the defense of freedom of inquiry in a state usually considered conservative in morals and politics.

Dorothy Richardson Buell

Dorothy Buell was born in Wisconsin and lived most of her life as a conventional homemaker. Nothing in her life before the age of sixty-five went beyond the ordinary. She and her husband Hal Buell seemed destined for a placid retirement. In 1949 Dorothy Buell happened to notice a poster announcing a meeting to "help save the Indiana Dunes" and the issue caught her imagination. At first she quietly attended meetings, but within a few years she emerged as the leader of what was already a prolonged campaign to preserve the remaining sand dunes at the southern end of Lake Michigan.

The effort to save the dunes from sand mining and industrial development had first flourished early in the twentieth century, involving chiefly persons associated with the University of Chicago. Only a few Hoosiers joined the preservation movement, and most who were not indifferent sought further industrialization on the Gary model. The first victory came in 1923 with the establishment of the Indiana Dunes State Park, which after ten years expanded to include about 2,000 acres and more than two miles of shoreline. Renewed efforts at industrial expansion after World War II revived the preservationists as well, and from 1952 the most active role was taken by Dorothy Buell's Save the Dunes

Council. She spoke at every opportunity to warn people of the dangers to the dunes and of the importance of preserving their unique beauty. She was an effective speaker and a remarkable organizer, although in appearance she was as traditional as could be: white haired, small in stature, and always formally dressed in hat and gloves. Her true strength became apparent as she fought year after year to preserve the duneland for future generations.

Dorothy Buell did recruit some Hoosier supporters for her Save the Dunes Council, but the political and business leaders of northwestern Indiana opposed her at

Dorothy Buell emerged in her retirement years as the leader of a prolonged campaign to preserve the remaining sand dunes on Lake Michigan's Indiana shoreline. Her Save the Dunes Council is still active today in promoting the conservation of a unique natural environment. Courtesy, Save the Dunes Council

every turn, as did most state and federal officials. Most people thought of national parks as dramatic canyons or soaring mountains in the West, not sand dunes from which Chicago skyscrapers might be seen on those rare days when strong winds cleared away the industrial smoke and dirt. Her greatest ally was Senator Paul Douglas of Illinois, who fought gallantly in Washington to stop the destruction of the dunes.

Douglas was accused of interfering in Indiana's affairs, and he was opposed by Charles A. Halleck, the Republican leader in the House of Representatives whose district included most of the dunes area. The arguments and the political infighting in Washington grew more intense, and the battle was often put in terms of jobs and development against frivolous parkland, with the usually unspoken implication that many of the park visitors would be "undesirable people" from Gary and Chicago.

In the end it proved impossible to delay "progress" entirely, and there is no doubt that most of the residents of northwestern Indiana favored further industrial development. Nevertheless Doro-

These bathers enjoy a run up one of the dunes at Indiana Dunes State Park in Porter County in 1929. In the background the pavilion and arcade, the first building in the development of the park, is seen under construction. The Save the Dunes Council sought to limit development to preserve the dunes in their natural state. Courtesy, Indiana State Library, Indiana Division

thy Buell and Paul Douglas were able to prevail in considerable part, with assistance at critical moments from presidents John F. Kennedy and Lyndon B. Johnson, and the somewhat reluctant support of Senator Birch Bayh. Today the Indiana Dunes National Lakeshore stretches from Michigan City on the east to the edge of Gary on the west, and inland to include several small areas of exceptional ecological value,

particularly Cowles Bog. The critical legislation passed in October 1966, but the park was not formally dedicated until 1972.

By then an aged Dorothy Buell had finally retired to California, Paul Douglas had been rejected by the voters of Illinois, and hundreds of thousands of tons of sand had been moved to make way for a new steel mill and a state-financed harbor. Nevertheless, thanks to Dorothy Buell's energy and Paul Douglas' political courage, more than 6,000 acres of sand dune, marsh, and bog have been preserved for all of the people to enjoy. Dorothy Buell died in 1977 at the age of ninety, secure in the knowledge that the great cause of her life had ended in a limited but significant success.

Eli Lilly

Eli Lilly was born in Indianapolis in 1885 and spent his entire life there except for two years at pharmacy school in Philadelphia and summers at Lake Wawasee in Kosciusko County. Lilly was named for his grandfather, Colonel Eli Lilly, a Civil War artillery commander and the founder of the pharmaceutical company. Young Eli followed his father J.K. Lilly, Sr., into the business and began at the age of ten by grinding herbs. He worked full time from the completion of his pharmacy studies in 1907 and maintained regular office hours well into his eighties. "Mr. Eli" as he was always known to employees, invariably arrived at nine o'clock sharp in the morning and the firm was very much a family concern until the 1950s. He was president of the company from 1932 until 1948, and chairman of the board until 1961. Lilly was very proud that no employee was laid off or reduced in pay throughout the Depression.

The Lilly firm made its reputation early for exceptionally high-quality pharmaceutical preparations, but rapid growth came only after 1922 with the manufacture of insulin. Mr. Eli was not a research chemist himself, but he continued the family tradition of supporting both basic and development research on a generous

scale. In time Eli Lilly and Company became one of the foremost ethical drug manufacturers in the nation and the largest corporation with home offices in Indiana.

Just as remarkable are the non-business achievements of Mr. Eli. He was deeply concerned for the responsible use of his great wealth, and contributed generously to the Episcopal church, to several Indiana colleges, and to the cultural institutions of his native Indianapolis. For many years he was the major supporter of the Indianapolis Museum of Art and the Indianapolis Symphony Orchestra, and his concern helped build the outstanding Children's Museum in Indianapolis. In cooperation with his brother J.K. Lilly, Jr., and their father, Mr. Eli took the lead in establishing the Lilly Endowment in 1937. Today it ranks among the wealthiest foundations in the nation, and its gifts have helped finance many of the remarkable public buildings which have altered the appearance of Indianapolis in recent years.

Amid all of his other business and cultural interests, Mr. Eli was most particularly concerned for the history of his native Indiana. From excavation of the Indian remains at Angel Mounds to the creation of Conner Prairie Pioneer Settlement, his money and

his leadership preserved the Hoosier heritage. For twenty years he was president of the Indiana Historical Society and in its modern form it owes its success and its generous endowment largely to him. He was also the founder and chairman of the Historic Landmarks Foundation of Indiana, and personally restored the Morris-Butler House in Indianapolis which is a showplace today. Mr. Eli also supported the restoration effort at New Harmony, in association with the remarkable Jane Blaffer Owen, a Texas heiress who married a descendent of Robert Owen.

Eli Lilly was far more than a financier of historical causes, for he devoted time and effort over many years to research. He is the author of such fine historical works as *Prehistoric Antiquities of Indiana* and *Early Wawasee Days*, and together with his brother financed the publication of R. Carlyle Buley's monumental *The Old Northwest* which received a Pulitzer Prize even though commercial publishers had rejected it. J.K. Lilly, Jr., was a noted collector of rare books and manuscripts and he presented most of his collection to Indiana University, where he built the Lilly Rare Book Library to promote research and to display a few of his treasures.

Eli Lilly was a remarkable businessman and philanthropist as well as a fine historian and a dedicated historic preservationist. His fortune made it possible for him to finance any project which caught his interest, and Hoosier history is richer as a result. He died in 1977, respected and active to the last, at the age of ninety-one.

Eli Lilly is seen here while chairman of the board of Eli Lilly and Company. He joined his family's pharmaceutical firm in 1907 after receiving his education as a pharmacist. From Indiana State Library, Indiana Division, Courtesy of Eli Lilly and Company

CHAPTER X

This early view of a street scene in Richmond, which prominently features a
haywagon, was painted by the English
painter Lefevre J. Cranstone during his
winter stay in 1859-1860. It is considered
one of his finest watercolors. Courtesy,
Indiana Historical Society

Partners in Progress

When Indiana's legislators selected "The Cross-roads of America" as the official state motto in 1937, they were combining a statement of fact with a prophecy for the future. The state had been naturally blessed with a location within America's industrial and agricultural heartland, and the hardy and industrious Hoosier spirit would ensure Indiana's future as an integral part of the nation's progress and economic growth.

Nearly a half-century later the state has fulfilled its promise as a crossroads. Indiana claims more miles of interstate highway than any state of comparable size, with eleven of these routes serving Hoosier cities. Its central location and access to the rest of the nation has made Indiana ideal for manufacturing, warehousing, wholesaling, and distribution.

Although ranking only thirty-eighth in size (Indiana is the smallest state west of the Alleghennies), it is ninth among all states in agricultural sales ($4.3 billion a year) and also ninth in industrial output ($63.4 billion annually.)

Agriculture, which was once the basis for the state's economy, continues to play an important, though not dominant, role. Seventeen million acres, or 73 percent of the state's landmass, contain its 89,000 farms, the overwhelming majority of which are owned and operated by farm families.

While most Hoosiers have no direct connection to agriculture (despite the image sometimes held by those in other areas of the nation), the hard-working, God-fearing, conservative qualities of the farmer continue to permeate the Hoosier character. Although the focus of Indiana's economy had already moved to manufacturing prior to World War II, Hoosier business and industry has continued to reflect a strong commitment to community service, an exciting spirit of entrepreneurship, and a pride in being the best.

Being the best often leads to being the biggest, and such has been the case with several Indiana industries. From an area located in the northern part of the state that is first in the production of travel trailers and campers to southern Indiana's ranking as America's premier producer of wood kitchen cabinets, vanities, and other cabinetwork, Indiana claims a long list of blue ribbons. The state's 2.5 million workers are America's largest suppliers of such diverse products as cut limestone, raw steel, vehicle lighting equipment, radio and television receiving sets, and musical instruments.

While the vast majority of Indiana's workers continue to produce manufactured goods, the state is reflecting the current national trends toward greater concentration in the service industries and in high technology.

No matter what the future holds, the people behind Indiana's businesses will meet the challenges with optimism and determination. In every part of America, indeed in every part of the world, people benefit from the efforts of those living and working at "The Crossroads of America."

The organizations whose stories are detailed on the following pages have chosen to support this important literary and civic project. They illustrate the variety of ways in which individuals and their businesses have contributed to the growth and development of Indiana. The civic involvement of the state's businesses, learning institutions, and government, in partnership with its citizens, has made Indiana an exceptional place to live and work.

HISTORIC LANDMARKS FOUNDATION OF INDIANA

Kemper House, an 1873 landmark of Victorian architecture, is home to Historic Landmarks' Indianapolis office. The foundation also maintains offices in South Bend, Cambridge City, Jeffersonville, and Greencastle. Photo by Darryl Jones

There are many facets to the heritage of Indiana—the recorded history of its people, the artifacts that reflect their life-styles, and the arts that preserve their dreams. Interwoven into each is the architecture—the homes and shops, churches and factories that sheltered the progress of the Hoosier State.

It was only after many historic buildings had been demolished, however, that the citizenry began to recognize the significance of these landmarks. Their concern was organized when a group of prominent citizens, led by Eli Lilly, joined together to form Historic Landmarks Foundation of Indiana in 1960. Later Lilly's generous contribution established the foundation on firm financial ground, and it has since grown to become the largest and most active statewide preservation organization in the nation.

The group's focus is somewhat unique as well. Rather than using its resources to directly initiate historic preservation throughout the state, Historic Landmarks has chosen a supportive role to the more than sixty local organizations in Indiana. Operating under the premise that individual communities are in the best position to identify, protect, and maintain significant architecture, Historic Landmarks has fostered the creation of local programs and has offered expertise and financial support to strengthen them.

Historic Landmarks' Statewide Revolving Loan Fund was established in 1977, enabling local groups to borrow the funds necessary for the purchase and stabilization of endangered properties. Thus far this financial support has resulted in the preservation of more than thirty landmarks. The Affiliate Program, launched a year later, offers additional support, fostering preservation at the grass-roots level through shared information and experience.

The administration of these and other programs is accomplished through regional offices in Indianapolis, South Bend, Jeffersonville, and Cambridge City. In addition, a regional representative in Greencastle oversees activity in western Indiana.

Since 1970 the statewide headquarters has been housed in the elegantly renovated 1885 Waiting Station of historic Crown Hill Cemetery, a tangible example of the value of preserving the talents of nineteenth-century craftsmen. Additional properties owned by Historic Landmarks include the Kemper House and the Morris-Butler House, both Victorian-era residences in Indianapolis, the Grisamore House in Jeffersonville, and the Huddleston Farmhouse Inn Museum, an 1840s farm complex in Cambridge City.

It is not in museums, but in adaptive reuse, however, that Historic Landmarks Foundation of Indiana sees its future. Reid Williamson, president of the organization since 1974, explains that the emphasis of the future will be on mainstreaming historic properties to the needs of the day, integrating the best of the past into the promise of the future.

Landmark Tours, the foundation's tour service, uses all means of conveyance in showing off Indianapolis' architectural achievements and cultural attractions. Proceeds help fund Historic Landmarks' statewide preservation programs. Photo by Darryl Jones

BLUE CROSS AND BLUE SHIELD OF INDIANA

An integral facet of Indiana's character has always been a strong attitude of self reliance, a pride in carrying one's own weight, and providing for the needs of family and community.

This individualism may have delayed the creation of a major health insurance program in the state until 1944, but this same spirit has fostered the success of Blue Cross and Blue Shield of Indiana, one of only seven mutual Blue Cross/Blue Shield Plans in America that are organized as mutual insurance companies.

The company traces its roots to 1929, when Justin Ford Kimball at Baylor University devised a plan for prepaid hospital expenses for Texas schoolteachers. The concept flourished, and within a few years similar programs were in effect across the nation.

Not until 1944, however, did the idea find fertile ground in Indiana, when concerned citizens met to discuss the difficulties associated with health care. Doctors frequently went unpaid for their work and hospitals could neither upgrade equipment nor fund adequate staff without assurance of payment for their services. Of even greater consequence was the

economic disaster that often occurred in families when the breadwinner was stricken with illness or injury.

The solution was the creation of Blue Cross of Indiana (Mutual Hospital Insurance, Inc.), followed two years later by Blue Shield of Indiana (Mutual Medical Insurance, Inc.). True to the spirit of community, both programs were organized as mutual insurance companies—owned by the members and operated for their benefit.

The first day of operation for Blue Cross, November 1, 1944, was also the day Horace Irving of Indianapolis became the first member hospitalized; four days later the first Blue Cross baby, Ruthann Day, was born. In less than six months Ray Blackford of Elwood became the 100,000th member, and arrived in Indianapolis with his wife and eleven children to commemorate the event.

When Blue Shield was created in 1946, it was as a separate and distinct corporation. The two companies worked cooperatively, although each had its own founders, employees, and areas of responsibility—Blue Cross to cover hospital costs and Blue Shield to provide for medical expenses.

The old Traction Terminal and Bus Station (above left) occupied the site of the present Blue Cross and Blue Shield of Indiana headquarters (above). The corporation occupied the older building while the new offices were being constructed in 1970-1971.

In 1972 the two boards of directors approved a joint operating agreement that lasted until June 1985, when the two companies made the next logical move—merging into a single business entity. The corporation resulting from the merger is Associated Insurance Companies, Inc., doing business as Blue Cross and Blue Shield of Indiana.

Lloyd J. Banks, who served as president of Blue Cross of Indiana since 1967, became chairman of the board of directors and chief executive officer of the single corporation. Richard C. Kilborn, president of Blue Shield of Indiana since 1966, became president and chief operating officer. The corporation also encompasses three subsidiary companies and a work force of 2,800. In 1984 Blue Cross and Blue Shield of Indiana paid more than one billion dollars in health care claims on behalf of its customers—a concrete example of Hoosiers taking care of their own.

THE LAFAYETTE LIFE INSURANCE COMPANY

On the day after Christmas in 1905, several of Lafayette's business leaders gathered to form The Lafayette Life Insurance Company. Months earlier they had recognized the need for a sound and dependable insurer to serve the residents of Tippecanoe County. They had worked to find 250 individuals who would each purchase a $1,000 policy and, this challenge accomplished, they met to officially initiate the business. They selected their name not only after their community, but after Revolutionary War hero General de Lafayette, whose service had been a source of inspiration to both the city fathers and the company founders.

The founders' purposes were clear. They would offer the best possible life insurance protection at the lowest reasonable cost. They would provide dependable service to their clients, and while they were interested in growth, they were much more interested that this new company

The firm's first offices consisted of one small room on the second floor of the Winski Building (top), once located at Fourth and Ferry streets. In 1906 larger quarters were secured at 326 Ferry Street on the ground floor of the old Wallace Building, now the Kettlehut Building (middle). In 1909 the second floor of the Emsing Building (bottom) was occupied and was to remain "home" for ten years.

maintain a sound and secure financial foundation.

The articles of incorporation established that the new venture would be a mutual insurer, and the dividends from profits would thereby be returned to the policyholders. A perpetual charter was granted to the firm, and operations were begun from one room in the Winski Building. Within a few months Lafayette Life had outgrown its space. In 1906 it secured larger quarters in the Wallace Building, and in 1909 the company relocated again, this time occupying the entire second floor of the Emsing Building.

The growth that was occurring was not merely in terms of space requirements, but in sales volume as well. In January 1912 agents met and set a goal of nine million dollars of insurance in force by year's end—a goal that was achieved.

The need for more and more space prompted the eventual purchase of land on the northeast corner of Third and Main streets, and the construction, in 1918, of a ten-story building. The June 27, 1919, issue of the *Tippecanoe County Democrat* announced the open house with the headline: "Lafayette's New Skyscraper is Thrown Open to the Public," and for nearly fifty years the Life Building remained the tallest in the city.

One of the reasons for the young insurance company's growth was its sincere desire to be of service, and

The first real home of LLIC shown here in 1919. This building housed the company for forty of its eighty years. Constructed by Lafayette Life in 1891, it still remains the second-tallest building in the city.

this priority is well illustrated by the actions of its board of directors following World War I. The original life policies excluded liability for death incurred in military service during time of war. When these deaths were reported, Lafayette Life would refund the premiums paid plus any dividends that had accrued. When peace was restored, however, these war claims were reviewed, and it was determined that they could have been paid while still maintaining a lower mortality rate than expected. After receiving this report, the directors requested that all war claims be reopened and that the beneficiaries be paid the face amount of the policies. A similar concern was demonstrated during the Great Depression, when every effort was made to help policyholders keep their insurance in force and to keep their real estate as well. The firm was flooded with letters from insureds who had no money to pay their premiums. At the same time, requests poured in for policy loans to be used for mortgage payments. Many insurance companies faced with the same situation

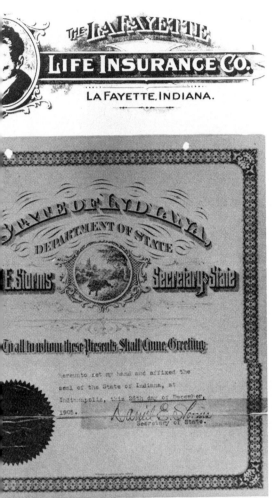

These articles of association were the original instrument on which the founders associated themselves together to form a life insurance company on the mutual principle, named The Lafayette Life Insurance Company.

suffered tremendously and some collapsed under this double financial pressure.

Lafayette Life, however, saw to it that every policyholder received a personal reply to his request. In cases where there was no policy cash value above premiums or accumulated dividends that could cover the premiums due, the company offered a special agreement whereby insurance could be kept in force by a nominal payment of one dollar per thousand per month. In addition, Lafayette Life met all applications for policy loans, and came through the Depression without borrowing a dollar or sacrificing an investment and never failing to pay dividends to policyholders.

The sound financial basis insisted on by the founders three decades earlier had served the firm well. By 1946 Lafayette Life had $50 million of insurance in force and by 1960 it had quadrupled to $200 million. During the early 1970s the company

reached the billion-dollar milestone, and by 1985 that figure had leaped to $5.6 billion.

The growth once again brought the need for more office space and a new home office was constructed on twenty acres at the corner of Eighteenth Street and State Road 25 in 1958. Under the leadership of Robert M. Whitsel, Lafayette Life's eighth president, a committee was appointed in 1976 to study long-range space requirements. As a result of the committee's recommendations, the east wing was added in 1978, more than doubling the available space.

The current facility is a testimony to the foresight of the company's founders and to the capable leadership Lafayette Life has enjoyed during the past eighty years. More than 230 employees work in the home office and over 600 agents serve in forty-eight states. They are aided by an up-to-date, modern data-processing center, which provides much faster response and more accurate reports in handling the day-to-day operations of management, agents, and policyholders. An in-house print shop produces reams of policies and support material for the firm, and an auditorium equipped with state-of-the-art audiovisual capabilities serves during seminars and training sessions.

As in the early years, expansion of facilities has gone hand in hand with expansion of services. Sales reached a record high in 1981, and in 1982 a subsidiary stock life company, Lafayette National Life Assurance Company, was formed. As this firm was being licensed in an increasing number of states, Lafayette Life introduced its first Universal Life policies in 1983.

No amount of progress, however, can detract from the purposes of the men who met to serve their community in 1905, even though that service has grown to include Americans everywhere.

The present home office.

ARVIN INDUSTRIES, INC.

Indiana residents readily recognize the name Arvin, but few may be aware of the enormous strides—in terms of both size and location as well as product diversification—this Indiana-based corporation has made in its 65-year history.

During the Columbus-based corporation's first forty years—from 1919 to 1959—all of its employees lived in Indiana and worked primarily on items for the automotive and home consumer markets. Today nearly 13,000 employees are working in twenty-nine locations in sixteen states as well as in Brazil, Mexico, West Germany, Canada, and Taiwan. While they continue to produce the well-known portable electric heaters and automobile exhaust systems, they also supply products as diverse as compact stereo systems, cable television converters, and security systems for nuclear power plants, as well as vinyl metal laminate stampings and precoated coils of steel and aluminum. They also offer research, development, and testing services to the U.S. government and private industry.

The product that will forever hold the place of honor in this *Fortune* 500 company, however, is the hand-operated tire pump—the first and very successful item produced for the fledgling automobile industry in 1919.

During his childhood on a Bartholomew County farm and later as a young man entering the Columbus job market, Quintin "Q.G." Noblitt had always demonstrated a marked mechanical talent. At the age of twenty-one he left for Indianapolis to seek his fortune, and during the ensuing ten years held a variety of positions connected with the young automotive industry. At one point, Q.G. ventured into producing his own automobiles and later he teamed with Frank Sparks to open a school for auto mechanics.

In 1919 a second business partnership was formed, this one to utilize

Today Arvin Industries has facilities in sixteen states plus Brazil, Mexico, West Germany, Canada, and Taiwan but, in 1919, this was the firm's original location in Indianapolis, Indiana.

Noblitt and Sparks' wide experience in automobile production and to fill a void in this new market.

Auto tires of the day were unreliable, and only the foolhardy ventured out without a tire pump on board. Q.G. Noblitt designed a pump far superior to those available, Al Redmond was brought into the partnership to head production, and Frank Sparks prepared to market the end result. They named their firm the Indianapolis Air Pump Company and realized a $10,000 profit the first year.

The company has never stopped growing. In 1920 car heaters were added, and a tire pump contract with Ford in 1921 began a working relationship that would one day include every major auto manufacturer. Within a few years Noblitt and Sparks (Redmond sold his interest in 1922) were expanding into related products including foot accelerator pedals, jacks, brake liners, hubcaps, and rear-vision mirrors. A logical expansion from automobile to home heaters was initiated, beginning the present consumer housewares business, and, later, car radios carried the company toward today's consumer electronics operations.

Frank Sparks' successful salesmanship opened doors for his firm that remain open today, but by 1929 he

Arvin Industries founders Frank H. Sparks (left) and Q.G. Noblitt.

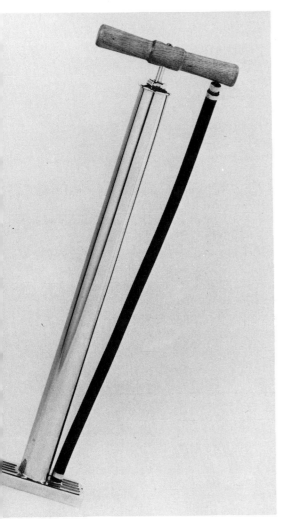

decided to pursue his dream of becoming a college president. Eleven years and a B.A., M.A., and Ph.D. later, he became the eighth president of Wabash College.

Q.G. Noblitt was the sole founding partner left to lead his enterprise, now located in Columbus, and lead it he did. The dynamic president successfully guided the business through the Great Depression, oversaw the opening of additional plants, and began a logical diversification of products that continues today.

Noblitt's influence on his company (the name was changed to Arvin in 1950, named for the inventor of the firm's first heater) is still in evidence today. Although he would no longer recognize the products or physical facilities, Q.G. would find the same atmosphere of quality and dedication he had fostered.

One facet of that dedication has always been to community service, particularly in the area of education.

Only the foolhardy would venture out without a tire pump back in the early days of the automobile. Q.G. Noblitt designed a pump superior to anything on the market and it became the company's first product.

It was prophetic that Noblitt and Sparks' first venture together was a school, for Arvin is dedicated to its involvement in quality education. Q.G. built five elementary schools and donated them to Bartholomew County. In addition to his tenure as president of Wabash College, Frank Sparks established Associated Colleges of Indiana, still one of the nation's most successful fund-raising organizations for private education.

Glenn Thompson, Arvin's second president, was a former teacher who had sold car heaters for Frank Sparks during his summer vacations. He later served as interim president of DePauw University and is remembered for spearheading a fund drive to build Memorial Gym at Columbus North High School, enlisting over one million dollars in contributions for the building, which was constructed without tax dollars.

Arvin Foundation gifts helped establish Ivy Tech in Columbus and supported the IUPUI library. In addition, the foundation recognizes teaching excellence in the communities Arvin serves through a series of Outstanding Teacher of the Year awards. The Q.G. Noblitt Chair of Business and Finance at DePauw University, the Sparks Student Union at Wabash College, and the Yandell Cline Library at Franklin College are all namesakes of Arvin leaders.

President James K. Baker, himself a former Arvin scholarship recipient, continues the tradition of service to education by serving as a trustee for DePauw University and has served as chairman of the board of governors of the Associated Colleges of Indiana.

Today Arvin Industries, Inc., supplies products and services to the automotive industry, the consumer appliances markets, government and utility customers, and commercial and industrial entities. The path traveled from the tire pump has been a spectacular one, but one consistently bolstered by a dedication to excellence and service.

HOOK DRUGS, INC.

The year was 1900 and John A. Hook had just earned his diploma from the Cincinnati College of Pharmacy. Though only nineteen, he had already gained practical experience during his apprenticeship to an Indianapolis druggist, and he was confident the time was right for him to open his own drugstore.

The son of German immigrants, he located his store in the heart of a strongly German neighborhood at 1101 South East Street, on the southeast edge of Indianapolis. He billed himself a "Deutsche Apoteke"—German Apothecary.

Pharmacists of the day competed not only with each other, but with mail-order patent medicines and homemade remedies. John Hook's reputation for integrity fostered his success. In 1908 he opened his second store and hired Edward Roesch, another young pharmacist, as its manager.

The outgoing Hook and the serious Roesch complemented one another, in both personality and business acumen, and in only four years Hook's chain had grown to twelve stores. The young pharmaceutical team weathered the shortages of two world wars and the Great Depression, and by the end of the first half-century the firm had grown to fifty drugstores.

John Hook died in 1943, and Edward Roesch succeeded him, leading the drug chain into the era of

John A. Hook (left) poses with his staff in his first store, located at 1101 South East Street in Indianapolis. Photo circa 1905

self service and suburban shopping centers. When his long career was tragically ended in an automobile accident in 1956, Hook's son, August F. (Bud) Hook—a 27-year veteran of the pharmacy operation—became president and Edward Roesch's two sons, Edward and John, ably served in top executive roles in merchandising and finance, respectively. Norman P. Reeves, who had worked his way up from store pharmacist, was chief of corporate operations.

This second-generation team instituted a revolution in store operations and locations. By 1972 all but two of the pre-1950 stores had been phased out and more than 150 new ones had been opened. In 1963 a giant home office and service center was built to serve the outlets scattered throughout the state, a facility

that has now grown to 596,470 square feet on thirty-three acres of land on Indianapolis' far east side.

In 1978, at age seventy-one, Bud Hook became chairman emeritus of the Hook board, and Norman Reeves took over the duties as chairman. After his death in 1981, his son, J. Douglas Reeves, president, added chairman to his title. Under this third generation of leadership, Hook Drugs has expanded to include well over 300 drugstores in Indiana, Illinois, Ohio, and Kentucky. Hook's Convalescent Aids Centers offer home health care equipment and supplies to regional markets.

Hook's became a subsidiary in 1985 of The Kroger Co., Cincinnati, Ohio, the nation's second-largest chain food and drug retailer. Despite the size and efficiency of this innovative, contemporary corporation, Hook Drugs, Inc., has remained true to its heritage and basic service of health care.

Thousands of individuals visit the nationally acclaimed Hook's Historical Drug Store and Pharmacy Museum at the Indiana State Fairgrounds each year to see the dramatic contrasts in the progress of family health care. Furnishings from Hook's first store are also in use at the 1900 John A. Hook Drug Store in quaint Brown County.

A Hook's drugstore was an early landmark at this busy Indianapolis intersection at Washington and Illinois streets in the 1920s, a site later occupied by the L. Strauss Clothing store. Hook's once operated seventeen stores in the Indianapolis downtown. Two new Hook's stores returned in the early 1980s.

JAYCO INCORPORATED

Campers and travelers throughout the United States and in many foreign countries are familiar with the products of Jayco Incorporated. None would be surprised to learn that the company's camping trailers, motor homes, travel trailers, custom vans, and fifth-wheel trailers are produced in Middlebury, Indiana—Elkhart County is, after all, the major manufacturing area for recreational vehicles in America.

They might be surprised, however, to know that Jayco is the result of one man's dreams and remains one of very few privately owned RV manufacturers in the nation. The firm, which now produces nearly 10,000 units a year, began less than twenty years ago—in 1968—when 130 units were produced on Lloyd Bontrager's eighty-acre farm.

Bontrager, who had five years' experience working for another camper manufacturer, decided that he could use his expertise to produce camping trailers on his own. He developed a new lift system for crank-up trailers, "mortgaged the farm for as much as possible," and found four friends and neighbors who were interested in investing in the new venture.

As Jayco's production increased, new employees were hired, many of whom were members of the large Amish community in northeastern Indiana. That tradition has continued, and today approximately 70 percent of the company's 450 employees are members of this faith. Bontrager credits much of the firm's success to the Amish craftsmanship and pride in work well done that these individuals have brought to their jobs. He is also very proud that Jayco tends to keep its employees, many of whom have been with the company almost from its inception.

The agricultural community where Jayco began was not zoned to accommodate the growing manufacturer

Today the Jayco complex occupies fifty-five acres and is a major employer in the small, basically agricultural community of Middlebury. © Troyer Studios Inc.

and in January 1970 it was moved the short distance to Middlebury, where all operations are congregated on a 55-acre site. Each type of vehicle is manufactured in a separate building and additional structures house such operations as research and sewing.

Vehicles leaving the Middlebury facility are distributed throughout the United States and in Canada. In addition, Australia is home to an affiliate company, partly owned by Bontrager, and licensing arrangements in England and New Zealand further ensure the international recognition of Jayco campers.

Jayco has not gone untouched by the problems that have affected the entire recreational vehicle industry. During the worst of the recession and

energy crisis in 1973-1974, production suffered, and a shorter slump occurred in 1981 when high interest rates slowed sales. The present and future, however, appear bright for Jayco (sales for 1984 reflected a 50-percent increase from 1983, and 1985 promises to follow the same pattern), and Lloyd Bontrager states that "the cooperation of our employees has been a key" to this optimism. He has fostered a feeling of family among his employees, and thousands of additional families—those who are camping and traveling in Jayco's products—will benefit from their efforts.

Lloyd Bontrager's farm produced a bumper crop of campers during Jayco's first year of operation. © Troyer Studios Inc.

ST. VINCENT HOSPITAL AND HEALTH CARE CENTER

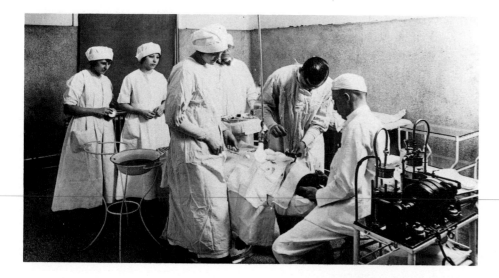

Surgeons and operating room staff perform a tonsillectomy in the third St. Vincent facility. Photo circa 1922

the process has proved to be a continuous one.

In 1977 the name was changed to St. Vincent Hospital and Health Care Center, and a commitment was made to community outreach. The first wellness center east of the Mississippi was opened to national acclaim. A sports medicine clinic was established to meet the needs of recreational and competitive athletes, and the St. Vin-

The *history* of the St. Vincent Hospital dates back to its opening in 1881, but the *heritage* of this institution can be traced to a much earlier time.

It was in 1633 that a parish priest in Paris, Vincent de Paul, organized an alliance of women to serve the sick poor. Under the leadership of Louise de Marillac, members of the Daughters of Charity were trained in religion and nursing, then sent to minister to those in need. Initially, the Sisters' work was confined to France, but as the order grew, their assistance was sought in other nations.

Bishop Silas Chatard requested that the order respond to the needs in Indianapolis, and in 1881 four women arrived to set up an infirmary in a vacant seminary building. The Sisters scrubbed and cleaned the facility, tended gardens and livestock, and looked after 109 patients during that first year. By 1855 the facility had fifty beds and a house physician—Dr. Joseph Marsee—who often donated his $25-a-month salary back to the hospital.

In 1889 a move to a new 150-bed building provided more room, but even that space was not enough and ten years later a second story was added to accommodate more patients. The most famous of those seeking aid was President Theodore Roosevelt, who visited for treatment of an abscess on his leg after delivering several speeches in the city in

The statue of St. Vincent and the Beggar at the entrance to the hospital testifies to the humanitarian atmosphere inside this modern, progressive health care facility.

1902.

In 1913 another move took place, once again in an effort to gain more space. During the sixty-one years spent at this location, medical science made enormous gains as new drugs and vaccines successfully fought many deadly diseases. In 1963 the hospital opened Indiana's first coronary care unit.

St. Vincent's fourth and present location is an ever-growing health care complex built on 114 acres on the north side of Indianapolis and administered by Sister Theresa Peck, D.C. Within a year after the opening, expansion was again taking place and

cent Stress Center opened in 1982 to provide care for incurable, mentally ill, and chemically dependent patients. Projects currently under construction include a satellite full-service hospital in Carmel, Indiana.

Despite its enormous growth, the 2,800 employees stay well aware of the original Sisters' compassion, evidenced by the hospital's theme, "We Treat You With Special Care."

MAYFLOWER CORPORATION

Times were good in 1927 and many Americans were celebrating their prosperity by leaving the farms and purchasing new homes along tree-lined boulevards in the cities.

Conrad M. Gentry, who made his living running a farm-to-market trucking service between Monrovia and Indianapolis, saw in this migration a need he might fulfill. Families were at the mercies of local haulers and railroad dockworkers when it came time to ship their precious household goods, and such items as furnishings and kitchenware were often demolished on their route from a local hauler to a railroad line to a second hauler to the new home.

Gentry envisioned a single carrier, a truck that would haul these goods from the old house directly to the new one, eliminating most opportunities for damage and loss. He convinced a friend, Don F. Kenworthy, to join him in his new venture, and reportedly chose the new company's name while dining in the Mayflower Café in Dayton, Ohio.

Gentry and Kenworthy secured padded vans and publicized their door-to-door pickup and delivery service. Their first year's revenues of $70,479 served as evidence of the timeliness of their idea and of the need to expand.

The following year the company reorganized, finding new capital from a group of investors headed by Burnside Smith, who became the firm's president and renamed it Aero Mayflower.

Smith, who would become the first of three generations of his family to lead the Mayflower Corporation, developed branch offices in every major city east of the Mississippi and north of the Ohio, and he entered into franchise agreements with nearly 300 local movers and storage warehouses.

A plane crash in 1935 resulted in Smith's untimely death, but his

dream for Mayflower lived on. Management, which now included son John Sloan Smith, continued to oversee the company's growth, and in 1940 Mayflower was granted the first nationwide operating certificate by the Interstate Commerce Commission.

Today grandson John Burnside Smith oversees the Mayflower Corporation and more than a dozen subsidiaries from the firm's international headquarters in Carmel, Indiana, just north of Indianapolis. Sophisticated computer systems keep track of over 1,700 vans, and innovations including "Air Ride," the use of soft rubber air bags in the vans, have enhanced the organization's image, making it—according to a Gallup survey—the

most recognized mover in America. Mayflower's traditional service of hauling household goods has matured, and today's fastest-growing operations center around the relocation of delicate electronic equipment, including computers.

Conrad Gentry would be amazed at today's complexity of operations, the innovative equipment, and the sophisticated cargo it carries. His original goal of moving belongings quickly and safely, however, is still very much in evidence during Mayflower's sixth decade of business.

The door-to-door delivery offered by these vans of the 1930s was a welcome improvement over the earlier options open to movers.

Today's vans are equipped to handle valuable possessions and delicate cargo with safety.

ELI LILLY AND COMPANY

Few Indiana firms have touched the lives of more individuals throughout the world than Indianapolis-head-quartered Eli Lilly and Company.

Nearly 30,000 employees are located around the world in the research, production, and marketing of human medicines, agricultural products, electronic medical instruments, and cosmetics. Products are sold in approximately 130 countries, and the company's astonishing research and development expenditure of $5.6 million each week testifies to its vigorous pursuit of products to benefit mankind.

Lilly pharmaceuticals have traveled to the South Pole with Admiral Byrd and to the moon with the astronauts. Within days of Lilly's first major scientific achievement, the production of insulin in 1923, the lives of diabetics were being saved, and the list of subsequent breakthroughs is long. In the late 1920s liver extracts were produced to fight pernicious anemia, and the 1940s brought vigorous work with antibiotics. During the mid-1950s Lilly was a major producer of polio vaccine, and in 1964 the company developed the synthesis of the first cephalosporin antibiotic. That same decade saw the development of two major cancer-treatment agents.

At the age of thirty-eight, Colonel Eli Lilly began his tiny drug company, which would grow to become one of the most prestigious pharmaceutical firms in the world.

More recently Lilly human insulin, a result of years of recombinant DNA research, was introduced.

Today's worldwide enterprise exists because one man, Colonel Eli Lilly, decided in 1876 to produce ethical drugs according to scientific standards in an age dominated by the flamboyant claims of patent medicine and traveling hucksters. The Civil War veteran invested $1,400 and hired two employees in addition to his fourteen-year-old son, Josiah Kirby "J.K." The young J.K. Lilly was put in charge of sweeping the floors, firing the boiler, and washing countless medicine bottles as the others labored at compounding medications for use by physicians.

J.K. Lilly became president in 1898, and continued his father's determination to align the firm's research with the latest advances in medical science. He oversaw construction of the first Lilly building devoted exclusive-

ly to scientific research and he saw to it that his two sons, Eli and Josiah Kirby Jr., earned pharmacy degrees from prestigious universities before joining him in a thirty-year alliance.

Together they developed a strong business structure (all Lilly employees were retained at full pay during the Great Depression) and oversaw important pharmaceutical contributions. During World War II the company supplied more than one million liters of blood plasma for the armed forces on a cost basis and provided enough typhus vaccine to immunize six million military personnel.

Today's management, led by chairman Richard Wood, is no longer based in the Lilly family, but the original philosophy has survived well into the firm's second century. "No business worthwhile," explained the colonel, "can be built upon anything but the best of everything."

In 1926 Lilly employees packaged the newly discovered insulin that would save the lives of diabetics throughout the world.

FARM BUREAU INSURANCE COMPANIES

Improving economic conditions were reaching Indiana's agricultural community in 1934, and farmers were facing the future with growing confidence. They did, however, share a common problem in the area of insurance for their trucks and automobiles, for affordable coverage was simply unavailable to them from existing companies.

The insurance then available to farmers was provided by an out-of-state company that did not meet the investment requirements necessary to promote continued growth of Indiana's economy. The directors of Indiana Farm Bureau, acting upon the wishes of their members, saw the need to start their own insurance company. As a result, the Farm Bureau Mutual Insurance Company of Indiana, Inc., was chartered on October 17, 1934, and licensed the following February.

The fledgling enterprise suffered the usual growing pains of a new venture, but despite a lack of insurance experience on the parts of management and agency personnel, policies were written on more than 5,000 vehicles during the first year.

That the new company was meeting a need was obvious; that it must find experienced leadership became just as clear when a tally of the first year's surplus showed an unimpressive balance of $148.01!

Once again, there was little hesitation in taking the necessary steps to remedy the situation. In 1936 the firm recruited individuals with expertise in property and casualty coverage, and at the end of the second year the surplus jumped to $9,300.

When the Hoosier Farm Bureau Life Insurance Company was established in 1937, the response was enthusiastic. More than 2,000 charter applications, amounting to over two million dollars, were received—a volume more than ten times the state's requirements.

The life insurance facet (now renamed United Farm Bureau Family Life Insurance Company) has continued to grow at a tremendous pace.

After stays in several smaller facilities, Farm Bureau Insurance purchased its present location—only two blocks from Monument Circle in the heart of Indianapolis—in 1950.

erages were being written. In 1981 a new firm, UFB Insurance Company, was established for marketing Individual Retirement Accounts and for other specialized needs.

Farm Bureau Insurance marked its fiftieth anniversary in 1984, celebrating the event with a pride derived from a job well done. The companies' staffs have grown from a mere handful of inexperienced people to more than 2,000 qualified professionals. While they have retained their close ties to the rural community, policyholders now represent all occupations and life-styles throughout Indiana.

"Our founders were people from

At the end of ten years insurance in force had increased to $47 million and in twenty it had grown to $181 million. By 1981 more than three billion dollars of life insurance was in force throughout the state.

The organization, soon referred to as Farm Bureau Insurance Companies, continued its innovative growth in insurance for rural policyholders. It was an early writer of farm liability policies and the first to offer farmers contingent workmen's compensation insurance. In 1946 fire and wind cov-

A portrait of Lewis Taylor, the first president of Farm Bureau Insurance, oversees company officers reviewing the more than 2,000 charter applications for life insurance in 1937.

the land who wanted a fair return for their insurance premium," explains a Farm Bureau Insurance spokesman. "They founded a company for that purpose—to get the best possible insurance at the lowest possible cost. Over fifty years later that idea lives on."

ECKHART & COMPANY, INC.

As his service during World War I drew to an end, Bill Eckhart planned his future. He had worked for an Indianapolis printer before the war and had learned the craft of directory printing and binding. Now he took his $900 mustering-out pay, acquired a loan on his life insurance policy, and rented shop space in the Hume Mansur Building in downtown Indianapolis.

His new business, Eckhart & Company, was purposely located near the Indianapolis Public Library's main branch, and young Eckhart specialized in the rebinding of library books. Soon libraries throughout central Indiana became clients. Eckhart would pick up damaged books, resew the pages and redo the covers, then glue the book back together for continued use.

In 1921 Bill was introduced to Mary Dooley, an event that would change both his personal and professional future. The young woman worked in the courthouse and she informed her future husband that libraries were not the only customers that needed quantities of books rebound. Before long Mary began doubling as an unofficial sales rep, bringing books from the courthouse to the shop for rebinding, and within a few months Bill had also begun to manufacture record books for the courts.

During the next three decades the company witnessed steady growth, a result of the young owner's dedication to customer service. He would list incoming jobs on a blackboard and complete them in order, considering each project an important assignment.

Son Bill Jr. took over the management of the firm in 1953, a few years before his father's death. Mary became more involved in the operations and continued to work on a regular basis until her retirement in 1982.

During the 1950s, Eckhart & Company gradually phased out the rebinding work to concentrate on its complete binding services for the

This page from the firm's ledger book for April 1922 shows an electric bill of $1.50 and a telephone bill of $4.80. Materials included two spools of thread at one dollar. Wages for two people totaled $93.18. April showed sales of $445.69 and expenses of $355.56, resulting in a profit of $90.13.

printing trade. A commitment was made to buy the best, most technologically advanced equipment available, and the founder's philosophy of quality service remained central to the operation. Within a short time services included cutting, folding, collating, stitching, punching, and drilling, as well as wire-o, spiral, and plastic binding.

A loose-leaf division was added during the 1960s, when the firm began production of customized ring binders. All operations are performed in-house for clients located throughout the United States.

By 1967 the growth of Eckhart & Company necessitated a move to larger quarters, and a 30,000-square-foot manufacturing and office facility was constructed near Indianapolis International Airport.

Today Eckhart & Company looks forward to its seventh decade in business and the family's third generation, grandson Brent Eckhart, now serves as vice-president. Office manager Rosie Bozell and plant superintendent Steve Newman oversee sixty employees, individuals who help to carry on the plans and dreams begun by the young veteran Bill Eckhart.

CROWN INTERNATIONAL

When the Indianapolis Colts are introduced to fans in the Hoosier Dome, and when the famous cry, "Gentlemen, start your engines," is broadcast around the world from the Indianapolis 500, the products of Crown International are at work. The sophisticated audio equipment produced by the Elkhart firm is used and respected throughout the world—in California's Disneyland, for instance, and at the concerts of the best-known rock groups. Twenty percent of Crown's production is exported, even to such leaders in the audio industry as Japan.

Crown's excellent reputation is no accident. The company has a strong tradition of quality workmanship and ethical business practices rooted in the Christian faith of its leaders.

Before founding his firm in 1947, Clarence C. Moore was active in the ministry, using his avocational interest in radios to help develop mission radio facilities in Quito, Ecuador. He invented the cubicle quad short-wave antenna—suited for the high altitudes in that country—enabling Radio HCJB to develop a worldwide ministry that is today the most powerful Christian broadcasting facility in the world.

Upon returning to the United

Evidencing Crown International's growth, the Elkhart facility doubled in size during 1984.

States in the mid-1940s, Moore pursued electronics and formed a new company, then named International Radio and Electronics Corporation. From his kitchen table "office" and his "plant" located in an old chicken coop, he manufactured open-reel tape recorders, designed to work reliably for missionaries in remote areas of the world.

Demand for Crown products grew rapidly, as did the innovations that kept the firm in a leadership position. A significant stride was taken in 1965, when Max Scholfield, then chief engineer and now president of the company, designed the first successful solid-state audio power amplifier.

Crown's spirit is evidenced by the events on Thanksgiving Day, 1971, when a fire completely destroyed the plant. All of the eighty employees reported to help clean up without a promise of pay. Within a week one line was back into production in a rented building nearby.

Founder Clarence C. Moore took a great deal of pride in the equipment his company produced, including these early tape recorders.

Today Crown International employs nearly 400 individuals, and sales have leaped from Moore's first year's production of forty tape recorders to twenty million dollars in annual revenues. Innovations have continued, and in 1979 Crown introduced the world's first power amplifier to use built-in computers.

The future appears unlimited for each of Crown's groups. The Commercial Sound/Pro Sound Division provides sound equipment for stadiums and auditoriums, traveling entertainers, and recording studios. Crown is one of two domestic manufacturers of sophisticated hi-fi equipment, and the Industrial Division supplies other manufacturers with components, including main power supplies and amplifiers to all the major producers of medical MRI-scan equipment.

What began as a strong interest in radios on the part of Clarence Moore is today a world leader in the science of audio technology.

DUNCAN ELECTRIC/LANDIS & GYR

Born into a prestigious Scottish family in 1865, Thomas Duncan could easily have lived the comfortable life his father envisioned. He did, in fact, initially follow that course, but at age seventeen Duncan's adventuresome spirit prevailed and he traveled alone to make his fortune in America.

Duncan's boyhood fascination with the developing science of electricity found fertile ground in his new homeland. Thomas Edison, who recently had invented the incandescent lamp, began New York City's first generating station shortly after Duncan's arrival. In 1884 George Westinghouse founded his enterprise and the General Electric Company was formed in 1892.

Young Duncan learned from the foremost authorities in this new field. As his expertise increased, he held key positions with electric manufacturing companies in the East and Midwest, and he developed many of the major innovations employed by the young industry. In several instances, however, these companies were acquired by larger interests, and Thomas Duncan was helpless as his life's work (including over 100 patents) was sold and no longer available for his use.

In 1901 he made the decision to enter the electric meter industry on his own. He chose Lafayette, Indiana, partly because of its proximity to Purdue University, and partly because the Lafayette Commercial Club offered him the free use of an existing building in exchange for promised job opportunities for local residents.

The new venture grew quickly as Duncan finally applied his talents on his own behalf. The versatile inventor obtained 152 patents for improvements to metering devices, and Duncan Electric established a significant share of the meter market, competing successfully with Westinghouse, General Electric, and Sangamo (then, as now, the only other U.S. meter manufacturers).

Thomas Duncan died in 1929, a few months before the firm's growth

Thomas Duncan, founder of Duncan Electric, was a major benefactor of the Lafayette Historical Association and the Tippecanoe County Art Association, and later left a bequest for the construction of an electrical engineering building and laboratory at Purdue University.

was halted by the Great Depression. Duncan Electric weathered the difficult times, however, and both the development of a successful new meter in 1934 and the establishment of the Rural Electrification Administration in 1935 aided the company's recovery. During World War II, when materials for meters were impossible to obtain, Duncan Electric turned its efforts toward aircraft instruments manufacturing, earning a prestigious Army/Navy "E" Award for outstanding contributions.

The firm resumed meter production in 1946, and in 1950 began construction of its present facility, which was expanded in 1966 and 1973. In 1976 Duncan Electric was acquired by Landis & Gyr, a multinational

Duncan's 350,000-square-foot facility was built in 1950 and houses the company's manufacturing, marketing, engineering, and administration departments. Subsidiary companies are located in Dayton, Ohio, and Miami, Florida.

corporation headquartered in Switzerland and the world's largest producer of electric meters.

Energy conservation concerns of the 1970s and 1980s prompted new developments, including the use of solid-state devices that replace the original principle developed a century ago by Duncan and his contemporaries. The founder's indomitable spirit, however, continues to live in the quality and service provided by the company's 900 employees.

HELSEL METALLURGICAL, INC.

"I'm a great believer in southern Indiana," explains Jess Helsel. "The people here are productive, and I'm convinced that small towns are the place to conduct business."

The explanation is frequently repeated to individuals surprised to find a thriving metalworking industry among the farms and small towns of Washington County—an area well known for its woodworking expertise. When Helsel first introduced the powder metallurgy operations in neighboring Salem in 1951, in fact, it was that community's first new industry in thirty years.

Helsel and three colleagues from a Kent, Ohio, plant arrived in Salem to implement an expansion of their employer's operations. As president, he oversaw the construction of an additional plant in 1968, and the company enjoyed industry-wide recognition for the development of technology that expanded the uses of powder metallurgy. He continued with the firm until 1973, when he opted for the freedom of directing his own operation. He purchased the assets of an Indianapolis-based metals concern, renamed it Helsel Metallurgical, Inc., and began operations on January 1, 1974. Two years later he moved his enterprise to Campbellsburg.

Jess Helsel, president.

After a decade in operation, the plant is undergoing its fourth expansion and the names on the payroll have more than quadrupled. Orders arrive from manufacturers throughout America and from overseas, and Helsel projects a doubling of the sales volume in the next three years.

Most often the orders are in the form of a need expressed by a manufacturer for a part to be used in its finished products. "We take an idea or a concept or a print," Helsel explains. "Then we design a material and a part to do the job."

Although automobile producers' needs dominate the powder metal industry, Helsel has purposely avoided that market, preferring to work mainly in the areas of hydraulics and appliances. The company has about 150 active customers, and the parts requested range from components for hydrostatic drive pumps to those for washing machines or computer printers.

When a part is requested, the formulation of powdered metals is engineered and machinery is tooled to shape the component. Presses delivering from four to 650 tons of pressure compact the powdered metals, then the resulting components go through a sintering process—heating to the precise temperatures that will meld the metals but retain the shape and size of the part. Finishing processes include coining and secondary machining and finishing operations.

Jess Helsel, who serves as a county councilman and chairs the state chamber's Small Business Council, takes pride not only in his company but in the positive impact the industry has had on the community. He notes that new businesses have begun to open, and he hopes others will recognize the advantages he has found in southern Indiana.

Larry W. Ooley (left), vice-president of manufacturing, and Jess Helsel, president, confer in front of a state-of-the-art control system for the powder metallurgy plant.

ST. ELIZABETH HOSPITAL MEDICAL CENTER

The small congregation of Sisters had been decorated for their service to the sick and wounded on the front lines of the Franco-Prussian War. Emperor Wilhelm awarded the Cross of Merit to the congregation and sent the Medal of Bravery to each of the twenty-three Sisters who had been on field duty—duty that had cost two of the young women's lives.

Within a year that same government, now under the influence of Bismark, inaugurated a persecution of the Roman Catholic Church so severe that it threatened the very existence of the congregation. In 1872 the May Laws were passed, and as a result the Sisters were prohibited from operating their orphan asylums and they were no longer allowed to teach. Requests from women to join the congregation were automatically denied by the government, and even the right to their own property was questioned in court.

Mother Superior Theresa, the order's foundress, was deeply concerned. She shared her fears with Bishop Joseph Dwenger of Fort Wayne, Indiana, who had made a pilgrimage to Rome and was visiting in Germany. She questioned him about the possibility of continuing in the United States, and she was assured that the Sisters would be made welcome in Bishop Dwenger's diocese.

As a result, six Sisters sailed for America on November 26, 1875. They settled in Lafayette and immediately set up a hospital in their home. The Sisters could not speak English, but their obvious devotion to caring for the sick and the poor needed no translation to the members of their new community.

As the city's health needs grew, so did the space requirements for the Sisters' hospital. On June 11, 1876, the cornerstone was laid for St. Elizabeth Hospital, and five months later it was opened to patients following a dedi-

The Sameday Surgery program, upgraded in 1983, is especially attuned to young children, providing them with individual attention and special care to allay their fears.

Since its establishment in 1879, the St. Elizabeth School of Nursing has graduated nearly 1,600 individuals to contribute to health services throughout the world.

cation ceremony complete with a parade of marching bands. An east wing was added in 1879 and the west wing followed four years later. Even a major addition in 1897 was not enough, however, and the part of the building reserved for the Sisters had to be converted to patient care.

During that same year the St. Elizabeth School of Nursing was begun as a training school for the Sisters. In 1937 the first lay students were admitted and in 1952 the school was among the first in the country to receive national accreditation. In 1980 the school became affiliated with St. Francis College in Fort Wayne, which enhanced the curriculum and the students' future career opportunities. Today's 200 students will join nearly 1,600 graduates who have served in health care professions throughout the world.

True to the directions followed by

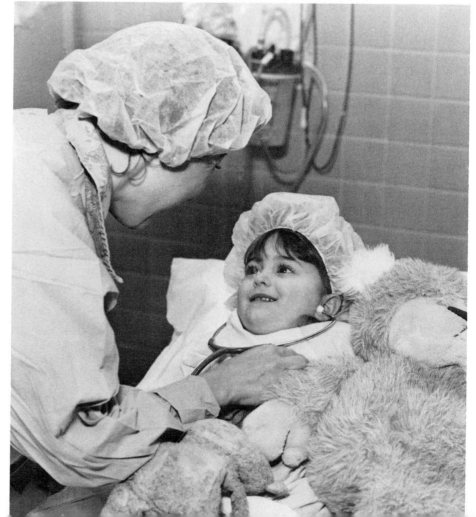

the first congregation in Germany, the Sisters have also been active in education since their arrival in Lafayette, and now administer both elementary and secondary schools in Indiana and in other states.

The tremendous growth of St. Elizabeth Hospital was but one of the results of Mother Theresa's wise decision to seek refuge for her order in America. By the turn of the century the Sisters had erected and managed twenty hospitals in the United States and staffed numerous schools, orphanages, and homes for the elderly. By the time of her death in 1905, the order had grown to include 870 Sisters in Germany and 600 in America. The compassion and dedication now offered at the St. Elizabeth Hospital Medical Center mirrors that provided by the Sisters more than a century ago. The medical care offered today's patients, however, could never have been imagined in those early days.

Administrator Paul E. Hess (the first lay administrator hired by the Sisters at any of their hospitals) and assistant administrators Sister M. Julitta Biegel and Sister M. Irene Schneidt oversee the 375-bed hospital, which has historically been a leader in new services.

In 1952 the first school of operating room technology in the nation began at St. Elizabeth, opening a new career field to those interested in health services. Cardiac care units were available to Lafayette residents

in the mid-1960s—before the hospitals in many larger cities made them available—and both the birthing room concept and an in-the-home hospice program gained early acceptance.

Statistics based on the results of open-heart surgeries in Indiana hospitals over the past three years reflect St. Elizabeth's impressive record and the addition of Percutaneous Transluminal Coronary Angioplasty (PTCA) has recently brought yet another current interventional therapy for coronary artery disease to the Lafayette area.

St. Elizabeth Hospital Medical Center is a vital part of the community it serves. A cross-section of the citizenry of Lafayette meets monthly for a luncheon at the hospital where a member of the staff discusses an aspect of health care and St. Elizabeth's

St. Elizabeth Hospital Medical Center offers a combination of the latest in medical technology with a tradition of genuine compassion for the residents of Tippecanoe and surrounding counties.

contribution. More than 450 volunteers and nearly 1,000 auxiliary members offer services and fund raising to benefit the hospital, and, in turn, St. Elizabeth provided nearly $2.3 million in hospital care to individuals unable to pay during a recent year.

Since 1983 a major upgrading of the Sameday Surgery program has offered many patients the option of high-quality surgical care at a more economical cost than a traditional hospital stay, and Alive and Well, a successful health-promotion service, is offered to area businesses, providing participants a thorough screening and education program which represents preventive medicine at its very best.

Lafayette and St. Elizabeth Hospital have shared more than a century of growth since the day the six Sisters first arrived from Germany. Both the city and the hospital look forward to the long and mutually beneficial continuation of that partnership.

The hospital, first opened for patients in 1876, expanded quickly. Wings were added in 1879 and 1883 and an addition was completed in 1897. Photo circa 1900

WILLIAM B. BURFORD PRINTING COMPANY

William B. Burford was the guiding force in both the excellence of craftsmanship and the significant growth of his company.

Henry Danner was a New York attorney when he married William Burford's daughter and went to work for his father-in-law.

Indiana was predominantly rolling prairie in 1870, and few railroads or even stagecoaches were available for transportation from one county seat to the next. William B. Burford remedied the situation by strapping his case filled with printing samples to his back and riding horseback from county to county, convincing seventy-two of the ninety-two local governments to choose his Indianapolis-based company for their printing needs.

His father, Miles Burford, had become a silent partner in Sheets and Braden, a bookbinding concern, in 1838, and the firm had expanded into printing in 1862. The name changed to Braden and Burford when William joined the business in 1867, and later became the William B. Burford Company when he bought out Braden in 1875.

The venture experienced rapid growth under the young president's vigorous leadership. To accommodate the increased volume, additional stories were added to the building located at 21 West Washington Street, and space was leased from adjoining firms as well.

The building housing the printing operation was constructed to include a 400-barrel reservoir on the roof that fed a unique iron pipe sprinkler system throughout the plant, and special fire walls were constructed at William Burford's request. Within a few months after completion, fire did break out in the plant, but although it lasted for two hours and destroyed everything in the room where it raged, neither the floor, walls, nor roof burned through. This extraordinary occurrence for that time was duly chronicled by the local paper.

By the turn of the century nearly 300 people were kept busy filling individual orders, which arrived from twenty-six states. Divisions included type printing, a bindery, and lithographing—an art at which the company's craftsmen excelled. William Burford was one of the first to import lithograph stones from Bavaria, and during the period before cameras were in use, men would draw intricate designs in reverse to be used on the stone presses.

In 1927 the business was incorporated and son-in-law Henry Danner became president, a position he would hold for over twenty years. By this time the William B. Burford Printing Company was the official state printer. When William died, the 75th Indiana Legislature adopted a resolution lauding him as a man who served the state with distinction and who took personal pride in his craftsmanship.

Henry Danner guided the firm until 1950, when a member of the fourth generation, Burford Danner, became president. Today both Burford Danner and his son, William Burford Danner, oversee operations at the plant, which was relocated to the Indianapolis south side in 1966. Cameras have replaced the meticulous work of the lithographers and there is no longer a great demand for the handmade leather bindings used by state and local governments for decades. The William B. Burford Printing Company, however, continues its tradition of excellence in the printing profession—a five-generation enterprise that has contributed to the progress of Indianapolis and Indiana for more than a century.

BALL STATE UNIVERSITY

"Ball State University began as a 'people's college,' and it's important that it continue to be a 'people's college,' serving the citizens of the state of Indiana—wherever they live," declared John E. Worthen, eleventh president of Ball State, shortly after his inauguration. "Our emphasis is upon excellent teaching, but the research and service provided by Ball State's very competent faculty serve a vast number of Hoosiers in communities large and small, in schools, businesses, industry, and government."

Ninety-three percent of Ball State's students come from Indiana's ninety-two counties. The third-largest university in the state, it also serves students from more than forty states and sixty foreign countries.

Originally a teachers' college—first as a private institution from 1899 to 1917—and as a state college from 1918 to 1965, Ball State became a university in 1965. Today Ball State offers a wide array of professional programs for career-minded students who will live and work in the twenty-first century.

Architecture, business administration, computer and actuarial sciences, human bioenergetics, art, music, the sciences, humanities, nursing, special

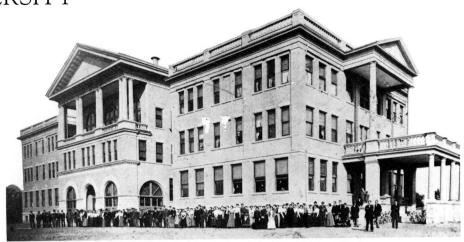

President F.A.Z. Kumler, the faculty, and students of the new Eastern Indiana Normal University in Muncie posed on August 28, 1899, for this dedication photo in front of EINU's only building. Today it serves as Ball State University's administration building.

education, and first- and second-year medicine are but a few of the 125 undergraduate, 85 master's-level, 18 doctoral, 14 education specialist degree programs, and more than a dozen two-year associate degree programs offered by the university's six colleges: College of Applied Sciences and Technology, College of Architecture and Planning, College of Business, College of Fine Arts, College of Sciences and Humanities, and the Teachers' College.

University College is Ball State's newest and most innovative program to sharpen and enhance essential academic skills, provide one-on-one tutoring, increase student retention, and provide career guidance and information for beginning students who are underprepared or undecided about career choices.

For the academically gifted and talented, Ball State has a challenging University Honors College program, plus the London Centre program and overseas study opportunities in France, England, Poland, Korea, Taiwan, China, Brazil, and Mexico.

From a small, floundering private institution—Eastern Indiana Normal University, which opened in the present administration building in 1899—through four more private attempts to operate a college, it wasn't until 1918, when the five Ball brothers bought the defunct school and gave it to the State of Indiana, that the Muncie institution began to flourish. First as the Eastern Division of Indiana Normal School at Terre Haute and then Ball State Teachers' College, the university owes much to the Ball family whose name it bears and to a loyal and supportive community that always has placed a high value on having a university in its city.

In 1984 Ball State University dedicated the Robert P. Bell building, the electronic nerve center of the campus, connecting by fiber optics all major buildings and academic departments with the university's computing services center.

BALL CORPORATION

The century-long history of Muncie's Ball Corporation provides a classic example of the American Dream. The story began with five brothers who shared a faith in each other and a strong belief in the value of hard work and ingenuity. Today the success of their early aspirations is evidenced by a prospering corporation that has reached one billion dollars in sales and employs more than 9,000 individuals in its twenty-five manufacturing facilities located in fourteen states and two foreign countries. The company's product line, which began with wood-jacketed oil cans and is perhaps most widely known for its glass home canning jars, has expanded and diversified to touch most Americans' lives.

The year was 1880 and Frank and

Ball's production of metal cans began in 1969 and has today grown into the company's largest product line with more than six billion cans produced annually.

Edmund Ball were searching for their future careers. Twice before they had left their home in Canandaigua, New York, to travel to Buffalo, where their uncle George, a Baptist minister, had located business opportunities for them. The first, a manufacturing operation producing crates for shipping fish, had been destroyed by fire, and the second, a carpet-cleaning operation, had proved unsuccessful. This time they borrowed $200 from their uncle and purchased a small part of an existing business, producing wood-jacketed tin cans to be sold to paint and varnish dealers.

The brothers perfected their own patents and the business grew rapidly. When fire once again destroyed their operation, they rebuilt. Soon after, brothers Lucius, George, and William, accompanied by their mother, moved to Buffalo to join the organization.

The five Ball brothers were constantly on the lookout for innova-

The five Ball brothers, who had been advised to stick together by their mother, each brought a special talent to their company. From the left, they are George A., Lucius, Frank C., Edmund B., and William C. Ball.

tions to their product line, and soon had added sixty-gallon kerosene tanks for customers including Standard Oil and one-gallon cans for home use. When competitors began making headway with glass cans, the Balls quickly adapted and, in 1882, built their own glass plant in East Buffalo. They found their new glass furnace was underutilized with the manufacture of oil cans alone, and corrected the situation by beginning the production of glass-top fruit jars. Despite fierce competition in this area, Ball created a substantial market and two years later expanded into the production of porcelain-lined, zinc-capped jars.

In 1886 fire struck once more, destroying the entire manufacturing operation. Once again the Balls would have to begin anew, but before doing so they decided to investigate reports that natural gas wells in the Midwest were providing a much cheaper source of fuel than the coal used by eastern manufacturers.

Frank Ball was touring potential building sites in Ohio when a telegram arrived from Muncie, Indiana, urging him to include that communi-

"Ball Mason fruit jars are the best," stated an advertisement in the 1904 Woman's Home Companion. *The familiar jar's popularity down through the years attests to this early claim.*

ty in his itinerary. He accepted and his arrival was greeted with an offer of seven acres, a free gas well, and $5,000 to cover relocation expenses. Never a company to back away from progress, Ball Brothers accepted, and the *Muncie Daily News* headlined "THEY COME," along with a six-column illustration of the proposed factory complex.

Frank and Edmund took charge of the new facility and continued Ball Brothers' quest for improvement. The company developed the first automatic glass machine, which revolutionized production throughout the industry. It began acquiring companies located throughout the nation to provide expansion and related products, and it established new facilities to provide avenues that are still being explored today.

In 1912, for example, a zinc mill was built to provide lids for Ball jars. By 1924 zinc battery cans had become a significant product for the company, and ten years later an expansion made the mill the largest of its kind in the world. Today Ball's zinc products division has moved into areas never dreamed of in 1912, including the production of the bulk of the zinc-copper penny blanks purchased by the U.S. Treasury.

Although the citizens of Muncie had rejoiced over Ball Brothers' arrival, they could never have imagined the positive impact the firm would eventually make on the community. When the only nearby institution of higher learning was ordered sold at public auction in 1917, the brothers purchased it. Sixty-four acres and new buildings were added and what is now Ball State University was begun. Edmund Ball had concern for his new hometown and provided funds through his estate to establish the Ball Memorial Hospital, which opened in 1929.

Frank Ball's presidency of Ball Brothers continued until his death in 1943. Sixty-three years of his guidance had provided the company a solid foundation and a wide name recognition among American consumers. The Balls' innovative spirit, however, was a legacy that would live far beyond the brothers' active leadership.

As Ball Corporation (which went public in 1972 and was listed on the New York Stock Exchange a year later) enters its second century, presi-

dent Richard M. Ringoen oversees products ranging from the traditional home canning jar (which now accounts for only 4 percent of Ball's revenues) to the ERBS, Earth Radiation Budget Satellite, which was deployed from the Space Shuttle late in 1984.

Packaging remains the largest operating segment, with cans for beer and soft drinks the principal product line. Plastics packaging, using newly developed co-extruded sheets, promises to take Ball into yet another era of food preservation. The firm's industrial products segment includes the zinc products division mentioned above, as well as the production of injection-molded and thermoformed plastics, and the technical products group continues impressive growth in electronics systems and aerospace.

Ball's pursuit of high technology and innovative product development is a logical extension of the dreams of the five Ball brothers. The wood-jacketed oil cans are gone, but the dedication and ingenuity of a century ago are still very much in evidence.

A composite of some of Ball Corporation's contributions to the American space program, from the early (1962) Orbiting Solar Observatory to the Earth Radiation Budget Satellite launched from the Space Shuttle in 1984.

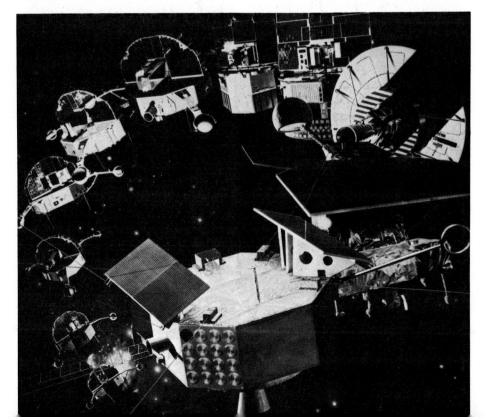

PERMANENT MAGNET COMPANY, INC.

Nearly every schoolchild has experimented with magnets in his science classroom, and nearly every one of the magnets used was produced by Permanent Magnet Company.

Education, however, is only one of several areas served by the Indianapolis firm. Permanent Magnet has designed and manufactured the magnets essential for such commonplace products as thermostats and hearing aids as well as the complex systems aboard guided missiles. The firm's products, which are totally manufactured at the Indianapolis plant, find markets throughout the world, and have even been transported beyond the earth as they have been utilized on every American space mission.

Founded in 1946, Permanent Magnet was the result of Stanley Malless' fascination with the mysteries and theories surrounding magnets. Malless, a graduate of Purdue University, had worked as a planning engineer for the Chevrolet Division of General Motors until his service in World War II. Following his duty he was asked to return to Chevrolet, and the Army also offered a career (he eventually achieved the rank of colonel), but Malless combined his interest in magnets with the knowledge that only half a dozen prime producers of magnetics existed in the United States.

He joined forces with Ralph M. Burns and Ora A. Hooker, and the three determined to make their operation the standard by which the existing companies would be judged. Before building a plant, Malless visited a large producer of thermostats in Milwaukee and came away with an order for 100,000 magnets. The business was under way, and Permanent Magnet's niche in the marketplace was established.

The metals most successfully converted to magnets must be imported from Africa, and Permanent Magnet's first stock of these raw materials

was of very poor quality. The inexperienced partners did not suspect the real reason for their lack of success and instead blamed their own procedures. They experimented dili-

Stanley Malless, president and chairman of the board, founded the firm in 1946.

gently until they had developed the process to produce the quality they desired. When good materials arrived and were put through these same processes, the surprising result was a higher-quality magnet than any of their competitors could produce. Customers raised their specifications, and Permanent Magnet was the only firm that could meet them—a situation that earned the company the nickname "jewelry manufacturers" within its industry.

From that auspicious beginning Permanent Magnet has grown, expanding its facility six times. The firm has no sales force, but relies on its fine reputation for specializing in complex work. Magnets of every size and shape are manufactured to customers' specifications and often the company is called upon to design the magnet to fit the buyers' needs.

Life without the use of magnets is inconceivable—it would mean the elimination of products from telephone receivers to phonograph needles to small electric motors. American industry without the aid of Permanent Magnet Company, Inc., is nearly as difficult to imagine.

Permanent Magnet Company, Inc., is situated at 4437 Bragdon Street, Indianapolis.

Patrons

The following individuals, companies, and organizations have made a valuable commitment to the quality of this publication. Windsor Publications and the Historic Landmarks Foundation of Indiana gratefully acknowledge their participation in *Indiana: An Illustrated History.*

AAA Hoosier Motor Club
Americana Healthcare Center
Nancy and Richard Andis
Architects Incorporated
Arvin Industries, Inc.*
Ball Corporation*
Ball State University*
Blue Cross and Blue Shield of Indiana*
Borden Inc./Dairy Division
Borns Management Corporation
Bowen Engineering Corporation
William B. Burford Printing Company*
Carroll County Wabash & Erie Canal
    Association, Inc.
Central Stainless Equipment, Inc.
The Clark Co. Historical Society/Howard
    Steamboat Museum, Inc.
The Corydon State Bank
Crown International*
CWY Electronics, Inc. (DST)
Kitty and Richard Dickson
Duncan Electric/Landis & Gyr*
Eckhart & Company, Inc.*
Elkhart County Ambulance Service, Inc.
Robert W. and Sharon C. Evans
Farm Bureau Insurance Companies*
FEPCO Tool & Supply, Inc.
Mr. & Mrs. John W. Fisher
Julie A. Gutwein
The Honorable Mitchell V. Harper
Hartzler-Gutermuth Funeral Home
Helsel Metallurgical, Inc.*
Historic Fort Wayne, Inc.
Mark M. Holeman Inc.
Hook Drugs, Inc.*
John E. Hurt
Indiana State University Alumni Association
Indianapolis Realty

L.E. Isley & Sons, Inc.
Jayco Incorporated*
Kunkle Valve Company, Inc.
The Lafayette Life Insurance Company*
Dr. & Mrs. Evan L. Lehman
David Leonards
David N. Lewis, A.S.I.D.
Eli Lilly and Company*
G. Linnemann
Local Beauty Supply Inc.
McAllister Machinery Company, Inc.
Dixie and James McDonough
Marion County/Indianapolis Historical Society
Mayflower Corporation*
Melvin Simon & Associates
Miles Laboratories, Inc.
The Mole Hole of Bloomington
Morrison's Management Services, Inc.
Mossberg and Company, Inc.
Newlin-Johnson Co. Inc.-Terre Haute
Odyssey Map Store
Permanent Magnet Company, Inc.*
The Portfolio
Quinlan Keene Peck & McShay, Inc.
James Whitcomb Riley Memorial Association
Susan Williams & David L. Rimstidt
St. Elizabeth Hospital Medical Center*
St. Vincent Hospital and Health Care Center*
Sales Research Corporation
Donald E. Smith
Sullivan State Bank
The Sycamore Group, Inc.
Terre Haute Convention & Visitors Bureau of
    Vigo County
Richard Vincent Interiors Inc.
Richard C. Walden
Waterloo Depot Foundation, Inc.
Marian E. White
Daniel E. Widner
Joseph L. Wisehart
WTHR-TV

*Partners in Progress of *Indiana: An Illustrated History.* The histories of these companies and organizations appear in Chapter 10.

For Further Reading

The basic reference for everyone interested in the history of Indiana is the multivolume series sponsored by the Indiana Historical Society. Four volumes are now available, and two more are still in preparation: John D. Barnhart and Dorothy L. Riker, *Indiana to 1816: The Colonial Period* (Indianapolis, 1971); Emma Lou Thornbrough, *Indiana in the Civil War Era, 1850-1880* (Indianapolis, 1965); Clifton J. Phillips, *Indiana in Transition: The Emergence of an Industrial Commonwealth, 1880-1920* (Indianapolis, 1968); and James H. Madison, *Indiana Through Tradition and Change, 1920-1945* (Indianapolis, 1982).

For the missing years between 1816 and 1850 the best work is Donald F. Carmony and John D. Barnhart, *Indiana: From Frontier to Industrial Commonwealth* (New York, 1954). For the period after World War II there is no systematic study yet available.

For all periods the *Indiana Magazine of History* provides a wealth of information, and some of its most significant articles have been collected in *"No Cheap Padding": Seventy-five Years of the Indiana Magazine of History* (Indianapolis, 1980), edited by Lorna Lutes Sylvester.

There are several anthologies of Hoosier literature, but the most accessible is Richard E. Banta's *Hoosier Caravan* (Bloomington, 1975). The many fine novels about Indiana provide an excellent way to understand its history, particularly the work of Edward Eggleston, Booth Tarkington, and Jessamyn West.

More specialized works describing various aspects of life in Indiana include:

Barnhart, John D. *The Valley of Democracy: The Frontier versus the Plantation in the Ohio Valley, 1775-1818*. Bloomington: 1953.

Buley, R. Carlyle. *The Old Northwest: Pioneer Period, 1815-1840*. Indianapolis: 1950; reprinted Bloomington: 1962.

Cleeves, Freeman. *Old Tippecanoe: William Henry Harrison and His Times*. New York: 1939.

Dorson, Richard M. *Land of the Millrats*. Cambridge: 1981

Edmunds, R. David. *The Shawnee Prophet*. Lincoln: 1983

—-*Tecumseh and the Quest for Indian Leadership*. Boston: 1984.

Esarey, Logan. *The Indiana Home*. Bloomington: 1976.

Fatout, Paul. *Indiana Canals*. West Lafayette: 1972.

Gray, Ralph D. *Alloys and Automobiles: The Life of Elwood Haynes*. Indianapolis: 1979.

Hilton, George W. *Monon Route*. Berkeley: 1978.

Hyneman, Charles D., et. al. *Voting in Indiana: A Century of Persistence and Change*. Bloomington: 1979.

James, James A. *Life of George Rogers Clark*. Chicago: 1928.

Martin, John B. *Indiana: An Interpretation*. New York: 1947.

Moore, Powell A. *The Calumet Region: Indiana's Last Frontier*. Indianapolis: 1959.

Peckham, Howard. *Indiana: A Bicentennial History*. New York: 1970.

Rowell, John A. *Yankee Artilleryman: Through the Civil War with Eli Lilly's Indiana Battery*. Knoxville: 1975.

Schneider, Allan F., ed. *Natural Features of Indiana*. Indianapolis: 1966.

Shumaker, Arthur W. *A History of Indiana Literature*. Indianapolis: 1962.

Stampp, Kenneth E. *Indiana Politics during the Civil War*. Indianapolis: 1949.

Welsh, Matthew E. *View from the State House: Recollections and Reflections, 1961-1965*. Indianapolis: 1981.

Wilson, William E. *The Angel and the Serpent: The Story of New Harmony*. Bloomington: 1964

—-*Indiana: A History*. Bloomington: 1966.

—-*The Wabash*. New York: 1940.

An itinerant German artist named
William Momberger painted this view of
the Wabash River near Vincennes circa
1860. Several years later it appeared as a
hand-tinted engraving in a book called
The National Gallery of American Landscape (1869). Courtesy, Indiana Historical
Society

Index

THIS BOOK WAS SET IN

GOUDY AND LYDIAN TYPES,

PRINTED ON

SEVENTY-POUND MEAD
OFFSET ENAMEL GLOSS

AND BOUND BY

WALSWORTH PUBLISHING COMPANY

ADVISORY COMMITTEE

LES RENARDS
les Mascoutens ou
Nation du Feu
les Quicapou
ILINOIS
LAC des ILINOIS
Miscouakimina
Chigagou
Missilimakinac
Lac aux Outaouacs
Lac des vieux Deserts
Ouisconsing R.
R. aux Renards
Mine de Plomb
Chemin des Voyageurs
Isles a Tessier
Isles aux Canots
Assenisipi ou R. ala Roche
Christal de roche
Ancien Villages des Ilinois 1679
Montagnes Pelees
Lac Pimitoüi
les Pimitoüi ou Peorra
Fort Crevecoeur
le Rocher
Riviere des Ilinois
Chasse des Amis des Francois
Tamarois et Caouquias
Cascaquias
Riviere d Oubache ou S Hieronyme
Desert de six vingt lieues d'e
ou les Ilinois font la Chasse d
Cap S. Antonie
Ancien Fort
Regio Metallorum
Metalla
LOUISIAN
Missouri R.
R. aux Boeuf
le Moingona R.
les Octotata
Saut de S. Antoine
Vieu Fort
Vieu Fort l'Huillier
R. S. Croix
Lac Pepin
Chicagou R.
Macopin
R. des Miamis
Poutouatami
Isle a la Son